VANISHING EDEN

In the series *Urban Life, Landscape, and Policy,*
edited by Zane L. Miller, David Stradling, and Larry Bennett

Also in this series:

Michael T. Maly and
Heather M. Dalmage

VANISHING EDEN

*White Construction of Memory, Meaning,
and Identity in a Racially Changing City*

TEMPLE UNIVERSITY PRESS
Philadelphia • Rome • Tokyo

TEMPLE UNIVERSITY PRESS
Philadelphia, Pennsylvania 19122
www.temple.edu/tempress

Library of Congress Cataloging-in-Publication Data

Maly, Michael T., 1968–
 Vanishing Eden : white construction of memory, meaning, and identity in a racially
changing city / Michael Maly and Heather Dalmage.
     pages cm. — (Urban life, landscape, and policy)
 Includes bibliographical references and index.
 ISBN 978-1-4399-1118-1 (hardback : alk. paper) — ISBN 978-1-4399-1119-8 (paper :
alk. paper) — ISBN 978-1-4399-1120-4 (e-book)
 1. Chicago (Ill.)—Race relations—History—20th century.   2. United States—
Race relations—History—20th century.   3. Whites—Illinois—Chicago—History
—20th century.   4. Segregation—Illinois—Chicago—History—20th century.
5. Discrimination in housing—Illinois—Chicago—History—20th century.   6. Ethnic
neighborhoods—Illinois—Chicago—History—20th century.   7. Sociology, Urban—
Illinois—Chicago.   I. Dalmage, Heather M., 1965–   II. Title.
 F548.9.A1M35 2016
 305.8009773'110904—dc23

                                                                    2015013702

♾ The paper used in this publication meets the requirements of the American National
Standard for Information Sciences—Permanence of Paper for Printed Library Materials,
ANSI Z39.48-1992

Printed in the United States of America

9 8 7 6 5 4 3 2 1

To our families and students

Contents

Acknowledgments

This project would not have been possible without the help of various people. First and foremost, as we look back on the path of *Vanishing Eden*, we are grateful to the fifty-three individuals who opened their hearts and shared with us their childhood memories, some wonderful and many quite difficult. We appreciate and respect the courage it took for folks to share moments in their lives that they regretted and experiences that cast them in a less than favorable light. We enjoyed the moments in the interview process when individuals spoke of the happiness in their childhoods, memories such as leaving the house in the morning and coming home when the streetlights came on; through these interviews our own memories of childhood were ignited. We are also grateful to the myriad other people who supported us along the way, particularly those who introduced us to the community, helping us understand related activism and actions. These people enabled us to enter their world and make sense of the history. Here we acknowledge Chip Berlet, James Capraro, Bob Gannett, Paul Green, James Keck, Christine Malcom, the late Jean Mayer, Dominic Pacyga, Mike Smith, and Monsignor Kenneth Velo.

We thank the Chicago History Museum for allowing us to access the files of the Southwest Parish and Neighborhood Federation. And we thank SAGE Publications for allowing us to reprint portions of Chapter 4, which were originally published in Michael Maly, Heather Dalmage, and Nancy Michaels, "The End of an Idyllic World: Nostalgia Narratives, Race, and the Construction of White Powerlessness," *Critical Sociology* 39, no. 5 (September 2013), by SAGE Publications Ltd. All rights reserved. Copyright © 2013 SAGE Publications, available at http://crs.sagepub.com/content/39/5/757.abstract.

We are grateful to the various Roosevelt University students who assisted with this project. In preparation for writing this book, we team-taught a course on neighborhood change and racial identity. We thank our students for reading with us, challenging us, and thinking critically about racial change and racial identities. We are also grateful to Shannon Kaneshige, Arthur Mitchell, and Joshua Reese for their help with transcription. We owe special thanks to one former student in particular: the very creative, insightful, committed, and hardworking Nancy Michaels. From the moment we introduced Nancy to this project, she got it. Nancy was working on her master's degree at the time, and she decided to embark on a thesis project that explored white flight and racial borders. She came on board as a research assistant and then as a collaborator. Chapter 3, on racial borders, is a direct outgrowth of her master's thesis and was co-written by her. Finally, we thank Roosevelt University for its support, including granting research leaves to allow us to work on this project.

We owe a debt of gratitude to Larry Bennett, one of the *Urban Life, Landscape, and Policy* series editors. His knowledge and insight, timeliness, editing skills, and general good humor made completing this book relatively painless. At Temple University Press, we thank both Mick Gusinde-Duffy and Janet Francendese for championing our project in its early stages and Aaron Javsicas for helping us shepherd the manuscript through the final stages.

Of course, we are deeply grateful to our families. Engaging in this kind of research and writing requires a dedicated amount of time. As writing deadlines approached, we sometimes had to push aside family time. For the understanding and space our families provided, we owe them a huge debt of gratitude. Mike Maly thanks Amelia Rulich and Thais Rulich-Maly for their patience, love, humor, and acceptance. Heather Dalmage thanks Owen and Mahalia Dalmage for being the light in her life and for not complaining too much about eating less than stellar meals as she focused on writing these words.

VANISHING EDEN

1

Racial Change, Neighborhoods, and Whiteness

In January 2006, the *Chicago Tribune Magazine* ran a story commemorating the fortieth anniversary of the Chicago Freedom Movement's march through Gage Park and Marquette Park on Chicago's Southwest Side. The article chronicles a march in August 1966 led by Martin Luther King Jr. and roughly six hundred civil rights marchers. Racial tensions were running high in Chicago that year, and everywhere the Chicago Freedom Movement's nonviolent marchers went that summer they were met with "rocks and rage" (Terry 2006). The August march was no different, as hundreds of whites met the marchers. Early in the march, counterdemonstrators hurled a rock "as big as a fist" at King, hitting him in the head. Another threw a knife at King, narrowly missing (Ralph 1993). Undeterred, King and members of the Chicago Freedom Movement continued, heading north from Marquette Park to Halverson's Realty, where they held a prayer vigil. Hundreds of whites filled the street attempting to halt the march, tearing up an effigy of Dr. King, smashing windows of cars driven by blacks, and yelling, "We want Martin Luther Coon—kill those niggers—send them home" (Roberts 1966). Following the vigil, the marchers made their way back to Marquette Park, where they were met by a mob of four thousand hostile whites. The mob attacked the nonviolent marchers with rocks, fists, eggs, bottles, and cherry bombs. The presence of approximately 960 police officers prevented King and the marchers from being injured. The marchers made their way to their buses and cars with whites chasing after them, breaking windows and battling the policemen. White hostility to the marchers stunned even seasoned activists there. Andrew Young famously remarked that far from being a "rabble element," hostile whites were "women and children and husbands and wives coming out of their homes [and] becoming a mob" (quoted in Ralph 1993: 123). A reporter on the scene noted that "men, women, and children sat on their front steps yelling 'Cannibals' and 'Savages' and 'Go Home, niggers'" (Roberts 1966).

Clearly, many people recall the tumultuous 1960s as a time that the Civil Rights Movement and other groups pressed for social change. In the summer of 2006, as part of an event marking the anniversary of the Chicago Freedom Marches, we boarded a tour bus to visit important sites for the movement on the city's Southwest and West sides. Given how much has been written about the Civil Rights Movement and the Chicago Freedom Movement, the tour provided context for those stories (see Garrow 1989; Ralph 1993; Anderson and Pickering 2008). For those new to the city, Chicago neighborhoods, particularly on the Southwest Side, are visually striking in appearance, with decidedly low-rise and residential landscape. It is difficult not to be impressed by the leafy and green streets of neatly packed, impressive bungalows, both solidly built and welcoming. The front stoops on each street recall a time that social life was more local and immediate, not spread over electronic devices. Visiting Marquette Park is particularly memorable, as its sheer size and activities (e.g., baseball games and people walking dogs) are a reprieve from the hustle and bustle of city life. Traveling east from the park, we pass several impressive Catholic churches that remain central to the fabric of the community. Finally, our tour ends along the faded commercial strips that connect the residential streets, reminding us that before large department stores one rarely found the need to leave the neighborhood.

The tour, albeit brief, covered only the story of the civil rights marchers. For us, however, another story lingered. It is the story of the lives of the lower middle-class and working-class whites who would have been most affected by the reforms that open housing marchers were seeking. Beyond the angry faces represented in pictures of the more violent clashes between marchers and whites, it seemed important to understand what was going on in the lives of those whites living in these neighborhoods. Lost in the headlines and stereotypes of white working-class communities were real people who went about the mundane aspects of their lives, going to work and church, tending to their homes, participating in their communities, and loving and caring for their children and families. The experience of whites living in segregated neighborhoods raises important questions. What did racial change represent to whites? What did it threaten? How did they make sense of the Civil Rights Movement vis-à-vis the potential for integration in their neighborhoods? How did whites organize themselves and their identities, roles, and emotions as racial change began to threaten their neighborhoods? Finding answers to these questions became the heart of our study.

Scholars have begun to answer some of these questions, focusing on why whites reacted so forcefully to the threat of integration and racial change. Although it was the marches that earned Marquette Park and the Southwest Side the reputation as an epicenter of northern racial hatred (Warren 2010; Pacyga 2010; Meyer 2000), there is ample evidence of white violence against blacks in the decades leading up to the marches of 1966 (Diamond 2009). Clearly, there were some hard-core racists fighting integration on the Southwest Side during the 1950s and 1960s, and for those whites the presence of blacks in their neighborhoods was too much to bear. For these and other whites, externalized anger toward blacks was a central response. Fear of integration seemed to permeate every conversation on the Southwest Side during the 1960s and early 1970s (McCourt 1977). For these whites, integration meant losing everything they had worked for: their home. The bungalow belt represented lower middle-class folks who "scrimped and saved and sacrificed" to own their own homes in "good" neighborhoods (Ralph 1993). Whites in these neighborhoods—labeled by some the "have-a-little-want-mores"—were working-class people striving for a better life for themselves and their children (Green 1988, 1990). Stock and retirement plans were not options for them; thus, a home was their principal investment. For this reason, property values were a frequent topic of discussion when referencing racial change. And given that property has always been racialized in the United States, a discussion of property values was inherently a racialized discussion (Harris 1993). Beyond the home, however, racial change also threatened their community or "turf," as well as a significant element of their identity. Thus, economic concerns were only one part of what whites were fighting for; owning a home in a stable white neighborhood for many first- or second-generation individuals was symbolic of social achievement and becoming "white" and "respectable" (Hirsch 1983: 195; Guglielmo 2004; Sokol 2007).

For many whites in these neighborhoods, the challenge to segregation was an attack on their community that left them feeling victimized. A resident responding to an editorial to the *Southwest News Herald* captured this when she claimed that King and his followers were the aggressors, suggesting that King "had nothing but hatred and vengeance in his eyes" when he came into their community.[1] Residents were also quick to blame outsiders for explicit expressions of hatred and violence, often suggesting that whites who were protesting the King marches were "greasers" from other parts of Chicago or that outsiders seized on the marches to display their racism, and regular people were not involved. Southwest Side residents felt victimized and resentful of government, intellectuals, wealthier North Side residents, and suburbanites, who they felt were hypocritical in condemning white resistance to integration while wealthier whites were able to prevent integration by maintaining higher property values (Kefalas 2003). The populist rage that emerged on the Southwest Side focused on both civil rights organizations and their allegedly well-off white supporters, none of whom, to their mind, were from the neighborhood. Also, many whites had fled integration previously—usually one or two parishes to the east, an experience that cost them a great deal economically and emotionally. Thus, as Mike Royko noted, "When they see someone marching in their direction saying, 'I want mine,' they say: 'You mean you want mine.'"[2] While there is likely some truth to these claims, there is no shortage of evidence to suggest that hostility toward blacks ran deep in working-class and lower middle-class communities in Chicago (Hirsch 1983; Ralph 1993; Seligman 2005). Some residents in the community were clearly loath to acknowledge the racism that was present.

The civil rights clashes happening in Chicago during the 1960s and those that people remember or visualize through press accounts, history, or media images were complex. For blacks, a history of containment, violence, and discriminatory housing practices that limited residential and social mobility options fueled the open housing movement. For whites, outside the more famous clashes, such as the one in Marquette Park, there was an everyday, block-by-block, intense tension with racial change. Our project documents white neighborhoods from the standpoint of the people who lived through these changes and experienced the loss of community, and their dreams for the future as a result. We seek to make sense of what it was like for whites growing up and living in racially changing—or, at least, racially charged—environments. Through this analysis we hope to illuminate and deepen the understanding of the ways in which race operates in everyday life. Thus, as we examine the stories whites tell of racial change and how it relates to their present lives, it is our aim to understand the changing contours of whiteness,[3] white privilege, and efforts to maintain positive white racial identities. We wish to avoid reducing the attitudes and behavior of whites to simple racism. We likewise are not interested in serving as apologists for white racism or attempts to push white people to the center of race studies. Rather, we seek to capture the complexities of racism and whites while strengthening race scholarship through an erudite analysis of how race, whiteness, and privilege are understood and enacted over time.

We developed several general questions about the nature of their neighborhoods and the resulting change. What was it like to live in racially changing communities? How did whites interpret and act on the threat of or actual racial change that was occurring? What did children hear and learn in the community and from their parents about race, integration, and humanity? And importantly, how did living through the process of racial change affect their understanding of community and race? Answering these questions leads to a story, for whites, of loss, change, racism, and racial formation. Undoubtedly, racial change signaled a loss of a neighborhood, a shifting sense of community, and unraveling social networks many have yet to find again. The immediate threat was also tied to larger changes. The city that whites were living in was shifting from industrial to postindustrial, white to minority, and urban to suburban. The country was shifting economically, ideologically, and politically, buttressed by the Civil Rights Movement and a decade of intensive social and political upheaval. The aim of our book is to understand racial change by attending to not only the immediate concerns of families living in neighborhoods but also how whites understood themselves and discussed their place in a shifting social landscape. Thus, as we examine the stories whites tell of racial change, we not only learn how whites understand themselves and their neighborhoods racially; we also begin to see the changing contours of whiteness, white privilege, and efforts to maintain positive white racial identities.

Our analysis is situated at the intersection of urban studies and whiteness studies. Thus, we examine race as it is constructed through discourse and action and how race is a central organizing principle in social institutions, such as housing, education, and employment. We use the urban studies literature that examines the shifting racial structure and dynamics in urban areas starting around 1950, with particular attention to cities in the urban North. Several demographic and structural shifts altered the racial dynamics in almost all of the big cities in the North after World War II. White flight and resegregation often followed a block-by-block pattern in most cities. The foundation of such shifts is rooted in numerous overlapping and complex social processes, with ties to religion, the economy, housing policy and suburbanization, racial identity, and political party restructuring. And at the same time, the Civil Rights Movement was attempting to alter the racial hierarchy in the United States. Thus, when looking at white flight, it is important to bear in mind that these shifts cannot be reduced to individual predispositions and prejudice. Rather, they are the result of a larger set of struggles over space, resources, and ultimately, racial power. Understanding this context, then, serves as an important touchstone as we examine how race shapes the lives and experiences of whites and, in turn, how whites continue to bolster and shape white privilege.

We draw on the critical whiteness literature that focuses on understanding white identity as a racialized location of privilege, power, and property. The early whiteness literature was concerned, largely, with "outing" the invisible privilege and power of whites (McIntosh 1992) and flushing out the complexities of whiteness—for example, antiracist whites, white double consciousness (Winant 1997), whites living across the color line (Dalmage

2000, 2004), and gay and poor whites (Hartigan 1999). By the late 1990s, whiteness studies had gone global. Some of the most interesting literature on whiteness has come out of post-apartheid South Africa, as whites have begun to think about themselves in a context in which they have lost political, if not economic, power (Steyn 2001; Dolby 2001; Ballard 2004). Each of these literatures informs our research as we explore a time that lower middle-class and working-class whites living in segregated Chicago neighborhoods faced the loss of political and social capital and the decline in the economic value of their largest asset: their home. Looking at the upheaval on Chicago's West and Southwest sides as a result of racialized battles provides an opportunity to examine how whites consciously do race work as their relatively stable identities have been shaken up. We explore institutional and ideological mechanisms that held racial borders in place before civil rights gains in the housing market. Thus, we track how racial borders were understood and transformed by whites in a way that allowed them to maintain a sense of white superiority, even as they experienced the end of what had been their way of life, their Eden.

Neighborhoods, Race, and Racial Identity

The emotion generated around the Marquette Park marches was emblematic of larger trends in urban neighborhoods throughout the country. In the post–World War II decades, patterns of racial residential settlement were altered and fortified through the dynamics of neighborhood change (Taub, Taylor, and Dunham 1984). In Chicago during this period, the tight boundaries of the so-called black belt expanded, and racial boundaries or borders on the South and West sides were destroyed; this was caused by a combination of forces that included remarkable black population growth, pent-up black demand for good housing, discriminatory actions by speculating realtors, redlining by banks, and white opposition to integration (Ellen 2000; Hirsch 1983; Jackson 1985; Levin and Harmon 1991; Massey and Denton 1993; Kruse 2005; Seligman 2005). In cities across the country in the 1950s and 1960s, neighborhoods experienced rapid and often total racial transition, leading to an almost block-by-block pattern of racial transition, with many neighborhoods experiencing 50–90 percent white flight in less than a decade (Duncan and Duncan 1957; Goodwin 1979; Soutner 1980; Oser 1994). The changes illuminated the tenuous ties and sense of solidarity that bound white communities together. In fact, without institutional protections for housing segregation, whites attempted to hold the racial border through intragroup pressure. The pressure was strong enough that if a white family sold their home, they needed to do so surreptitiously. One of our informants, Jim, from the Auburn Gresham community, provides such an example: "The first person on our block that moved out moved out in the middle of the night. The next day they just weren't there. You know: a moving van pulling up, and a black person moving in. I would say after the first person left, you probably didn't have to move out at night anymore. It was just expected that everyone was going to leave." Whites, fearful of blackness and feeling abandoned by politicians, police, and the government, began to search for ways to regain a sense of safety and security. Until this time, many whites had passively accepted institutional support for their privilege. Now they were forced to actively think about how they would claim, maintain, and struggle for white privilege. Without a history of active solidarity, but with a pervasive fear of blackness and an overwhelming cynicism toward integration, unsuccessful attempts were made to hold the racial border through intra-community pressure. White flight was rooted variously in deep-seated racism against blacks, fear of losing communities and newly achieved "white" identities, and a fear that property values would decline precipitously as blacks moved in.

When white flight did not immediately occur, resistance to racial change included efforts by various actors to mitigate the perceived negative effects of racial transition (Molotch 1972; Taub, Taylor, and Dunham 1984; DeSenna 1994; Keating 1994; Wiese 1995; Seligman 2005). Many residents organized to "defend" their communities from racial change, using a variety of tools to "stabilize" their communities and keep blacks from moving in. The defending organizations perceived themselves to be guarding investments that whites made in their homes and upholding the values of self-government to preserve segregated housing and communities. Neighborhood defense took various forms. The most prominent from the 1920s through the 1950s involved hostility, harassment, and violence directed at blacks who attempted to move into white neighborhoods (Hirsch 1983; Sugrue 1996; Kruse 2005; Seligman 2005). Another form that emerged in a small number of neighborhoods is best described as "managed integration" (Molotch 1972). Unlike the small number of communities that attempted to pursue integration (Saltman 1990; Maly 2005) actively, in these "managed" communities the first goal was to intervene in the process of racial change to stabilize communities, not welcome African American newcomers. For example, Seligman's account of Chicago's northwestern Austin community shows how whites employed the "language of stabilization" in its attempt to shut down panic-peddling real estate agents by banning for-sale signs (Seligman 2005: 184–185). Although the efforts varied, the common response involved residents focused on the institutional practices working against stable communities. On the whole, the defensive stabilizing efforts did not hold; in the three decades following World War II, millions of whites fled central city neighborhoods for the suburbs or neighborhoods on the central city's periphery.

As scholars have analyzed the factors accounting for the rapidity of racial change in the urban North, the practices of religious institutions have received much attention. In the urban North, and particularly on Chicago's South Side, neighborhood boundaries were intimately tied, and almost equivalent, to the borders of Catholic parishes. In fact, the parish grounded residents' sense of place. "The one thing you always noticed about the South Side of Chicago," notes a member of the St. Sabina parish on Chicago's Southwest Side, is that "people always talked in terms of what parish do you belong to and not what street that you are from. Nobody would say, 'I live around so and so park,' or 'I'm a South Sider' even. They would just say, 'I'm from Sabina's' . . . because they were proud of it. Because it was something special to them" (quoted in McMahon 1995: 71). Family, neighborhood, and parish were tightly woven together in the lives of both adults and children. Strong ties between the local parish and the community were surely recognized even by those non-Catholic residents, if for no reason other than that friends organized their lives around parish activities. And while the Catholic church was important in its provision of religious functions, it also ensured cohesion of various white European ethnic groups. For the Irish, as one example, who were often not welcome in Anglo-Protestant communities, the church provided support as well as an anchor for their identity (McGreevy 1996). This strong communal tie was in part a function of Catholicism's traditional emphasis on the importance of community. Catholic devotionalism stressed examining one's sins within a community setting, elevating the community (and the priest) and diminishing the individual (McMahon 1995).

The church's accent on community, however, was tested when it came to race. As John McGreevy (1996: 177) notes, the Catholic church in the 1960s had two cultures, or two "Catholic worlds"—one working toward integration and one opposed to it. The former included Catholic liberals seeking to integrate church institutions and organizing programs to deal with the issue of race. In the late 1950s in Chicago, the church formed the Organization for a Southwest Community (OSC) to confront the issue of integration on Chicago's South Side. The OSC was born in part out of an effort to stem demographic change in heavily Catholic parishes and prevent parish decline (Frisbie 2002). Joining in anti-blockbusting campaigns, the OSC implemented an ambitious plan for building a stable integrated neighborhood on the Southwest Side. As redlining prevented young white couples who wanted to live in the St. Sabina community from obtaining long-term mortgages with low down payments, the OSC responded by creating a home loan program. The OSC worked with three banks to provide low-down-payment loans on the Southwest Side, leading to almost five hundred loans. The OSC also initiated an anti-blockbusting campaign aimed at uncovering and prosecuting real estate speculators who spread rumors and fear with the aim of profiting from massive turnover of property. St. Sabina parish also turned to Friendship House, a movement aimed at creating interracial understanding, to help deal with the race issue (McGreevy 1996). With the guidance of Friendship House, the parish sponsored a program that encouraged white and black parishioners to meet and socialize with the hope that this would discourage racial stereotypes. These programs did appear to calm whites' fears of racial change as more whites took their homes off the market and pledged to "stick it out" (McMahon 1995: 151–152). However, the OSC began to decline, due in part to a lack of a strong organizer (Frisbie 2002). Another aspect was the shooting of Frank Kelly, who was white, by a black youth, across the street from St. Sabina. According to the late journalist Robert McClory, this event more than anything else tipped the community. Within the span of a few years, two thousand white parishioners had left (McClory 2010).

Such efforts at interracial interaction stand in contrast to the substantial numbers of Catholics who were opposed. Survey data show that in the 1960s, white Catholics were the American group least likely to see integration as acceptable; for many, integration meant losing their communities and churches (McGreevy 1996). For whites who were veterans of racial transition (i.e., having fled from one or two parishes to the east), experience suggested to parishioners and some priests that integration was not possible. This "world" in the Catholic community included bitter parishioners who were becoming increasingly hostile to any sermons that contained the theme of "love thy neighbor," not wanting to be lectured on racial tolerance (McGreevy 1996). Many white Catholics felt abandoned by the church's stand on integration, while others rejected priests and nuns who supported the Civil Rights Movement. Within the church itself there were priests who were openly opposed to integration, even working to keep whites in the neighborhood and maintain the status quo, with little actual concern for integration (McMahon 1995: 145).[4] A clear example of this sentiment was Father Francis X. Lawlor, a Catholic priest and science teacher at St. Rita High School. Lawlor believed that without intervention, racial transition would result in the loss of Catholic schools and churches on Chicago's South Side. His plan was to "hold the line at Ashland Avenue" by creating a network of 186 block clubs to "promote the cultural, social and economic cohesiveness of the community" (in McCourt 1977). Lawlor generated a significant following in Chicago largely because he tapped into the fears and frustration of whites living in the path of racial change.[5] Invoking solidarity among white ethnic groups, Lawlor gave voice to whites who felt they were a "forgotten minority" without any programs "sponsored on their behalf by the government or the churches or civil rights groups" (McGreevy 1996: 232). In doing so, Lawlor echoed a sentiment that would form the basis of the white reaction to the Civil Rights Movement, one that parallels the language of rights.

Compared with other religious groups, members of the Catholic church historically have remained in their neighborhoods and resisted integration and racial change. White Protestants and Jews were more likely than white Catholics to flee their neighborhoods. For example, in 1950 the solidly Jewish area of North Lawndale was home to 87,000 whites, as well as forty-eight synagogues. By 1960, all but 11,000 whites had left, and all forty-eight synagogues had closed (fifteen in one year), while the more Catholic South Lawndale remained white during this period (McGreevy 1996). As Gerald Gamm (1999: 55) notes, "Arson, banking programs, and blockbusting targeted Jewish and Catholic neighborhoods without discrimination, but Jewish neighborhoods succumbed to the urban exodus more easily, more rapidly, and more thoroughly than Catholic neighborhoods." Looking only at the response of individual members of programs sponsored by the Catholic church, however, obscures the structural reasons that white Catholics resisted integration and did not flee as readily as their Jewish neighbors. Comparing the structure of Jewish synagogues and the Catholic church reveals different institutional rules surrounding membership, rootedness, and governance of each church. The Catholic parish system defines membership geographically. Churches are viewed as permanent structures that root parishioners in that place. Jewish synagogue membership is seen as voluntary and tied more to the Torah than to a geographic location. In addition, the Catholic church's rules on authority follow a hierarchical structure of governance, where the parish "does not exist apart from a priest and a hierarchy" (Gamm 1999: 19). In comparison, the Jewish synagogue is structured around congregational authority, within which the rabbi and religious hierarchy are subordinated. Understanding this structure provides a deeper understanding of the serious commitment white Catholics had for their neighborhoods, as well as their fear of integration.

Beyond individual and institutional structures, racial change and white flight were tied to the broader structural shifts that began in the 1960s and 1970s. Indeed, the popular narrative about racial change in northern cities involves a small number of blacks moving into the neighborhood, concerned whites beginning to panic about housing values or the prospect of black neighbors, and moving within a few years. While this did occur in numerous northern neighborhoods, complex changes occurring in urban America were also at play. A generalized urban crisis emerged during this time that originated not just in white antipathy toward black neighbors or the wave of black mobilization and uprisings of the late 1960s. Instead, urban historians point to long-simmering issues surrounding deindustrialization, racial segregation, and declining housing that entangled to set the stage for urban crisis (Sugrue 1996). Beginning in the late 1940s and 1950s, manufacturing industries started to automate production and relocate plants to suburban and rural locales. Thus, the once dependable urban jobs that helped thousands gain a foothold in the middle class started to become less plentiful. Also, the lines of racial segregation were formed and shored up in these decades, as migrating blacks from the American South came to northern cities (Massey and Denton 1993). In Chicago, incoming blacks were packed into a narrow band of streets in the black belt, creating pressure on the borders of white neighborhoods, as well as an economic incentive for blockbusters to exploit white fears of integration (Hirsch 1983). As the formerly tight racial lines began to break up, whites who had previously given little thought to how institutional racism protected their segregated white spaces began to feel abandoned. Finally, decline of urban neighborhoods did not occur simply when blacks moved in. Cities across the country suffered a blight problem after decades of untouched deterioration during the Great Depression and World War II. In her research on Chicago's West Side, Amanda Seligman (2005) notes that concern over blight dates to the 1950s, with the city enforcement of building codes making it very difficult for new black families to afford or maintain their houses.

As whites began to flee their neighborhoods, federal intervention created pathways for flight by placing a high value on suburban housing while devaluing much of the older city stock of housing (Lassiter 2006). With the onset of the Great Depression and, in particular, the collapse of the home finance sector, the federal government intervened by creating the Home Owners Loan Corporation (HOLC) to revive financial institutions, stimulate the market for homes, and reform the mortgage process. The HOLC also used a color-coded ranking system for neighborhoods that favored new, white, and middle-class areas and marked in red (for least desirable) older and minority neighborhoods.[6] Accepting existing racial segregation and prejudices, the HOLC applied notions of ethnic and racial worth, perpetuating segregation and generating a new market that discriminated against nonwhites (Jackson 1985). Assessing the intervention of the federal government in the housing industry, David Freund (2007: 133) notes, "The new federal presence in housing markets did not merely institutionalize segregation by putting state authority and state resources behind the impulse. It codified and then administered a racially exclusionary system of housing economics." These institutional practices, seemingly designed to protect property rights for whites, ended up creating chaos and disadvantage for whites who lived on the racial borders. In fact, this social location is one that many of our respondents look back on and describe as "traumatic."

The HOLC's appraisal logic had a lasting impact on the housing industry. Private lending institutions and other government programs adopted the agency's residential security maps, its appraisal system, and the definition of "minority homeownership as an actuarial risk to white people"

(Freund 2007: 118). The HOLC's impact was greatest on the Federal Housing Administration (FHA). The FHA was designed to stimulate private investment in home mortgages by insuring them against losses. Between 1934 and 1968, the FHA revolutionized the home finance industry by reducing down payments, extending the repayment period, establishing minimum construction standards, and shrinking interest rates by reducing risk to lenders (Jackson 1985). Yet because of the underlying logic, the FHA also invested in segregation and suburbia over integration and cities. For example, the FHA favored single-family homes over multifamily units. Also, in establishing construction standards, the FHA established minimum requirements for lot size, how far the house was set back from the street, and separation from adjacent structures, all of which favored the suburbs. Finally, the "unbiased professional estimate that was a prerequisite for any loan" was often biased against diverse environments, dense areas, and "inharmonious racial or nationality groups" (Jackson 1980: 435–436). Thus, the estimated $119 trillion provided by the FHA in its first four decades went largely to white, middle-class residents who chose to live in the suburbs. Suburbanization furthered the urban crisis, deepening the problems of cities and encouraging decline in many neighborhoods. Robert Beauregard (2002:94–95) notes, "The departure of the white middle class left the cities with lower property assessments and lower tax revenues, increased crime, poorer health, greater social and economic dependency, more family instability, and larger governmental expenditures." As middle-class families fled, cities felt the effects of fewer individuals paying property taxes, the speed-up of deindustrialization, and the beginning of widespread neighborhood deterioration. For many whites, these factors remained invisible, while blackness was seen as the cause of the deterioration. In short, while these institutions created the context in which integration was undermined through economic practices, most whites blamed blacks for declining property values. Between 1950 and 1970, large numbers of whites began to leave their old neighborhoods for the suburbs.

Whites fleeing central cities left not only their old neighborhoods and religious institutions but also their political identity. From the 1930s to the mid-1960s, a liberal governing coalition united disparate groups of working-class citizens (e.g., urban northerners, rural southerners, and blacks) by promising that the state would protect their economic interests and social security. The New Deal coalition, as it is known, stretched from Washington to the Deep South and to big cities in the North. As Thomas Sugrue (1996: 10) notes, "White and black Americans took the promise of liberalism seriously and mobilized in the 1940s and 1950s to assert their rights as citizens." Whites centered their organizing on the expansion of unions and workers' rights, but it also included mobilizing around protecting their class positions and racial identities. The New Deal coalition, however, began to seriously fray in the 1960s around issues of race. Jonathan Rieder (1989: 244) notes, if there was one "single source of displeasure that shook the New Deal Coalition to its core, it was the civil rights revolution." Working-class urban ethnics, Catholics, and northern whites, who were loyal to the Democratic Party, felt threatened by the "broad array of social and cultural changes" occurring during this period (Formisano 1991: 236). Such feelings are understandable, given that working white men and women were the main beneficiaries of this coalition. Thomas and Mary Edsall (1991: 30) note, "By the 1960s, . . . liberalism had begun to press an agenda that increasingly targeted benefits to minorities and provoked often divisive reactions—including cultural and racial antagonisms, anger over reverse discrimination as well as over threatened white hegemony, fear of crime, and distress at continued family dissolution. The struggle to expand and enforce citizenship and constitutional rights became, by the late 1960s, a source of bitter, often subterranean, conflict, dividing rather than strengthening the once-powerful political coalition dominated by those at the bottom." Race became a wedge issue as whites interpreted civil rights gains—from fair housing to school desegregation, busing, and affirmative action—as having gone too far. Whites began to see themselves as negatively affected by race and race politics, choosing then to flee their neighborhoods and abandon the Democratic Party to be "re-born right" (Nicolaides 2002: 285).

The Democratic Party struggled to find answers to white discontent, while politicians attempted to exploit the concerns and fears of the white lower middle class. The emergence of the white ethnic voting bloc in the late 1960s was one part of this story. White ethnic politics during this time centered on fighting off perceived threats to group status, complete with resentment toward government programs favoring blacks and a concern over crime. Rather than joining blacks in their struggle, whites began to claim that as white ethnics they were also victims (Sugrue and Skrentny 2008). The Republican Party, for its part, sought to build a new coalition around taxes and race in an attempt to break up the liberal coalition that had unified the economic interest of the poor. Edsall and Edsall argue that the GOP attempted to divide this coalition by drawing in disaffected whites through a divisive rhetoric of loss and victimization. For example, the GOP framed the issue of taxes in terms of what government takes from whites, not what it provides to various groups. This focus on the costs of liberalism resonated with whites who experienced "loss of control of school selection, union apprenticeship programs, hiring, promotions, neighborhoods, public safety, and even sexual morals and a stable social order" (Edsall and Edsall 1991: 11). The GOP also framed the emergence of black power and the urban riots that occurred in cities across the country in the late 1960s as the failure of liberal social policies (e.g., school desegregation and busing) and embraced law-and-order rhetoric (Formisano 1991; Sugrue and Skrentny 2008). By the late 1960s, what has been termed the "white backlash" had picked up steam as many northern urban whites were drawn into the Republican Party, whose leaders capitalized on white fears of crime, busing, housing integration, and a loss of rights.

As whites pushed back on the Civil Rights Movement, the language of rights became a powerful organizing tool. For many whites living in urban neighborhoods, homeowners' rights were counterpoised to the Civil Rights Movement, as it was perceived that civil rights were helping blacks by eroding the privileges whites had worked so hard to attain. As whites pushed back on the Civil Rights Movement, the language of rights became a powerful organizing tool. In the 1950s and 1960s whites began to move away from an old narrative that centered on race toward one that centered on "a person's relationship to place and to property" (Freund 2007: 18). This narrative, complete with racial codes, suggested that whites had consistently shown superiority in owning, maintaining, and protecting their property; thus, they had the right to secure their houses and neighborhoods from threats. Sugrue explored this notion when looking at the rise of the homeowners' rights movement, in which whites began to couch their claims in terms of entitlement and victimization. He notes, "Some defined homeowner's rights as an extension of their constitutional right to freedom of assembly. They had a right to choose their associates. That right would be infringed if their neighborhoods were racially mixed" (Sugrue 1996: 219). Undoubtedly, class resentment fueled white mobilization during this period, as whites expressed a populist rage not only against civil rights groups but also against wealthy, and liberal, whites. Often on the front lines of the black struggle for social justice, lower middle-class and working-class whites viewed calls for integration as hypocritical and dismissive (Podair 2004). In the 1970s, whites in Boston complained bitterly that busing was singling out working-class communities and avoiding wealthier and suburban areas (Formisano 1991). In Los Angeles, suburban whites evoked the rights language to claim their right to control their community, property, and schools (Nicolaides 2002). In most cases, whites portrayed themselves as victims of the media, politicians, and "knee-jerk" liberals who were playing "race politics" with their legitimate concerns, dismissed as just a "bunch of mindless, unfeeling racists."[7] In evoking these rights, whites often positioned themselves not as whites, but as victims of a government that had "elevated minority rights over the rights of the majority" (Sugrue 1996: 227).

For hardworking whites in lower middle-class and working-class neighborhoods, social and racial changes, fueled by the HOLC practices, must have felt like a bait and switch. Having worked hard, scrimped and saved, and endured doubling up in houses, they had finally made it; now they found the rules were changing. Segregated white spaces were being threatened by real estate firms, lending institutions, and government—that is, the very institutions that once supported these neighborhoods. As the Civil Rights Movement pressed the state for change and the state responded, whites living in segregated working-class communities felt abandoned (Hirsch 1983; Sugrue 1996; Nicolaides 2002; Kefalas 2003). Writing about Chicago neighborhoods in the 1950s and 1960s, Andrew Diamond (2009: 226) posits that "many whites in the Bungalow Belt perceived" the building of public housing near white working-class neighborhoods "as a state-driven integration initiative, [and] the *Brown* decision struck working-class whites as further proof that the government, federal or local, was clearly not looking out for their interests." Once their segregated white neighborhoods were no longer "protected" by the state (see also the Fair Housing Act of 1968), whites felt they had few choices if they wanted to continue their way of life. Becky Nicolaides (2002: 6) notes that from the 1950s through the 1970s, "Property relations became the primary mediator of class and racial power." Thus, one's home and, by extension, one's neighborhood represented much more than housing; they represented social power. And importantly, the social, cultural, and economic struggles behind the Civil Rights Movement led to several significant shifts in the U.S. racial landscape, altering the foundation of how whites understood themselves.

The varied social, religious, economic, political, and racial factors that engendered racial change and reshaped urban areas throughout the United States are well documented. We know less about the legacy of racial change.[8] In this study, we focus on this legacy, building on the well-documented research on the events, processes, and institutions involved as whites defended their communities, fled, and reconstructed new ones. To understand this legacy, however, it is important to attend to the complexity and shifting meaning of race and racial identity. As we examine the experience of growing up in racially changing neighborhoods on Chicago's Southwest and West sides from the 1950s through the 1970s, we focus on a time and space that offers a lens to understand how whiteness shifts over time. Whites born in Chicago during this time grew up in a city in which race was explicitly lived and openly talked about. In response to Civil Rights Movement victories, the state began moving toward color-blindness in legislation, actions, and words (Omi and Winant 1994). Thus, whites' experiences were grounded in particular spaces and an understanding of race that shifted over time. Such changes allow us to explore the ways in which racial privilege, or whiteness, shifts across different eras and maintains itself as a powerful force in the lives of people. Our focus is on investigating these shifting understandings, demonstrating how whiteness works to remain strong and powerful, protecting the privileges afforded to whites and working to frame whites as good, moral, and righteous.

To understand the nature of race and racial identity, it is important to clarify the meaning and landscape of race. We start with the assumption that race is a social and cultural construct, not an essence that is fixed or grounded in biology. And while race is socially constructed, what race means and the importance of the various categories are fluid, shaped by social, economic, and political forces. Within this context of shifting racial meanings, individuals learn to interpret those meanings through their daily interactions. As Michael Omi and Howard Winant (1994: 60) argue, we learn "some combination, some version, of the rules of racial classification, and of [our] own racial identity, often without obvious teaching or conscious inculcation." Through socialization, then, race becomes a common sense or a manner of knowing, explaining, or operating in the world. Part of this common sense relates to social hierarchies. Patricia Hill Collins (2000: 284) argues that we create hierarchies based on values and power so that one group is dominant and other groups are subordinate. The dominant group also creates a system of "common sense" that justifies its "right to rule." Given the presence of such a hierarchy, it is best to see race as a social fact, something that is indeed constructed (rather than inherent) but real in its consequences (Anderson 2003). Thus, while race may be an idea that is constructed by people, it is grounded in material, political, and social realities (Guglielmo 2004; Lipsitz 2006). In short, race may be in our heads, but it has measurable effects in the world.

Being on top of the racial hierarchy is tied to access to valued resources. Folks defined as white receive privilege and power for no reason other than being part of the group defined as white. Whiteness is not simply about the lack of melanin. It is about the way in which power and privilege operate in the world and is clearly linked to a struggle over desired resources (Steyn 2001). Maintaining access to resources often requires that subordinate groups be excluded. Margaret Anderson (2003: 33) has noted that race both can be constructed and "[result] in a specific distribution of differential resources." This unequal distribution of resources is not natural. It requires effort—or, to quote George Lipsitz (2006), a "possessive investment in whiteness." Lipsitz argues that conscious, deliberate, and systematic attempts to institutionalize group identity and power have provided whites with structural advantages that affect individual and group life chances and opportunities (e.g., FHA/Veterans Administration appraisal and lending practices, urban renewal efforts, lending and real estate discrimination, segregated education, and tax policy). In this way, whiteness can be understood as a process of asset accumulation for whites (Leonardo 2004). Racial identity is thus inextricably linked to a form of political behavior that is achieved through everyday processes (Boyd 2010).

Nevertheless, many whites do not recognize this privilege. Undoubtedly, as Amanda Lewis (2004: 626) notes, in a racialized social system all "actors are racialized, including whites." Most whites, however, tend not to see themselves as being racialized, having shared race-based concerns, or acting in racially motivated ways. Thus, many scholars have concluded that white racial identity or whiteness is "invisible," even an "unacknowledged norm," a "hidden identity," or an "unmarked category," masking the privileges of being on top of the racial hierarchy (Frankenberg 1993; Dyer 1997; Doane 2003; McIntosh 1992). The cultural hegemony of whiteness is maintained by making whiteness appear normal, thereby mystifying or not calling into question the racial order. In fact, most whites appear relatively unaware of the role race plays in shaping their lives or the advantages that come with white racial identity. One reason for this is that most of us see social life as a "sum total of conscious and deliberate individual activities" (Lipsitz 2006: 21). As a result, "discourse on privilege" leads many whites to view racism as individual in origin (e.g., a few bad apples) rather than exploring the structural nature of race or the systemic nature of racial privilege and disadvantage (Leonardo 2004: 140). The power of whiteness, then, results not so much from individual animus as from individualistic notions that preclude apprehension of the collective efforts made to sustain white privilege. The fact that the legal system has formally equalized individual access to resources (e.g., housing) furthers this dodging of the structural nature of race, as any "unequal group results" can be explained by individual or cultural factors (Collins 2000: 279).

White identity is more than an individualized process. It "involves the formation of social groups organized around material interests with their roots in social structure, not just individual consciousness" (Anderson 2003: 29–30). Whites may not see themselves as racial actors; however, they are racially interested and do act in racially motivated ways that serve to protect their racial interests (Hartigan 1999; Lewis 2004). This becomes clear when white interests and power are threatened. Whites claim that they are now an aggrieved group that has suffered disadvantage from "reverse" racial discrimination (Gallagher 1997; Bonilla-Silva, Lewis, and Embrick 2006). Whites explain or defend social relationships and social practices using a racialized language (Bonilla-Silva 2001b; Doane 2006). Scholars have looked at such racialized language in various ways, examining "discursive repertoires," racialized storytelling, race talk, "sincere fictions," testimonies, frames of understanding, and cultural practices (Frankenberg 1993; Delgado 1999; Myers 2005; Bonilla-Silva, Lewis, and Embrick 2006; Lipsitz 2006; Vera, Feagin, and Gordon 1995). Underlying these disparate examinations is a focus on how racial discourse shapes our common-sense understandings of the world and thus reinforces "ways of knowing" that support the racial hierarchy. As Ashley Doane (2006: 256) notes, it is through racial discourse that individuals or groups frame "racial issues as they strive for ideological and political advantage." In other words, rhetorical strategies allow whites to make racial claims that promote a particular, and privileged, position.

Examining these strategies is particularly important, given relatively recent and substantial changes in the racial structure. The Civil Rights Movement, other social movements, and legislation reframed racial politics in the United States, altering how race operated, challenging white dominance and racial exclusion (e.g., housing and schools), providing legal protection for basic civil rights, and challenging white hegemony surrounding culture and national identity. Woody Doane (2003: 15) has argued that "implicit in this process was a challenge to the historical foundations of whiteness; that is, an attack on the legitimation of white identity grounded in claims to white supremacy and the casting of whiteness as a positive and normalized alternative to a negatively defined 'racial other.'" In short, the gains of the Civil Rights Movement made it more difficult for whites to claim they were the unexamined core of U.S. culture. Yet the movements in the 1960s did not overturn racial supremacy. While the civil rights struggles challenged legalized segregation and widely held beliefs about the innate biological inferiority of blacks, a new racial democracy failed to emerge (Omi and Winant 1994; Bonilla-Silva 2001a; Forman and Lewis 2006). In fact, equality was "reinterpreted, rearticulated, reinserted in the business-as-usual framework of U.S. politics and culture" (Winant 1997). Starting in the late 1960s and early 1970s, a racial reaction movement rearticulated the meaning of race in the United States, creating a new racial common sense (Omi and Winant 1994). A new sensibility emerged that reproduces racial inequalities and protects white privilege through an alternative set of discursive strategies (Bonilla-Silva, Goar, and Embrick 2004).

These discursive strategies have altered how we talk about race, particularly how racial antipathy is expressed. The shift in racial discourse is generally described as the "color-blind era." However, the moniker should be understood as the prevalent form of racial discourse rather than as an indication that a state of racial equality has been achieved. Unlike previous periods in which racial prejudice was more overt, today whites are more likely to express such sentiments in covert, contradictory, and subtle ways (Bobo, Kluegel, and Smith 1997; Bonilla-Silva and Forman 2000; Sears and Henry 2003; Myers 2005). In a color-blind era, white stories often extol "non-racial" positive virtues of white residents and neighborhoods, with little acknowledgment of how institutions have supported whites and ignoring or discriminating against others (Feagin 2010). Other themes of color-blind discourse involve naturalizing segregation and expressing the interconnected themes of racial resentment and white victimhood (Bonilla-Silva 2009). The rise of color-bind discourse is intimately tied to the period from the late 1960s through the 1980s, when the United States experienced the rise of the "new right," an authoritarian, resentment-fueled, and right-wing populism that sought to curtail the progressive civil rights gains of the 1960s (Kazin 1995). The new right "rearticulated" such gains through a façade of racial neutrality while using racial coding or "phrases and symbols which refer indirectly to racial themes, but do not directly challenge popular and democratic or egalitarian ideals" (Omi and Winant 1994: 123). Coded terms, including "busing," "welfare," and "affirmative action," suggest that blacks do not try hard enough to overcome difficulties; that they take what they have not earned; and that the playing field is tilting away from whites (Kinder and Sanders 1996: 105–106; Wellman 1997). By the early 1980s, at the national level, the Reagan administration was borrowing from the new right, arguing that racial discrimination had been eliminated and, as a result, civil rights remedies were now working against whites and group-based rights should be challenged.

Studying Race, Studying Whites

It is in this context that we began our study with the 1966 Freedom March. Our original goal was to understand the experience of racial change for whites living in neighborhoods where the marches were held. However, a lapse of forty years made this focus impractical. An opportune meeting with the son of a leader of a Southwest Side community organization led us in the direction of looking more broadly at the legacy of racial change, particularly youth who grew up in such neighborhoods. Few studies of residential segregation and racial change have focused explicitly on youth; fewer still have looked at the legacy of racial change on the lives and racial identities of whites growing up in racially changing neighborhoods. Most studies have focused on the usual suspects—institutions (e.g., banks, real estate agents, and insurance companies), government policies, the media, and community organizations—and their role in either perpetuating or disrupting racial segregation. When youth are discussed, they are presented in two broad but uniform ways. First, they are represented as the reason that people move (e.g., safety and school quality) or as examples of racial tension when racial change occurs, particularly in schools. Second is a popular image of youth as "protectors" when they seek, often violently, to maintain the color line and their communities (Diamond 2009).[9] We seek to extend these representations by exploring the experiences with racial change and asking, "What was it like for young people to grow up in spaces that were obviously racially charged and threatened by change?" By focusing on individuals who grew up in Chicago communities that either felt threatened by or experienced racial change from the 1950s to the 1980s, we examine how young people made sense of what was occurring and how this experience affected their lives. Understanding several key issues focused our study—in particular, how our respondents saw their neighborhoods before racial change; their experience with integration or racial change; information they received from their parents and friends about race; interactions they had with blacks during racial change; and how racial change, or the threat of racial change, affected their racial worldviews and residential choices years after racial change.

These issues became the heart of our multiyear, multi-method research project to understand the experience of racial change through the eyes of former white residents. Our project focused on neighborhoods that were undergoing racial change in the 1960s, 1970s, and 1980s, focusing on learning "what was going on" or how whites growing up in neighborhoods before and during racial change made sense of their experiences and memories of that time. Our research design initially focused on several of Chicago's Southwest Side neighborhoods (i.e., Gage Park, Chicago Lawn, West Lawn, and West Elsdon), an area that experienced racial change starting in the 1960s. We recruited respondents who grew up in these communities from 1955 to the late 1970s to ensure a range of experiences with racial change. A snowball sampling technique was used to recruit a total of fifty-three respondents for semi-structured, qualitative interviews.[10] In the end, twenty-seven respondents came from the Southwest Side. We expanded our reach by including residents who grew up in other Southwest Side communities that were undergoing racial change or were adjacent to communities undergoing racial change. Nine respondents were added from the Southwest Side neighborhoods of East Beverly, Auburn Gresham, and West Englewood. Midway through the data collection phase, an informant led us to former residents of the West Side neighborhood of Humboldt Park. We focused exclusively on a community near the Catholic parish of Our Lady of Angels, an area relatively close to Madison Street, the site of riots by blacks after the assassination of Martin Luther King Jr. in 1968 (Coates 1968; Seligman 2005). Seventeen more respondents came from this area. The design incorporated respondents representing varied experiences with racial change—specifically, proximity to and pace of racial change, as well as whether and when families moved. Approximately twenty-three respondents came from areas such as Humboldt Park, West Englewood, Auburn Gresham, and East Beverly, where racial change was occurring rapidly, with parents of children from these areas eventually moving out of the neighborhood. The other respondents lived in areas where racial change occurred more slowly. The two sets of respondents, however, shared experiences and memories that were strikingly similar. A more detailed discussion of the methods and methodology is in the Methodological Appendix.

The two broadly defined geographic areas known as the Southwest Side and West Side represent large areas within Chicago. These labels include a range of smaller neighborhoods, each with its own character, churches, geography, organizations, and challenges. We use these labels to describe the areas, acknowledging that the character of each space was distinguishable. And although separated geographically and unique in character, the two sections of Chicago have common features. Both areas are best described as entrenched communities or places that had a strong sense of place. People moving to these communities were not transients. Expecting to stay for years to come, residents invested in these spaces, meticulously maintaining their homes and gardens. And they were family-oriented spaces: people knew one another well. Shelia, who grew up in Gage Park, notes, "You knew everybody on your block . . . everybody!" The front porch or stoop was a centerpiece of community life in the 1960s and 1970s, serving as a social and an entertainment space, particularly on summer evenings. Such a communal existence led to one's private life bleeding into the public. It also led to a strong sense of security and solidarity for residents. Residents recall leaving doors unlocked, with little care for safety. Patricia, who grew up on the Southwest Side, recalls, "We always felt like we were secure and part of a group, part of a neighborhood; it was great." Others recall "everyone looking out for one another."

For children, these Southwest and West side neighborhoods were marked by friendship, exploration, and security. Blocks had dozens of kids, most of whom played sports or games in the streets or in the alleys behind the houses. Former residents recall summer days when they would leave their houses in the morning and their parents expected them in at dinner and again when the street lights came on. Play during this era was informal, orchestrated by kids. "When you were a little kid, you didn't need to be driven to any parks," Dave remembers. "You didn't have to be involved in organized sports. . . . [I]t was always neighborhood kids." Outside sports, kids in these neighborhoods felt the freedom to explore their neighborhoods, particularly on bikes, without a lot of restriction. These neighborhoods also allowed kids to walk short distances to neighborhood dime stores, local markets, or ice cream and pizza shops. The abundance of children and general sense of security were supported by a strong sense of shared parenting; adults did not hesitate to tell kids how to act. As Betty, who grew up in West Englewood, notes, "It was one of the neighborhoods that if your mother didn't catch you doing something, somebody else's mother would, and they would tell you [they]'re going to tell your mother. Or 'Hey, you stop that.'"

Chicago neighborhoods during this time were akin to urban villages, small towns in a major city. These areas, on the West Side and Southwest Side, were a "community of neighborhoods, with bungalows and duplex homes, neighborhood stores, and many schools and churches to meet the needs of its large families" (McCourt 1977: 32). While likely unfamiliar to kids today, neighborhood life functioned as relatively contained areas. Tommy notes, "Living in the neighborhoods of Chicago was the best of both worlds. In the neighborhoods there was a small town atmosphere, but then you were living in the great city of Chicago." On the Southwest Side, Western Avenue was the commercial hub. Businesses catering to particular ethnic groups dotted these locations. On the West Side, Chicago Avenue was the hub. David Cowan and John Kuenster (1998: 9–10), writing about Chicago Avenue in the late 1950s, describe the street as having "a mix of businesses sprinkled with Italian names. Bakeries and butcher shops, cafes and produce stands were jammed among an array of small grocery stores, dime stores, drugstores, clothing stores, barber shops, pool halls, social clubs, restaurants, taverns, bowling alleys, and two movie houses." Donnie, who lived only a few blocks from Chicago Avenue, says, "All our safeguards were in that neighborhood, the stores, all the Italian stores. Every store you wanted on Chicago Avenue. Anything you wanted." With such a rich neighborhood life, many former residents do not recall leaving the neighborhood until high school. Phil from the West Side states, "I don't ever remember being downtown. I remember we went to Harlem Avenue. My mother had a friend who lived out there. We thought we were going so far."

From early in its history, Chicago has been defined by a patchwork of ethnic neighborhoods. And while sections of the city have been ethnically identified—the Italian Taylor Street, the Czech Pilson, the Polish West Town, or the Irish parts of the South Side—these spaces were never ethnically segregated. The neighborhoods on the Southwest and West sides were similar, as both communities were made up of second- and third-generation immigrants, largely from Europe and primarily Catholic. On the Southwest Side, the area consisted of numerous small ethnic enclaves where one could still find "Polish, Lithuanian, German, and Italian neighborhoods with their own bakeries, grocery stores, and restaurant" (McCourt 1977: 32). This was particularly true of the Lithuanians, who moved to Marquette Park beginning in the 1940s, setting up major institutions (e.g., Holy Cross Hospital and Nativity Blessed Virgin Mary Church) and an ethnically themed section near Marquette Park appropriately named "Lithuanian Plaza" (Cutler 1982). While ethnic mixing had occurred by the late 1960s due to intermarriage and mobility, many residents had parents or grandparents who spoke only limited English. Yet these different groups were rarely concentrated on specific blocks. On the West Side, the neighborhood surrounding Our Lady of Angels parish was more than half Italian, with a sizable Irish population and a smaller Polish group (Cowan and Kuenster 1998). Residents were first-generation Americans, their parents having arrived in America from Italy; many of them spoke only Italian in the home.

For immigrants in Chicago, moving to single-family homes in neighbor-hoods on the Southwest or West side was intimately tied to class status and social mobility. Undeniably, to be a resident on the Southwest or West Side in the 1950s and 1960s likely meant that one's life was caught up in one of the great periods of economic growth and prosperity in the United States. Expectations were high. In the twenty-five years between 1948 and 1973, the country emerged as the dominant world power: its economy was expanding; incomes were rising for most people; and more and more people were begin-ning to own their own homes (Patterson 1996). Things were looking up for urban residents, and further growth seemed inevitable (Beauregard 2006). Having only recently escaped crowded and rundown apartment buildings in other parts of the city, where they often endured doubling up with extended family, dealing with renters, and less desirable conditions, this growth rep-resented for whites of the Southwest and West sides an ascent to the bottom rungs of the middle class. Considered upper working-class or, to be generous, lower middle-class, residents on the Southwest Side have been described as "policemen and firemen, pipefitters and steamfitters, workers in the Clearing railroad and at Midway Airport" or "Nabisco, at 73rd and Kedzie" (Ehren-halt 1996: 92).[11] Those on the West Side have been described as "ordinary hardworking people who cared deeply about their families and took pride in their community" (Cowan and Kuenster 1998: 9). In general, most of the men were blue-collar workers and usually wage employees, while others were policemen, firemen, or maintenance workers or owned and operated small shops and businesses. With these jobs, whites by the 1950s had achieved "bread and home" and a degree of economic security (Hirsch 1983: 195). Moving to these neighborhoods was a move away from past problems to a single-family home, the middle class, and, importantly, respectability.

The tree-lined, lower middle-class or working-class communities gener-ally referred to as the "bungalow belt" feature modest, well-kept homes inter-spersed with two- and three-flat apartment buildings. At this time, moving to the bungalow belt represented achieving the success, security, community, and achievement that embodies the American Dream. As Dominic Pacyga (2003: 134) notes, "The bungalow belt had always symbolized upward mobil-ity and middle-class status for Chicagoans. Home ownership, neat lawns, steady jobs, a fine education for children, consumer goods, especially an automobile, a particularly intense American patriotism has long been identi-fied with the city's outlying neighborhoods." In other words, homes in these areas were "monuments" to those hardworking men and women living there who "embrace 'American' values surrounding home, neighborhood, and nation" (Kefalas 2003: 153). Given their recent arrival in these neighbor-hoods and the middle class, whites, scholars have noted, "jealously guarded" their homes and their communities (McCourt 1977: 32). In these spaces, the home represented more than an individual achievement. It was a communal achievement, tied to the interrelated spheres of family, parish, and neighborhood (Sugrue 1996).

The role of the Catholic parish and the parish school in these neighborhoods was also significant. As noted above, Catholic parishes were a principal way life was organized in neighborhoods. In the 1950s and 1960s, this was certainly true on the Southwest and West sides. Numerous Catholic parishes served the Southwest Side, including St. Gall, Queen of the Universe, Our Lady Star of the Sea, St. Nicholas of Tolentine, St. Sabina, St. Simon, St. Adrians, and St. Turbius. On the West Side, Our Lady of Angels anchored the community in the 1950s and 1960s, becoming one of the largest parishes in Chicago, with roughly 4,500 registered families. The majority of Catholic families sent their children to the parish school.[12] The parish also was a center for community organizing. Many local community groups held their meetings at the church and received support from the priests. The Southwest Parish and Neighborhood Federation (Parish Federation), a powerful community organization discussed in Chapter 2, is one such example, having been founded through support from a "federation" of Catholic parishes.

Race was also a central feature of these communities. Although these areas contained a mix of ethnic groups, they were considered white, and that identity was defined in part by the threat to their way of life posed by proximity to black communities to the east. As racial change began to threaten these communities, race became a central lens for interpreting neighborhood life and action. In discussing her research on the Southwest Side in the early 1970s, Kathleen McCourt notes that "there has developed throughout the entire community an obsession with racial change and an atmosphere in which anything new in the community is viewed in terms of its potential for accelerating or slowing down ultimate racial change" (McCourt 1977: 44). Racial change became a common topic of conversation, including when it would occur and which neighbors might be moving. In many ways, these areas represented "defended communities," spaces that respond by attempting to "seal [themselves] off" as a response to "fears of invasion from adjacent areas" (Suttles 1972: 21). As racial change approached these neighborhoods, fear and anxiety was pervasive. For some, the fear came from a perception that they would not be safe if blacks moved in; for others, it was an indirect fear that they would be losing their community and "whatever cultural identity remain[ed] to them" (McCourt 1977: 40).

Chicago's Southwest and West sides are intriguing places to examine racial settlement patterns, given the extent and rapidity of racial change in the decades after World War II. To understand the memories and place attachments of our respondents, it is important to understand the context of the neighborhoods in which they grew up. This context includes institutionally rich, socially interconnected neighborhoods, where individuals and families felt grounded. Often populated by recent immigrants to the United States, these spaces served as important locations for social mobility. For residents, owning a home in the bungalow belt was not only an investment in their future; it was also a symbol of their worth, based on the values of hard work and connections to family, neighborhood, and the parish. Race and racial identity are also significant factors that are woven into this context. Racial change threatened not only the strength of these communities and the investment in their homes but also their identities.

Plan of the Book

We begin our analysis of the legacy of racial change by examining the social and economic context of Chicago's lower middle-class and working-class neighborhoods during the 1960s, 1970s, and 1980s. Appreciating these neighborhoods is important, given that such a context undoubtedly shaped how our respondents made sense of racial change, their social ties, and themselves. In Chapter 2, we begin by surveying the shifting social, economic, and racial context of the Southwest Side (specifically, near Marquette Park) during this period. In doing so, we explore how the contours of race and class at local and national levels shaped the organizing strategies of those whites who chose to stay as racial borders began to shift. Examining historical documents, we use the case of the Parish Federation to explore the most significant organizational response by whites as racial change threatened their neighborhoods. Founded in 1972 by the Catholic church, the Parish Federation aggressively sought to improve and stabilize white neighborhoods on Chicago's Southwest Side. Moving beyond the federation's intent, actions, and accomplishments, we explore the racial discourse that surrounds its organizing efforts. As we demonstrate, neighborhood attachments were crucial to the lives of white Chicagoans, and in the postwar period race was the lens through which they understood the strength of those bonds. On the Southwest Side, whites perceived that the tables in the city had turned by the mid-1970s, leaving them feeling abandoned, ignored, and even targeted by the government and financial institutions. Early in its history, the Parish Federation organized as whites, but by the early 1980s they realized the importance of ethnic identity as a basis for organizing, self-consciously referring to themselves as white ethnics. In their defensive efforts to remain "good" in their own eyes as well as others' (i.e., the media and wealthier North Side and Lakefront whites or in the suburbs), they publicly framed their actions in non-racialized terms and at the same time (re)claimed their own white *ethnic* identity. The switch to "ethnic" allowed whites to make claims to a racialized group identity while simultaneously asserting that their neighborhood battles were not racially based. In other words, instead of fleeing, the Parish Federation began a fight for whites' neighborhoods, and ultimately their group position, by drawing on the theme of whiteness as liability while avoiding consideration of shared obligations to nonwhites.

In the next two chapters, we move from the past to the present, using data from our respondents to explore the stories that whites tell about their experience with racial change. Attending to the memories whites have of a racially explicit time provides great insight not only into the legacy of racial change and the white reaction to integration in urban America but also into how constructions of race are tied to racial identity construction. As we lay out our respondents' recollections, we are cautious to neither read their memories as "fact" nor refute specific memories of the time of racial change. Instead, we focus on understanding how whites frame their memories and make sense of their experiences. All memory is framed in a social context, and here we look to understand how memories are racialized. Indeed, racial narratives or stories are crucial for bolstering white racial identity, privilege, and racialized solidarity. In a racialized culture, it is difficult to see the racialized other as one of us. Through discourse and action, whites create and maintain racial borders, both physical and ideological, that preclude them from seeing shared obligations with nonwhites. In these chapters, our focus is on the use of racial discourse and memory to bolster white racial identity in ways that limit the ability of whites to disrupt racial inequality and subordination.

In Chapter 3, we specify the ways in which whites made sense of the racial borders in their everyday lives. We begin with an analysis of the physical layout of the areas and agree with Jane Jacobs's idea that "a border exerts an active influence" (Jacobs 1961: 256). Major streets on the Southwest Side (i.e., Western) and West Side (i.e., Chicago Avenue) share the distinction of being well-known physical borders that served as barriers, not seams, between the white neighborhood on one side and the black neighborhood on the other. These avenues were fixed, stable barriers against which whites could situate their lives and identities. The closer to the border they lived, worked, shopped, or played, the more aware they became of the threat to their segregated "idyllic" world. In addition to physical borders, other, less tangible racial borders existed, including those that defined acceptable choices for marriage and family, friendship networks, schools, and leisure spaces. Reinforced through racial socialization, these other borders strongly mediated how individuals defined themselves in the world. In fact, the borders were pervasive enough that most believed them to be a reflection of a natural order of human communities. As the physical borders began to shift through fair housing demands, legislation, panic peddling, and mortgage discrimination, the "way of life," the idyllic world, was threatened. At the same time, televisions were now sitting in most living rooms projecting, in living color, images of a world of protests, interracial couples, riots, drugs, and myriad other threatening images. The physical and ideological border, now breached, meant that these now vulnerable whites needed to respond. A central piece of the response was a tightening of racial borders through an engagement in explicit racialized discourse and action.

In Chapter 4, we pay particular attention to how memories are racialized by examining the stories white residents tell of the period prior to and after racial change occurred in their neighborhoods. Racial change did alter the place attachments for many respondents, unraveling the knitted nature of the community, generating varied emotions, and altering identities. Our respondents frequently spoke nostalgically of their old neighborhoods and a time that life seemed good—that is, orderly, friendly, safe, and homogeneously white. Nostalgia narratives are an important way individuals react to social disruptions, framing memory in such a way that one selects positive elements from one's personal history, scrubbing away memories that are unpleasant. Here we explore the use of nostalgia narratives and race talk by whites to construct, maintain, and repair a positive white racial identity through color-blind discourse, even when facing social contradictions (e.g., victims who are engaged in violence and a feeling of powerlessness amid recollections of "flight" and "fight" responses). Recalling racial change through a nostalgic lens and using color-blind language, whites claim to be victims of overwhelming circumstances (e.g., institutional practices and state-based changes) or "others" (i.e., unruly blacks) and are rarely able to see other alternatives (e.g., integration) or the actions of whites that hastened racial change or impeded integration. In the process, we see that nostalgia narratives of the old neighborhood serve as a strategy to regain white ownership, provide common-sense understandings of how to achieve a good life, and validate a social hierarchy of white as good and justifiably dominant. These memory-making activities illustrate another possessive investment in whiteness and are the foundation of contemporary white racial discourse.

Finally, in Chapter 5 our focus turns to exploring racial knowledge and ignorance as connected to whites' ability to empathize (i.e., walk in another's shoes) and build genuine relationships across race lines. Racialized knowledge is the "what" and "how" whites know, ultimately shaping the ways whites are able to imagine how others experience the world. For example, we found that many whites "know" white racism as an individual failing. For our respondents, that failing or flaw can be understood, and thus tolerated, based on their knowledge and empathy for a history in which whites suffered from racial change. For example, we find that whites extend empathy for racist individuals, given their experience with racial change (for some, the loss their neighborhoods). Thus, in this case, whites empathize with the other whites who hold racist views while ignoring black pain and suffering. Here racialized knowledge impedes the empathy that whites feel for other groups. In short, the empathy is bounded by race. When asked how to overcome racism, respondents claim that education and exposure to other racial groups are key. In exploring these claims, our data demonstrate that whites had very little exposure to blacks growing up, a reality that led to many distorted images of blacks and ultimately to general ignorance of how racial change and continued segregation affect the lives of blacks. And while exposure and education are important first steps, they are clearly not enough to shift racialized boundaries between whites and blacks. Instead, what is required to create solidarity across racial boundaries is structural change that creates equity, fair housing, access to inclusive education, and a cultural shift in which exposure, education, trust, and an explicit discussion of empathy are central.

The common thread, woven through the various chapters of this book is that whites put a fair amount of effort into creating and maintaining racial solidarity and whiteness, often in subtle and unreflective ways. Our interviews reveal the ways in which whites were socialized to recognize and protect racial borders, lessons that stayed with them throughout their lives. Clearly, both racial socialization and whiteness influence how we remember our past. In this case, via the sharing of memories, our respondents continue to reinforce whiteness through efforts to naturalize racial boundaries and specific attempts to bolster group position. Here we see the process of whiteness, woven through the structures of society and evident in racial discourse, creating racialized ways of knowing and leading to bounded empathy. Through these efforts, racial solidarity and group identity are strengthened as whites continue to recognize racial differences and boundaries. In the end, racial solidarity and bounded empathy limits one's capacity for humanity.

2

Controlling the Change

White Ethnics, White Victims

O n April 29, 1984, after a long process of community organizing, whites from working-class neighborhoods on Chicago's Southwest and Northwest sides staged an official convention to explore issues important to the people of the neighborhood. The Southwest Parish and Neighborhood Federation (Parish Federation) joined with the Northwest Neighborhood Federation to form the Save Our Neighborhoods, Save Our City (SON/SOC) coalition. The coalition opened its "White Ethnic Convention" with the following words: "Ladies and Gentlemen, I say to you now that we are tired of apologizing for being white. We are tired of having to pay for the protection that should be ours by right. The time has come for neighborhood change to end. The city must once again become a healthy and secure place to live that our families can be proud of."[1] Using the language of loss and victimization, the coalition framed its grievances in racial language. Central to these concerns was the use of "white ethnic" as a self-descriptor. As with neighborhood groups from across the country, the white ethnic response centered on destabilizing forces, such as real estate and Federal Housing Administration (FHA) practices, schools, crime, economic development, scattered site public housing, and protecting their home values. Underlying the white ethnic response was insecurity about the changes in the racial, class, and social structure of the city and, ultimately, the larger nation.

For working-class residents of urban neighborhoods, the moorings of the racial and class structure were breaking free. Deindustrialization, suburbanization, racial change, and white flight were reshaping cities. In addition, the successive events of Martin Luther King's civil rights housing campaign of 1966, the race riots on the West Side after King's assassination, the disturbances at the Democratic National Convention in 1968 , and the murders of members of the Black Panther Party elevated race as a central issue in the city. As Larry Bennett (2011: 4) notes, Mayor Richard J. Daley's "'city that works' had suddenly crashed. In its place was a racially divided, economically crippled emblem of the soon to be dubbed Rust Belt." At the neighborhood level, the institutions (e.g., banks, real estate, and government) that once shored up segregated housing markets began to turn their backs on those they had once protected: white residents. A pattern of redlining, panic peddling, and blockbusting led to a predictable pattern of block-by-block racial transition along the edges of the ghetto, creating a good deal of insecurity and fear among whites. All of these changes left working-class whites feeling squeezed from the top and the bottom, leading many to organize to protect what they now framed as "group-based" interests and to give voice to their collective concerns.

The Parish Federation was founded in 1971 through Catholic Charities, which in the early 1970s funded professional organizers to work in a number of Chicago neighborhoods that faced deterioration and the deleterious outcomes of economic and racial change.[2] The Parish Federation's organizing reflected a "neighborhood-based, participatory politics" that began to emerge in the 1970s, particularly in working-class white neighborhoods (Bennett 1987). This "backyard revolution" or "urban populism" included a varied mix of groups on the right and left that campaigned against, among other things, "downtown interests," "city hall," and "power brokers" (Boyte 1980; Swanstrom 1985; Osman 2008). Emerging out of Alinsky and neo-Alinsky traditions, the neighborhood movement held to a steadfast belief that neighborhood action is a starting point for social change and attempted to challenge "power relations within and beyond the neighborhood" (Fisher 1994: 146). Across the country, such group activities ranged from protesting urban renewal and highway construction to preventing redlining, panic peddling, and blockbusting. From this movement emerged white ethnic leaders who took on downtown interests and powerbrokers while "eulogizing safe, white enclaves, demanding community control over schools, and calling for neighborhood preservation" (Teaford 1990; Formisano 1991; Osman 2008: 112). Emblematic of this movement, the Parish Federation did not seek broader goals (e.g., economic restructuring), focusing instead on family and neighborhood and on protesting corporate and government practices (Bennett 1987; Squires et al. 1987). The Parish Federation got to work quickly in giving the Southwest Side a chance for neighborhood preservation and stability, trying to halt white flight and neighborhood deterioration. In the process, it framed its efforts in the language of grievance that highlighted whites' precarious racial and class position.

In this chapter, we examine how changes in the racial, class, and social environment in cities intersected with a larger movement that sought to rearticulate the meaning of race through color-blind discourses. The year of the SON/SOC convention marked Ronald Reagan's second term as president, with a continued agenda toward creating color-blind discourses undermining civil rights legislation. By 1984, the Civil Rights Movement was viewed as history by many whites and some blacks, who saw the passing of the major pieces of legislation as leveling the playing field—or moving us in the direction of a leveled playing field. Whiteness as a form of social privilege was increasingly visible, and whites would either have to acknowledge this privilege or develop new strategies to maintain it (Doane 2006). As whites fought to protect their slipping privilege and power, they used racialized language at a time that racialized language, in its explicit form, was losing favor in dominant discourse. We argue that white residents of the Southwest Side, close to the racial and economic borders, were caught up in the turmoil of institutional practices that were shifting or morphing to comply with the new civil rights legislation and still uphold whiteness. These men and women chose to mirror the tactics of the Civil Rights Movement through claims to a shared white ethnic identity—a group-based claim—to have a voice and press the state for protection. After presenting the context for their organizing, we trace the narrative presented by the Parish Federation as it toiled to stabilize its neighborhoods. This setting is important to understanding the social forces that shaped the neighborhoods in which our respondents grew up.

Not Tennis Country

Mike Royko once described the working-class nature of the Southwest Side by claiming, "That's not tennis country."[3] Royko's apt description signifies the tenuous class structure of Chicago's outlying neighborhoods in the decades after World War II. For whites in the 1960s and 1970s, owning a home represented economic security and a foothold on the American Dream. A bungalow, for first- and second-generation immigrants on the Southwest and West sides, was a step up from poorer neighborhoods, representing a lifetime of work, sweat, and sacrifice. For the aspiring class, their home was their retirement plan. The city in which they lived, however, was both unsettled and uncertain. As in other major cities, particularly in the urban North, complex, numerous, and overlapping factors were reshaping Chicago. For many working-class to middle-class whites, these changes created a fair amount of concern and led many to question whether their homes, neighborhoods, and ways of life could be extended to the next generation (Bennett 2013). Racial shifts in population and geography, economic restructuring, and suburban growth all weighed heavily on the minds of residents. These changes not only threatened their social status but also challenged dominant forms of white political power and cultural dominance.

Clearly, race was a central concern and a driving force for reshaping northern cities in the 1960s and 1970s. The interrelated forces of white flight and suburbanization dramatically reshaped residential neighborhoods throughout the urban North. From 1940 through the 1970s, roughly four million blacks left the rural South for urban areas, dramatically increasing the black population share in most northern and western cities (Massey and Denton 1993). Robert Beauregard (2002: 137) notes that "the rate of growth of the African American minority in nearly every one of the fifty cities [in the United States] was greater than that of the white majority." Beauregard goes on to report that between 1960 and 1968, the white population shrank in absolute terms in every central city on this list while the minority population increased. In Chicago between 1940 and the late 1960s, the black population increased by 600,000 residents, and by the late 1960s one in four Chicagoans was nonwhite (Abu-Lughod 2000). In most northern cities, the incoming blacks were confined to specific neighborhoods, or "black belts." As the densities grew in these neighborhoods, blacks began to look for housing in white neighborhoods, and various institutional agents sought to exploit white fears for profit (Frey 1979). As a result, a period of rapid racial change began in many formerly white neighborhoods. Chicago was no different. As Bennett (2013: xviii) notes, "From the mid-1950s until the 1970s, the ultimate source of tension in Chicago was the battle over residential space."

As was occurring in many cities, as blacks were moving in, whites were moving out. Between 1950 and 1970, roughly 900,000 whites left Chicago, with many relocating just beyond the city limits to the suburban rings of Cook County, and others to the metropolitan "collar" counties. The influx of black residents and the potential expansion of the black ghetto was a central concern for white residents. The black ghetto for many whites symbolized declining property values, poverty, and social disorganization, threatening their recent arrival to the privileges of whiteness (Hirsch 1983; Guglielmo 2004). The influx of blacks began to change the racial geography of the city, and whites fled. For middle-class and working-class residents on the South and West Sides, the new and shifting racial boundaries left many feeling "under siege," and they organized to resist these and other changes, such as public housing projects (Pacyga 2010: 307). Integration was not seen as an option. While some whites did resist, others chose to leave. Some moved a neighborhood or two to the west; others left for the suburbs. As Janet Abu-Lughod (2000: 230) notes, "If ever there has been a classic case of white flight, it happened in Chicago."

The flight from cities was obviously more complex than simple racial prejudice. A variety of institutional decisions were influential in pulling whites to the suburbs. One of the pulls was industry. In the nineteenth century and early twentieth century, industry centralized in urban areas because they provided easier access to transportation, raw materials, and workers. American cities began to shift shortly after World War II to a pattern of decentralization as the movement of industry and jobs dramatically reshaped the residential landscape of major northern cities. Thomas Sugrue (1996: 127–128) notes that the so-called Rust Belt in the North "lost hundreds of thousands of manufacturing jobs beginning the 1950s, as firms reduced employment in center-city plants, replaced workers with automated technology, and constructed new facilities in suburban and semirural areas, in medium-sized cities, often in less industrialized states or regions, and even in other countries." By the 1970s, many commercial and industrial businesses—and, increasingly residential investors—viewed central cities as undesirable locations to do business. The cost of industrial disinvestment went well beyond lost wages, seriously affecting the well-being of many workers and the fiscal stability of municipal governments, and heightening tension between central cities and their suburbs (Bluestone and Harrison 1982; Beauregard 2002).

The city of Chicago was typical of these broad trends, although it did fare a bit better than other Rust Belt cities such as Detroit and Cleveland. Chicago witnessed a tapering off in industrial employment following World War II, with about 250 plants leaving Chicago for the suburbs in the first five years after the war (Rast 1999). The truly sharp decline in manufacturing jobs, however, did not occur until the late 1960s and early 1970s. Between 1967 and 1982, Chicago lost 250,000 jobs, approximately 46 percent of its "former industrial might" (Pacyga 2010: 366). Many of these jobs moved just beyond the city limits, undermining the economic viability of working-class central city neighborhoods in the 1970s. Municipal decisions made matters worse by neglecting such neighborhoods, instead focusing on transforming the downtown core into spaces for corporate expansion and upscale residential communities. By the 1970s, the city had invested capital in and around the Loop (e.g., everything from streets to sewers), hoping to leverage private commercial and residential investment and restructure the city's economy from manufacturing to services (Rast 1999). A heavy commitment of public funds led to a downtown rebirth of sorts in terms of increasing the number of office buildings and raising property values, creating a sharp contrast with the downward path of outlying and working-class neighborhoods.

Expanding ghettos and shifting industrial locations were not the only factors leading to the ascendance of the suburbs. As in most other cities in the United States, in the Chicago suburbs a program of massive housing construction began, with approximately 700,000 new homes built in the fifteen years after World War II (Pacyga 2010). As noted in Chapter 1, federal housing initiatives such the Home Owners Loan Corporation and programs sponsored through the FHA and Veterans Administration (VA) fueled a boom in housing construction by favoring suburban locations and providing incentives to banks to lend money to families looking for homes in the suburbs. In Chicago, the 1950s signaled the decline of the city and the ascendance of the suburbs. Across the nation, suburban growth accelerated in the 1960s, growing by eleven million people in the first six years of the decade (Beauregard 2002: 135). By 1960, only 62 percent of Cook County's residents lived within the city of Chicago, a percentage that would decline in subsequent decades. By 1970, nearly half the population of the Chicago metropolitan region was living in the suburbs (Abu-Lughod 2000). Most of the new suburbanites were white, as the suburbs were largely closed to blacks. Suburban growth shifted the dynamic in urban America; the suburbs became more influential in the political, economic, social, and cultural life of the metropolitan region.

On the Southwest Side, these structural shifts were accompanied by the specter of racial change. As white lower middle-class and working-class neighborhoods lay in the predictable path of racial change, residents feared that integration meant neighborhood deterioration, including the lowering of property values and deterioration of community cohesion. Such fear was not unfounded, given the workings of the dual housing market in Chicago. Like that in other large cities, Chicago's pattern of racially segregated housing produced two housing markets: one for whites, and one for blacks. The dual housing market, a principal engine of racial change and ghettoization, worked in a predictable manner. As blacks moved north, discrimination restricted housing options to a narrow set of neighborhoods (e.g., a black belt), particularly Bronzeville on the South Side and parts of the West Side. Restricted supply for blacks and incredible demand due to migration from the South inflated rents for blacks (Hirsch 1983). Overwhelming demand for housing, a willingness by blacks to pay inflated prices to escape the black belt, and the flight of whites living in neighboring communities to the suburbs helped create a pattern of racial transition from the 1950s through the 1970s. The dual housing market both thrives on and reinforces the geographic separation of racial groups in U.S. cities.[4]

The dual housing market is not a natural occurrence. Interrelated and overlapping institutional actors contribute to its existence. In the 1960s and 1970s, real estate firms and the home finance industry were key actors. Racial change created fear and despair for many whites, and real estate brokers capitalized on these emotions in various ways. One way was by steering potential white homeowners to white areas and blacks to transition areas.

An Urban League study indicated that such steering was common on the Southwest Side in the 1970s (Fox and Goldman 1977). In particular, whites living in the Bell-Oakley-Claremont area on the eastern edge of Marquette Park reported receiving calls from realtors offering instant cash payments for houses and being warned to sell before their houses became worthless.[5] Another method was to use the specter of racial change to obtain listings from white homeowners and then scare them to sell. Brokers used a variety of tactics to solicit property listings, including repeatedly soliciting home-owners through phone calls and letters, spreading false stories about black crime, and even hiring blacks to walk through neighborhoods (Seligman 2005). Two reporters studying Marquette Park in 1976 found so much illegal racial steering and blockbusting that they concluded that real estate agents played the biggest role in encouraging racial change.[6] While this study high-lights the pervasiveness of the practice in 1976, archival data show that as early as 1971 residents had organized an anti-solicitation drive to stop real estate agents from soliciting their neighborhoods, even delivering anti-solic-itation lists by hand to more than two hundred real estate offices.[7]

Real estate agents often partnered with banks in supporting the dual housing market. Key to this process was a tiered home finance market in which banks denied conventional mortgages and home improvement loans to residents who lived in racially changing areas. In the late 1960s and 1970s, banks routinely redlined areas of the city that they deemed financially unprofitable. As FHA and VA loan programs shifted course and began to provide mortgage insurance for loans in urban areas, many home buyers and sellers unable to obtain conventional financing relied on these programs. They required little or no down payment and lower credit standards than conventional loans, often attracting home buyers with little homeownership counseling and incomes that were just sufficient to cover expenses (Fox and Goldman 1977). For brokers who found it difficult to obtain conventional mortgages due to redlining, FHA financing was a risk-free way to boost profits. Widespread fraud involving the use of FHA insurance programs was reported in Chicago during this time. Banks were accused of helping unqualified buyers obtain mortgages through fictitious down payments, inflated home appraisals, and false credit information, as well as paying a prearranged fee to real estate agents to direct FHA home buyers to them (Boyer 1973; Ziemba 1975; Collins 1985).

An audit study of 275 homes sold between 1974 and 1976 in the Chicago Lawn area on the Southwest Side revealed that 82 percent had been financed through FHA or VA loan programs, and only 15 percent were secured through conventional mortgages (Fox and Goldman 1977: 34). Real estate agents steered blacks into buying houses through the FHA and VA, either indicating to buyers that conventional loan money was not available or specifically advising buyers that FHA/VA financing be used (Werelo 1974). The typical result was foreclosure if the buyer missed a payment and the boarding up of the home, a signal of neighborhood decline. Importantly, banks were giving conventional mortgages during this time, yet those mortgages were going to lakefront or suburban buyers. For example, Talman Federal Savings and Loan reported to the Parish Federation that from 1970 to 1974, it had invested $22.8 million locally while investing $363.9 million in the suburbs and $77.9 million in the rest of the city.[8] As Greg Squires and his colleagues (1987: 108) point out, the concentrated use of FHA mortgages in Chicago during the 1960s and 1970s was a strong indicator that a neighborhood was declining and "had essentially been written off by the city's lending institutions."

With real estate agents peddling fear, banks lending money to only the least-qualified home buyers, and the savings and loans sending their money to the suburbs and wealthier parts of the city, it is little wonder that white residents organized to stabilize their communities. On Chicago's Southwest Side, two organizations emerged to deal with racial change. The first, the Southwest Community Congress (SCC), was founded in 1969 to deal with fear and anxiety surrounding racial change and to work toward peaceful integration (Squires et al. 1987). The SCC was "virtually invisible" in the mainstream press and worked from a face-to-face approach rather than issuing manifestos or holding big events (Berlet 2001: 147). The larger and somewhat more prominent group was the Parish Federation. While quite different in their approaches, the two groups shared a goal of attempting to stabilize their neighborhoods by challenging the institutional forces supporting the dual housing market. In this chapter, we use archival data to explore the storylines used by whites of the Parish Federation as they organized to navigate the various changes that were occurring. (For a discussion of the methodology, see the Methodological Appendix.) Focusing on the federation, the larger of the two main organizations, we explore the stories that whites tell as they struggle to stabilize their neighborhoods. The storylines in the data give us insight into how whites understood themselves and their communities at the intersection of race and class as they worked to protect their way of life against racial change within a changing city.

The Parish Federation's organizing represented a common-sense understanding that the world was spinning out of control and that ordinary folks and their neighborhoods were being ignored, and even run over. Using stories of innocence, virtue, loss, and abandonment, the Parish Federation drew on racially explicit language to frame grievances through an intersecting lens of class and race. Its members were recent arrivals to the white lower middle class, and racial change threatened their foothold on both class and racial privilege. Thus, as the dominant racial discourse was moving toward color-blindness, whites from the Parish Federation were living in racially explicit space. They organized to defend not only their homes and neighborhoods but also their identity. In their defensive efforts to remain "good" in their own eyes, as well as in the eyes of others (e.g., the media and wealthier whites along the lakefront or in the suburbs), they publicly framed their actions in non-racialized terms and at the same time (re)claimed their white *ethnic* identity: the switch to "ethnic" allowed whites to assert a racialized group identity while still making public claims that their neighborhood battles were not racially based. Self-consciously referring to themselves as white ethnics, the group evolved to pursue a white ethnic commercial district, a white ethnic annual convention, and a home equity insurance program. The label positioned these whites as an aggrieved and powerless group defending their rights. In the end, the Parish Federation's position limited its ability to reach across the borders of racial solidarity to establish common cause with other aggrieved groups.

White Ethnic, White Victim

The Southwest Side of Chicago became a symbol of northern racism in the 1960s and 1970s. Across the United States, viewers of evening news broadcasts contemplated the images of whites reacting violently to Martin Luther King's march through the neighborhood. A few years later, some twenty members of the American Nazi Party opened an office on Seventy-First Street, a few blocks east of Marquette Park. Hoping to capitalize on the attention that Marquette Park was getting, the Nazis held rallies and handed out flyers on Saturdays at the commercial hub of Sixty-Third and Western.[9] The Ku Klux Klan (KKK) also began to be active in the community during this time. As powerful as the racial symbolism of swastikas and the KKK tends to be, it masks a deeper complexity, as the community was never as unified in accepting these provocations as the media suggests. Indeed, there were several reactions to the civil rights era. One reaction was the organizing by a group of whites not necessarily to keep anyone from moving in but, rather, to press the state for protection against institutional practices that were destabilizing the housing market. These racial moderates neither took up the cause of integration nor outwardly supported the American Nazi Party.[10]

The cause the Parish Federation took up was against the various institutional actors that supported the dual housing market and racial change. Southwest Side whites felt that elites in the city had turned away from them, leaving them clearly abandoned and ignored or, conversely, actually targeted by the government and financial institutions. Residents expressed this sentiment in a variety of ways. A common narrative was one of the old neighborhood now overrun, deteriorated, and infested with crime. This narrative of loss hints at the depth of the place attachment that residents developed for their neighborhoods. As one leader proclaimed during the White Ethnic Convention of 1984, "When we moved from St. Justin Martyr parish, we left a once proud house [that is] now surrounded by boarded-up and vacant buildings. We left a yard where my children could no longer play without the threat of harassment. We left a neighborhood where my children could no longer walk safely to school. We were constantly endangered. We could not even go as far as the corner store. In fact, by the time we moved from that community, there was no corner store left to go to."[11] Another leader echoed this sentiment at the convention: "The old neighborhood calls up a rich family history. The old parish our parents belonged to, the social clubs, the schools our grandparents helped establish, the parks, the cultural monuments. . . . [U]nfortunately, many cherished neighborhoods can only live on in our memories. Today these empty shells only hint at past beauty. Row upon row of buildings carry the scars of deterioration, neglect, and crime."[12] Similar nostalgic stories, highlighting "cherished" and "once proud" neighborhoods that had declined, reinforced the notion that constant danger "forced" whites to leave their neighborhoods when blacks entered. Whether residents truly were endangered or not, whites perceived that they were unsafe and that blacks were the cause of neighborhood decline.

Supporting such compelling stories of loss is an analogous story line extolling the virtues of Southwest Side residents and neighborhoods. An editorial from the Parish Federation publication captured this narrative:

> Our communities are worth fighting for. Our safe, prosperous, well-maintained communities are a pleasure to live in. Our traditions and institutions provide a slice of Old World culture deep in the heartland of America. Our values of diligence and family, church and community make this city work and provide encouragement for those ambitious enough to reap the bounty this nation offers. The successes our people have enjoyed and the communities we have built are accomplishments we should all be proud of. We have every right to work together to preserve and protect what we have worked so hard to achieve.[13]

Other claims of hard work, strong values, pride, and determination punctuate much of the Parish Federation's materials. Claims of virtuousness frame whites as justified in their aggrieved assertions and arguments for redress. Using clear, exclusive "us" language, leaders presented themselves as the virtuous holders of values that set them apart from other groups, values that are central to what makes a good neighborhood good. Such claims are designed as clear "social markers" that rhetorically establish and protect their social status (Kefalas 2003). Left invisible is the group that is deemed as not virtuous, those who apparently are not ambitious enough to succeed. Indeed, also left out are the institutions that, until this point, had supported the success of individuals and the larger community.

The positive and virtuous narrative sets the stage for a set of stories highlighting the group's aggrieved status. A language of abandonment was apparent when Southwest Side whites discussed threats to their neighborhoods and the institutions responsible for destroying those neighborhoods. Real estate agencies, financial institutions, government, and politicians received the greatest condemnation. Indeed, the evidence reveals that abusive real estate and lending practices did target the Southwest Side. As they were for whites in other such areas across the country, property values were a central concern for the Southwest Side's lower middle-class whites. For them, neighborhood stability was necessary to protect their single biggest investment. Jean Mayer, chairwoman of the Parish Federation during the 1980s, noted, "We want to make sure the house we have sunk our money into won't lose its value through forces beyond our control. All we want is to hold onto something we have struggled so hard to achieve" (quoted in Ring 1984). Many on the Southwest Side had lost money or knew people who had lost money. Another leader of the movement said, "Many of us, our friends and relatives[,] have moved from neighborhoods abandoned by financial institutions and abused by realtors and mortgage bankers. We lost thousands of dollars on our homes. And it took everything we had to relocate to where we live now on the Southwest Side. The experience taught us that we have to think carefully about investing in repairs and improvements in our homes. New roofs, siding, gutters, basements and porches, too often get put off because we fear that we might not get back what we put into our home."[14] It is important not to underestimate the importance of property values, given that the house represented the retirement savings of many working-class to lower middle-class families.[15] Homeownership also meant respectability and stability. Thus, concern over property values became a central organizing position. Implicit in this complaint is also an understanding and warning to the city that the loss of people who put resources into communities ultimately will be bad for everyone.

The Parish Federation was especially attuned to outside forces complicit in neighborhood decline. Evidence of redlining, blockbusting, solicitation by realtors, biased FHA practices, and plans to locate scattered site public housing left them feeling victimized. In a speech at the first SON/SOC convention, a leader stated: "Up to now, we have been at the mercy of unscrupulous realtors, mortgage bankers, and politicians. All these outside influences have contributed to neighborhood change and we have . . . been victims."[16]

Residents believed that institutions that had once supported aspiring whites and their communities had turned their backs on Southwest Side neighborhoods. In many ways, the privileges whites had come to expect were under attack for the first time. As a result, residents felt under siege and ignored and portrayed themselves as "victims rather than obstructionists of unplanned racial integration" (Dold 1984b). As victims, residents began claiming that they deserved attention and even legal redress. At the 1984 SON/SOC convention, a leader reported: "Each of us is here today to confront neighborhood change. We read so many newspaper stories about the first black family to move into a neighborhood, but nothing about the last white ethnic family to move out. Although we are all victims when neighborhoods change, the same cries of outrage are silent when our children are encouraged to move only to the suburbs. The same access to legal action that is readily available to black victims of steering is non-existent for white victims of redlining."[17] Claiming discrimination from outside influences that look at their neighborhoods "only in terms of dollars and cents," leaders of the Parish Federation searched for ways to fight back. In this way, whites were experiencing the kind of institutional neglect that many nonwhites have long experienced.

While property values and the negative actions of various institutional actors were key concerns, more was at stake. Residents of the Southwest Side felt that their voices were not being heard in the changing city. A common theme in the Parish Federation's discourse was that government and other institutional actors were disrespectful of or ignored the concerns of its members' neighborhoods. For example, in mayoral candidate forums held on the Southwest Side during the late 1970s and early 1980s, Parish Federation members called for answers to their concerns. An editorial published in 1983 noted, "The Candidates Forum is designed to get straight answers to real and immediate problems facing our community. We all know that our Southwest Side neighborhoods have been written off for years and ignored by City Hall for the past many years."[18] Parish Federation members also organized to fight what they viewed as a pattern of neglect in terms of city services and police. When the Chicago Housing Authority purchased two buildings in the 1970s intended for scattered site development, opposition to locating public housing in the community began in earnest with claims that the Southwest Side, for many whites, was their "last ditch stand." With the real estate and financial institution abuse, community residents were reeling and sought to protect a sense of economic *and* social security in the world.

In many ways, the Parish Federation's sense of not being heard extended to a more general reaction to liberalism and the Democratic Party, resentment of federal power, left-wing activism, and the Civil Rights Movement in particular. As did lower middle-class whites in other cities, the Parish Federation activists viewed Democrats and liberals as promoting the rights of minorities at the expense of whites who worked hard to achieve a small amount of financial security (Rieder 1985; Fisher 1994; Kazin 1995; Wilson and Taub 2006). An editorial in the Parish Federation publication echoed this new populist discourse of resentment, asserting:

> The people of our predominantly white ethnic communities are not against decent housing and Federal subsidies for the poor. We take grave exception, however, when such programs are administered in a way that harms and destabilizes our own communities. The Democratic Party has yet to recover from the many excesses and abuses that were inflicted on our neighborhoods in the name of the Democratic Party's "Great Society." Today, in the 1980s, the campaign to end the slums ought to begin right here in our peripheral middle-income communities, communities that have been built by the hard work, perseverance, and generosity of our country's white ethnic immigrant population. The Democratic Party must be concerned with the plight of hard-working middle-income people as it professes to be about the poor.[19]

Having only recently climbed up to the lower rungs of the middle class, the Parish Federation's whites reacted against liberalism and the Democratic Party in a way that represented their concern with ebbing economic and social status (Jacobson 2008).

The Parish Federation's concern about being overlooked coincided with a strong resentment toward more affluent whites in other parts of the city and region. The federation often articulated discomfort at being trapped in the middle. Defensive of not only its neighborhoods but also its organizing, the Parish Federation positioned itself on one flank by stating, "What we have achieved is the result of hard work, perseverance, frugality, and sacrifice. We condemn this ready characterization and dismissing of whites as racist, because we struggle to preserve and protect our middle-income neighborhoods from the ever-encroaching expanse of the city's ghettos and slums." On the front lines of blacks' struggle for social justice, these lower middle-class whites also viewed calls for integration as hypocritical and dismissive. These whites took issue with claims by wealthier white liberals that their concerns and organizing were rooted in racism. They believed that downtown, lakefront, and suburban whites came by their "progressive views on race on the cheap" because they lived in wealthy communities and were able to carefully control who moved into their neighborhoods (Kefalas 2003: 7). For many whites, black neighborhoods were easily equated with decline, crime, and the underclass. Wealthy groups avoided poor groups in subtler ways (e.g., through zoning), and Southwest Siders contended that it was hypocritical to object when they organized to protect their neighborhoods. While not every white resident felt this way, such sentiments affirmed local discussions of their collective situation and served as the basis for what they worked to prevent from happening to their neighborhood.

For members of the Parish Federation, the city and other institutions had turned on them, leaving them without protection or voice. Using their position as homeowners, members of the Parish Federation battled against big business and government forces that impersonally worked against their community. A Parish Federation publication captured this: "We represent a crucial tax base, a tax base that the city depends on for its operation. . . . No! The Southwest Side will not be written off! Together, we can base our efforts on a principle as old as the country in which we live . . . NO TAXATION WITHOUT REPRESENTATION!"[20] Claiming their rights as taxpayers, residents expressed a frustration not only with the workings of the dual housing market but also with the city government's focus on downtown development at the expense of neighborhoods. "If downtown developers can't afford to contribute to the neighborhoods," Mayer remarked, "then subsidizing downtown development should stop, because the taxpayers can't afford it" (quoted in McCarron 1987). In this manner, the Parish Federation captured the broad spirit of the neighborhood movement of the 1970s that represented an attempt by Americans to "regain some measure of power over a world seemingly out of control" (Boyte 1980: 2). A general mistrust of big institutions led leaders to more direct forms of democracy and advocacy to soothe their class and race concerns.

The White Ethnic Organizational Response

The Parish Federation used the narrative of victimization and abandonment as an inspiration for action. Over slightly more than a decade, whites on the Southwest Side built a formidable organization that worked on several fronts in their efforts to stabilize their community and prevent exploitation from institutional and governmental actors. Early efforts targeted predatory real estate agencies through the creation of anti-solicitation lists of residents to present to real estate agencies. The creation of these lists was a labor-intensive affair, often involving door-to-door canvasing and obtaining information and signatures from residents who objected to real estate agencies' solicitations to sell their property. The Parish Federation's efforts in this regard were extremely important in defending against panic-peddling and blockbusting practices. Often hand-delivering these lists to agencies, the Parish Federation resorted to picketing and pressuring agencies into signing non-solicitation agreements. Over the course of a decade, the Parish Federation established more than fifty voluntary non-solicitation agreements with local real estate firms.[21] This organizing was among the most important in stabilizing the neighborhood.

The Parish Federation's organizing strategy also focused on the home lending industry, particularly patterns of redlining and abusive FHA mortgage practices. From personal experience residents knew that financial institutions were targeting their communities. Rates and terms on home mortgages fluctuated based on where one lived. Home improvement loans were hard to come by, particularly if one lived east of Western Avenue. The Parish Federation's efforts attempted to force local financial institutions to disclose their lending practices in the community. When banks resisted, the Parish Federation employed a "greenlining" strategy in which local residents with savings accounts signed pledges to withdraw their money. Scared of losing millions of savings dollars, the banks began to comply, including the biggest bank in the community, Talman Federal Savings and Loan. When banks began to disclose their records, a clear pattern of redlining on the Southwest Side emerged. Getting banks to disclose their lending records helped: in a few years, the banks began to meet mortgage demand in the area. The other fight was with FHA abuse, particularly the use of kickbacks to mortgage brokers and fast foreclosure schemes. Joining forces with groups from the Austin neighborhood, the Parish Federation targeted a notorious mortgage banking firm known for financing rapid racial change across the city. The campaign involved asking the firm to disclose its lending record to the public and the FHA to review the records of the firm and of other unscrupulous mortgage bankers. When this did not work, the Parish Federation turned to attorneys and, eventually, the U.S. General Accounting Office. By 1977, the state of Illinois had passed legislation banning mortgage bankers with high rates of foreclosure from conducting business.

While these victories were noteworthy, they were not enough to combat fears of racial change on the Southwest Side. Hubert Connolly, a one-time president of the Parish Federation, remarked, "Our neighborhood is adjacent to a racially changing community east of Western Avenue. Consequently, homeowners here fear that their property values may one day depreciate if racial change occurs" (quoted in Ziemba 1978). As documented, the eastern of edge of Chicago Lawn, near Marquette Park and Western Avenue, had experienced an array of illegal real estate practices and the beginnings of racial change. With residents worried that they would "lose their shirts" if they did not move, the Parish Federation turned to a home equity insurance program being experimented with in various communities across the country, including nearby suburban Oak Park.[22] Home equity insurance programs offered residents in targeted areas reimbursement for 100 percent of any losses they incurred when they were forced to sell below the appraised value of their home. The hope of the program was that no one would ever need to use the insurance, as it removed the potential for real estate agents to create panic selling on the part of whites (Dold 1984a). Data on existing programs indicates that they had tremendous potential for stemming the flight of middle-income residents due to suburbanization and deindustrialization (Lyons, McCourt, and Nyden 1986).

The Parish Federation's focus on abandonment and victimization was clear in the discourse employed to advance its home equity insurance plan. The organization made use of racial codes to defend its need for institutional protection. At the SON/SOC's White Ethnic Convention, one member remarked: "While our neighborhoods are asked to bear the cost of badly-managed public housing, the government has done nothing to insure the stability of our neighborhoods. We need our own affirmative action program that protects our predominantly white ethnic neighborhoods. It's called Home Equity. If the government can underwrite housing programs that experiment with our neighborhoods, then it can underwrite a program to protect us against property loss and destabilization."[23] Clearly feeling that they lacked power and control over the fate of their neighborhoods, residents sought a way to alter the equation and safeguard their neighborhoods. The reference to public housing management and affirmative action programs suggested that Southwest Side whites were equally, if not more, deserving of government protection.

The reaction to the home equity proposal was mixed. Although it received support from aldermen and several mayors, the proposed program had a bumpy ride over a ten-year period. Black leaders had the strongest negative reaction. Aldermen from heavily black wards claimed that the program was racist. Alderman Marian Humes criticized the plan as a way to maintain all-white neighborhoods: "You are using code words that mean, don't let blacks in" (R. Davis 1979). An editorial in the *Chicago Tribune* similarly suggested that the home equity plan contained the "implicit assumption that black access inexorably causes lower property values" (Sulzer 1988). Mayor Eugene Sawyer shared this concern about the plan's "racial overtones," stating, "It's designed, in my opinion, to control integration" (quoted in Devall 1988). The Parish Federation fumed over the portrayal of home equity insurance as racist, feeling that its members' class-based concerns were being ignored. The reality was that black and white groups were both affected by the unscrupulous actions of various actors in the housing market. The different interpretation likely reflected the fact that the Parish Federation neither reached out to black groups in this process nor was willing to either endorse or reject integration, giving the impression that it was working only to protect its members' interests and not to build a coalition. When the home equity insurance ordinance came up for a vote by the City Council, not one of eighteen black aldermen voted in favor.

In the end, the home equity plan passed after a decade-long organizing effort. The program reflects an attempt by whites to challenge the institutional forces that were impinging on their neighborhoods. The housing
market in Chicago Lawn was volatile because of "the perceptions people
have of the future, based on their past experiences" (Lyons, McCourt, and
Nyden 1986: 243), and the steady diet of pervasive racism in the media, in
policing, in education, and in the housing markets. Their earlier experiences
made them susceptible to individuals or institutions that stirred up panic
and predicted negative outcomes. For Southwest Side residents, home equity
insurance provided a psychological breakthrough (Cuomo 1980), easing
their fears of declining property values. The Parish Federation's racial language and lack of reaching out to nonwhite groups, coupled with the pervasive racism across institutions, provoked the negative reaction from blacks.
This situation can be clearly differentiated from the situation in the village
of Oak Park, which established a similar program in the 1970s. Oak Park,
however, invested in creating the Oak Park Housing Center, which actively
promoted integration of the community. While the Parish Federation vigorously defended its program as not racist, class and race considerations clearly
intersected in this debate.

Rise of the White Ethnic and Pride of Origins

After several strong years of organizing, the Parish Federation had begun
using the term "white ethnic" by the late 1970s as a descriptor and a rallying
cry. Often referred to in the media by this descriptor, the Parish Federation
and its Northwest Side partner adopted the label "white ethnic" as a point
of pride. "Why is the phrase 'white ethnic people' used?" a letter from the
federation to another neighborhood group asked. "'White ethnic' is the label
that has been used to describe our neighborhood. We accept that label and
turn it into a badge of pride. Other communities talk a 'black' or 'Hispanic'
agenda—we're talking about a 'white ethnic' agenda which will address the
issues facing our neighborhood and our hopes for the future."[24] Taking a
page from the Civil Rights Movement, the Parish Federation had learned
that when institutions stop providing protection, people need to organize in
a group, identify how they are being harmed as group, and demand group-
based legislation and policies. Unfortunately, the federation's demands for
group-based recognition were solidifying as the broader discourse was
moving toward the protection of individuals' rights. Nonetheless, as members of the Parish Federation struggled to regain their rightful social position, they drew on race and ethnicity to legitimate their claims and recover
lost privileges. While the Parish Federation worked a variety of angles
to regain lost social capital, we focus on two that used the "white ethnic"

descriptor: (1) a proposal to bring new commercial development (i.e., an "Ethnic Village") to the racial border of Western Avenue, which divided the lower-income and black eastern areas from the whiter, lower middle-income areas, and (2) the buildup to the first SON/SOC White Ethnic Convention.

As early as 1975, the Parish Federation had identified commercial redevelopment along Western Avenue at Sixty-Third Street as a priority to stabilize the area. This intersection was considered a border between white Chicago Lawn and the black neighborhoods of Englewood and West Englewood. Frustrated by new construction and redevelopment dollars focused on the lakefront and downtown, residents started pushing for redevelopment on Sixty-Third Street. By 1983, the Parish Federation had catalogued forty vacant and abandoned storefronts along a six-block strip, approximately ten resale shops that had moved in, and an increase of arson in abandoned storefronts. Long-standing businesses began to move out.[25] Often referred to in the early years as an "economic buffer zone," the Parish Federation's proposal matured into a comprehensive development plan to bring private and public investment into the community through an "Ethnic Village" composed of ethnic shops, specialty shops, and cultural attractions, including converting an abandoned furniture warehouse into a museum or cultural center. The ethnicities emphasized in this plan were those of the older European populations of Chicago Lawn, including Polish, Irish, German, Lithuanian, Bohemian, and Slovak.[26]

The Parish Federation often defended the Ethnic Village by arguing that residential and commercial stability went hand in hand in middle-class communities across the city. Yet it is clear that more was at stake. A prevailing concern among Parish Federation members was whether whites would feel welcome and envision the shopping area as a place for themselves. A speech written for the 1984 convention noted, "The plan promises to be exciting and is just the kind of program we need in order to feel that we all have a future on the Southwest Side."[27] While other groups, including the SCC, claimed that the plan kept nonwhites out, the Parish Federation vigorously defended it: "The Ethnic Village is not exclusionary. . . . [T]he question isn't whether or not minorities can own or operate business along Sixty-Third Street. They already do. The question is, in five years will white ethnics feel they are still welcome in Chicago Lawn as well?"[28] Undoubtedly, the Ethnic Village was an attempt by white residents to secure a place for themselves as change threatened their cherished neighborhoods. Thus, at the convention, a speech calling for members to vote on the redevelopment plan noted that more was at stake than mere physical improvements: "We're not voting to see merely cosmetic improvements; we're voting for our future."[29]

The use of the "white ethnic" descriptor emerged in the run-up to the convention. As the Parish Federation organized to position itself as a rightful voice in the city, it drew on its members' immigrant past as a source of strength and unity. In the keynote address to the convention, Chairwoman Mayer stated:

> But who are we? . . . [W]e are all descendants of economic and political refugees of oppressive regimes and intolerable living conditions. When our people came to this country, they were virtually penniless, with suitcase in hand and ten healthy fingers, determined to reap the promise this country had to offer. Once here, our people suffered terribly from exploitation, discrimination and disease, toiled in unbearable working conditions and huddled in squalid slums. Yet, through diligence, drive and tenacity, our people have bettered themselves and have built happy, healthy, safe neighborhoods and rich cultural institutions. WE ARE AMERICA'S SUCCESS STORY![30]

The Parish Federation was not alone in sharing such ethnic tales of past suffering. And while ethnicity and ethnic differences were never far away for lower middle-class and working-class whites, the revival of ethnicity in the 1970s became a way not only to mobilize for collective identity and group rights but also to distance oneself from typical white privilege. Thus, by claiming "not quite whiteness" or using a "language of ethnic specificity," white ethnics found a way to declare rights at a time that it was not considered legitimate to make claims based on whiteness (Jacobson 2008: 21–22). While disavowing racial discrimination, many whites resented the militancy of blacks and felt that new government policies had gone too far. For white ethnic political claims to have merit, whites would have to reclaim a past of shared suffering and draw analogies to "officially recognized minorities" (Sugrue and Skrentny 2008: 178).[31] Harking back to past suffering offered the recently labeled white ethnics a new way to make seemingly non-racial claims based on their own group identities.

As the Parish Federation maneuvered to be recognized in a shifting city, the use of the "white ethnic" descriptor allowed them to assert a narrative of ongoing victimization and thus position themselves for redress. Expressions such as "having to pay for the protection that should be ours by right" gave white ethnics the rhetoric needed to demand remedial government action.[32] The label "white ethnic" did create a backlash from those who saw it as racist. The Parish Federation was particularly sensitive to accusations of racism. An editorial in the Parish Federation publication defended its group position: "If we refer to ourselves as 'white ethnics,' won't we be branded as racists? We must stop being made to feel ashamed or apologetic about being who we are. For too long, we have let others define 'white ethnic' as another name for 'racist.' Who gives any leader . . . the right to besmirch our good name, origins and accomplishments?"[33] The federation was thus clearly aware of the potential pitfalls of using this self-descriptor, a label that positioned it rhetorically as another group seeking recognition in an increasingly racially divided city. It also helped the federation press institutional actors for renewed attention. In particular, the Parish Federation's ire was aimed at liberals and wealthy whites living in the suburbs or on the lakefront, whom it accused of "reducing every issue in our community to a black-white issue" and of "playing race politics with our legitimate concerns."[34]

It was not coincidental that the "white ethnic" label was adopted with more fervor around the time Chicago elected its first black mayor, Harold Washington. The SON/SOC coalition's approach to Mayor Washington inverted the minority approach to the white establishment by blaming him for stirring up racial issues. In an editorial in the *Southwest Federation News* entitled "The Emperor Has No Clothes," members lamented:

> We are fed up with Mayor Washington's constant demeaning of our history, our values, and our aspirations as white ethnics. We reject his claims that we have advanced ourselves in this city at the expense of minorities. What we have achieved is the result of hard work, perseverance, frugality, and sacrifice. We condemn his ready characterization and dismissing of whites as racist, because we struggle to preserve and protect our middle-income neighborhoods from the ever encroaching expanse of the city's ghettos and slums. In this same vein, we condemn his persistent efforts to provoke animosity and hatred from blacks and Hispanics toward whites who choose to remain in the city.

Having long been on the receiving end of policies and practices that supported white, middle-class neighborhoods, the Parish Federation and its coalition partner resituated themselves and invoked what would become a central pillar of color-blind discourse: calling out reverse racism when white privileges were challenged. The SON/SOC went as far as to refer to Washington as a "cynical political opportunist, ready to exploit every racial fear and antagonism without regard to their dire consequences" (Rivlin 2013: 239).

The SON/SOC's reaction to Mayor Washington has to be understood in light of the shifting context of Chicago. The SON/SOC coalition was not alone in its public trepidation that Washington would turn his attention to minorities at the expense of whites (Rivlin 2013). The Washington administration's affirmative action measures, which were regularly portrayed in the media, did not help soothe white fears in this regard. The Parish Federation clearly read the Washington administration's commitment to shift municipal policy as an indication that its communities would lose out. Bennett (1987: 271) notes that "many white residents of Chicago's northwest and southwest sides assumed that among the Washington administration's intentions was a desire to drive them from their neighborhoods, thus opening up 'good' neighborhoods to the city's black population and assuring a black voting majority in Chicago." Shortly after Washington's election in 1984, the Parish Federation expressed concerns that he was "running City Hall with a vengeance," claiming, "The Mayor is banking on white flight to enhance his re-election chances."[35] Ironically, the Parish Federation and its Northwest Side partner had common ground with what Washington wanted to accomplish: stabilized neighborhoods, stemmed middle-class suburban flight, economic development through neighborhood initiatives, and enhanced citizen control over service delivery (Bennett 1987). This common ground was realized as Washington's advisers helped persuade him that the SON/SOC's commitment to neighborhood preservation was sincere. The mayor lit a "candle of understanding" with the SON/SOC, making a brief appearance at the group's second convention in 1985 and endorsing its home equity plan (Rivlin 2013: 238).

Race Is Always There

In the three decades after World War II, race and class politics were central in reshaping many U.S. cities. The intersection of race and class was particularly apparent on the Southwest Side. Class concerns were certainly important to understanding the racial worldviews of white residents. For example, Maria Kefalas (2003: 155) argues that the racial views of whites in the working-class neighborhood she calls the "Beltway" (several miles west of Marquette Park) were the result of efforts to "fortify the cultural and moral boundaries between themselves and more stigmatized groups" due to their working-class status. And, of course, race was always present, especially in a racially polarized city. As the Parish Federation argued that it was "gravely neglected" by institutions, it also defended its members as "unfairly maligned" as racists, a particularly vexing characterization. The Parish Federation's leaders argued that their organizing was about class concerns. Mayer, a longtime member and the Parish Federation's chairwoman in the 1980s, claimed that the federation simply wanted to "keep the neighborhood economically safe" and that "we just didn't want the neighborhood to become a slum."[36] A Parish Federation organizer reiterated these claims: "Every fight we had was about economics. It is not black people who destroy neighborhoods. It's redlining; it's FHA abuses; it's panic peddling. It is not black or white; it is green. And that is the Southwest Federation in a nutshell."[37] While this seems to be a legitimate characterization, class, as we have seen, was not always primary, as the Parish Federation changed its organizing strategy in the late 1970s by framing its members as an aggrieved ethnic group. This shift was likely rooted in several realities of the post–Civil Rights Movement era. First, while class politics seemed to gain in strength with the flight of capital, downsizing, and a declining standard of living (Winant 1997), public opinion moved to the right, and labor unions began to lose not only members but also credibility. Thus, political mobilization around class concerns was fading. Another reality involved the presence of extremist groups in the neighborhood. Nazi groups made it difficult for moderate groups such as the Parish Federation to organize explicitly around race. Class and ethnic claims proved a more suitable and legitimate route to distance its positions from such groups and from racial politics. Yet, as we explore below, the Parish Federation did not consistently follow through with the logic of its class-based claims.

When this strategy broke down over clear racial conflict, the Parish Federation often used a color-blind "It's anything but race" strategy to frame its work. In numerous documents outlining the federation's historical organizing, race was often portrayed as something outsiders brought into the community. Referencing the civil rights marches in the community, it stated: "We all remember that most difficult time fifteen years ago when our community inadvertently became a national battleground for varying proponents and opponents of the Civil Rights [M]ovement. As a result of the national publicity and media exposure that the late Dr. Martin Luther King Jr. received when he led marches and demonstrations in our community, other outsiders also thrust themselves upon our community seeking notoriety at our expense."[38] In other cases—particularly that of Frank Collins and his Nazi organization—the federation attempted to deflect negative press by discounting their presence and encouraging "homeowners" and other residents to ignore them and stay away from their rallies. Here the Parish Federation blamed the media for ignoring the homeowners who "maintain an active commitment to the community on a day-to-day basis."[39]

Although the Parish Federation sought to mute race and racism, race clearly was a persistent reality. In fact, even when the Parish Federation raised issues attuned to class concerns, it is difficult to assess whether class was the only issue. For example, the Parish Federation justified the Ethnic Village redevelopment plan to the publisher of the local newspaper as a way "to eliminate the malignant cancer festering on our Eastern periphery."[40] While it is safe to assume the federation was referring to blight, decay, and neglect by institutions, the racial implications are clear, given that the neighborhoods on the eastern periphery were all black. Another example involved organizing around FHA/VA loan abuse. The Parish Federation files indicated intensive monitoring of properties purchased by blacks through illicit FHA/VA loan programs. One case involved a black police sergeant named James Glover, who purchased a six-flat apartment building one block west of Western Avenue. The Parish Federation organized around this issue partly because it looked like a typical FHA/VA loan scam, given that Glover had purchased the building using a VA loan. The organization lobbied state representatives to change policy to limit such loans to single-family homes. Concerned that Glover was not personally living in the building he had purchased, the Parish Federation began tracking who did live there and expressed concern that black families were its only occupants. While the legacy of destabilizing FHA and VA loan activity was real, it is unclear whether preventing abuse was the federation's only motivation, an uncertainty reinforced by its failure to reach out to black groups on the matter.

And as loud as the Parish Federation's claims were that outsiders were bringing race and race politics into the discussion and the community, racial tensions in the neighborhood were inescapable. These tensions were very clear when it came to the issue of integration. For example, many residents strongly held the general belief that school integration leads to residential integration. In the fall of 1972, this anxiety played out dramatically on the Southwest Side over integration at Gage Park High School. Claiming that the school was overcrowded, white parents boycotted and filed a federal lawsuit against the Board of Education stating that the school was operating at 165 percent capacity.[41] The boycott involved parents and students staging a sit-in at the school and students not attending school. More than a thousand white students boycotted the school for about ten weeks. Picket lines formed. Fights between white and black students broke out (Neenan 1972). White residents supported a proposal to shift school boundaries so that roughly six hundred students would transfer to Englewood High School to the east. While white protesters claimed that this was a matter of school quality, not race, the students being asked to transfer were all black. Public officials, including Alderman Edward Burke, supported the plan to transfer black students to other schools. These officials also pleaded with residents to "tone down the racial aspects of the boundary dispute" and to "stay off that issue [race] here. . . . [T]he issue is education."[42] Black parents, however, clearly saw the dispute as a racial one. Most black students did not want to transfer to another school. Some black parents and students asserted that teachers at the school were openly discriminating against black students, and several students reported being attacked by white students (Neenan and Masson 1972; Kelly 1973). Blacks clearly did not feel welcome at Gage Park High School.[43] Although the students eventually returned to the school, no solution satisfactory to all parties was reached (McCourt 1977).

Relatedly, in the 1970s, when the first black family moved into the small area between Western Avenue and the community of West Englewood, whites expressed their opposition violently. Between 1974 and 1976, more than sixty acts of violence and vandalism were perpetrated against black families, including the burning of garages and even the firing of bullets through windows (Fox and Goldman 1977). Similar incidents of racial violence and attacks continued on the Southwest Side into the mid-1980s, including the throwing of Molotov cocktails at homes and the drawing of swastikas on doors (Davidson and Sullivan 1984; Tayler 1985). These stories are confirmed by former residents of the area. One respondent told us about a number of white youths who threw objects at the windows of houses known to be owned or rented by blacks, while local cops following close by were reluctant to arrest the kids. And while the majority of residents did not get involved in such actions, it is impossible to ignore the fact that many neighborhood residents expressed strong aversion to living near blacks, as is evident in the field notes taken by Parish Federation organizers. In an interview with the *Chicago Tribune* about arson attacks on blacks, one resident captured these views by saying, "They [blacks] don't belong here. . . . [T]hey knew they were asking for trouble" (quoted in Tayler 1985). While the Parish Federation publicly (and likely privately) condemned such actions and sentiments, the reality was that race and racial tension were a constant reality in the daily lives of whites living close to racial boarders.

The actions of the Parish Federation were at times, at odds with those of a smaller neighborhood organization, the SCC. Often derided by the Parish Federation as too liberal, the SCC focused on integration. In response to the racial incidents in the eastern section of Chicago Lawn in the 1980s, the SCC began reaching out and meeting with black leaders to collaboratively seek solutions. In one meeting, a black leader in the group asked several white SCC members, "I wonder if you know that there are a lot of black families that live on the other side of Western who take turns sleeping at night?" The question served as a watershed moment for members of the SCC. As a leader noted, "It was breath-taking, the realization that that was the single most important thing, to stop the fire bombings." Recognizing that white youth were behind many of these incidents, the SCC determined which houses or apartments were the easiest to target and through contacts in various parishes organized a neighborhood watch. The watch involved "old Catholic ladies" setting up lawn chairs near vulnerable houses to wait for white teenage kids to start throwing rocks or other objects. Given the insularity of the community, those involved in the watch generally knew the kids and called them out. Such informal pressure limited the provocations by young, racist whites in the neighborhood, according to Chip Berlet, a member of the SCC coalition. Eventually, a special police arson unit cracked two arson cases, arresting white neighborhood kids and "rebutting the claim that violence was carried out by 'outsiders' or 'extremists'" (Berlet 2001: 154).[44]

The presence and organizing of the SCC around integration highlights one of the more telling aspects of the Parish Federation: its stance on integration. For example, in a letter to a high-level aide to Mayor Washington, the federation stated, "The issue of the Southwest Side in 1983 is not integration versus segregation, rather it is neighborhood stability versus resegregation." While much of its work centered on fighting institutional practices that worked against middle-class residents of different racial backgrounds, the Parish Federation did not see integration as a workable strategy. In fact, many of its platforms seemed to skirt the issue of integration, looking to maintain the status quo rather than welcome any change. Parish Federation resident leaders and professional organizers argued that the group's members were political moderates, and while "integration wasn't their cause," they were "live and let live" people who did not want people getting hurt. Positioning themselves as the forgotten middle, the federation's leaders often claimed that their lived experience told them integration would not work. In many ways, this response is tied to the fact that for many the Southwest Side was a site of secondary settlement. Documents and several interviews revealed that many residents had lived elsewhere in the city, often in neighborhoods to the east, until racial change occurred there. "That is the irony," a community organizer told us. "A lot of times, these ethnics would move one neighborhood over. It wasn't like they were really fleeing . . . one parish over." Research on other communities facing racial change highlights both financial vulnerability of the residents and their frustration of having moved once before (Rieder 1985; Bell 2013). Thus, their perspective on integration was undoubtedly driven by feelings of having been displaced from elsewhere in the city, fear of losing property values, and the experience of witnessing neighbors flee as neighborhood demographics shifted. Both the Parish Federation's stabilization effort and the creation of a white ethnic identity can be interpreted through this experience.[45]

At the same time, while a social class interest was motivating the Parish Federation, it failed to follow the logic of its own "It's not black or white; it's green" stance. For example, this stance suggests finding common cause with working-class and lower middle-class Hispanics, poor whites, and blacks equally victimized by unjust institutional practices. Beyond the Southwest Side, the federation's collaborators frequently were the North Side "white ethnics" in the SON/SOC movement. In our interviews, some Parish Federation representatives claimed that the lack of partnerships with black groups was due to a lack of strong black organizations with which to work. This claim, however, was refuted by other informants, who indicated that not only black organizations but also middle-class black neighborhoods were close by, the latter a mere five-minute drive to the east in Chatham. As Bennett (1990: 123) notes, instead of aligning with these groups, the Parish

Federation and the SON/SOC upwardly aligned themselves with "suburban homeowners and other taxpayers threatened by crime, loss of home equity because of incompatible neighbors or land use, and local tax hikes." In this way, given the changes occurring in the city, the Parish Federation's position came across as defensive and dismissive of integration.

The Parish Federation's stance on integration also might explain why it sometimes was unable to see how other groups might interpret its rhetoric. Responding to the SON/SOC's claim that the white ethnic agenda celebrated the vitality and uniqueness of neighborhoods and exemplified the values of hard work, sacrifice, and decency, the newspaper columnist Monroe Anderson claimed, "Now, let me see, if the white ethnics from the Southwest and Northwest Sides have come together to celebrate this 'uniqueness,' I can only assume that the ethnics, the black ones, conversely must be a common people, with values of laziness, self-indulgence, and indecency" (Anderson 1984). Anderson was not alone in taking issue with the Parish Federation and its coalition partner's polarizing statements. Others read the Parish Federation's rhetoric as foregrounding race for political gain. A former Southwest Side organizer stated, "There was a period when the Southwest Federation wasn't doing this kind of thing. . . . [W]e'd show the economic causes of panic peddling—the enemy wasn't black people. . . . [P]eople are being led to think it is a black-white issue" (Grimes 1984: 3). In the end, it is safe to say that the Parish Federation's aggressive organizing and polarizing rhetoric seemed to limit its ability to build a coalition among groups that had similar economic interests and concerns with neighborhood viability.

For South Side whites in the 1970s and 1980s, the fight was on. What they were fighting against, however, had already happened. More affluent whites had left the city for the suburbs. The types of jobs that had supported single-earner working households were also leaving the city, the state, and, eventually, the country. City development had decidedly shifted toward the downtown and away from the outlying neighborhoods. In addition, the edifice of segregation had begun to erode as once supportive institutions were turning against white neighborhoods. At a national level, the post–Civil Rights Movement era had altered the status quo, leaving whiteness visible. These events left whites feeling insecure, without a voice, and abandoned. Thus, in a real sense, whites on the Southwest Side were reacting to a loss of privilege. The loss was related to both the shifting contours of class and race in the city of Chicago and broader shifts in the racial hierarchy and racial discourse. The privileges that they had come to expect—dependable and decently paying jobs, segregated white communities, and institutional support—were now eroding. The election of Mayor Harold Washington was particularly symbolic of these changes and the loss that they felt.

It is tempting through contemporary eyes to view the rhetoric and actions of the Parish Federation as matters of simple racism. And white ethnics have been portrayed as "urban rednecks," living in "provincial backwaters of prejudice and ignorance" (Formisano 1991: 234). The redneck image is often perpetuated by more privileged whites who employ subtler forms of racial antipathy grounded in social class. The story we present attempts to capture the complexity of the white response to these changes, focusing on the intersection of race and class. Lower middle-class and working-class white residents were living in a context in which past experience suggested that integration meant racial change, loss of property values, and neighborhood decline. Fear of neighborhood change was palpable, grounded in various preconceived pejorative notions of blacks and a parallel concern that their neighborhoods would deteriorate due to disinvestment. Southwest Side white residents were not alone in their concerns, and the concerns were not merely local. Like many northern whites, urban Catholic ethnics who were once loyal to the Democratic Party felt threatened by the social and cultural changes of the 1960s, particularly around race. Many whites saw civil rights gains for blacks as a loss, particularly for those socially and geographically close to blacks (Formisano 1991). Thus, as the Parish Federation organized to address the changes facing their neighborhoods, their rhetoric invoked both class-based complaints and—despite their protest—concern about the shifting nature of their racial identity. As the racial discourse shifted, they were left with few ways to legitimately make their case.

The Parish Federation was organizing to protect its neighborhoods at a time that whiteness was undergoing a transformation. The political and cultural mobilization of nonwhites forced whites to think about who they were in relation to other racial groups (Gallagher 1997). As David Wellman (1997: 321) suggests, "White men have discovered what nonwhites and women living in a predominantly white male (and heterosexual) world have always known: Life in a racial and gendered category is not always comfortable. Thus, white men are beginning to experience what they previously took for granted." White racial consciousness increased in the post–Civil Rights Movement era as whites experienced life as a "marked" category for the first time. White racialization occurred in a variety of ways (e.g., affirmative action debates); however, a central theme that had emerged by the 1980s was of whiteness as a liability. On the Southwest Side, whiteness became visible as institutions began to abandon white neighborhoods through disinvestment. The actions and rhetoric of the Parish Federation—expressing the beginnings of color-blind discourse—demonstrate an attempt to reposition its members as both white ethnics and victims to regain privilege. And the Parish Federation's failure to consider integration or reaching out to non-white groups demonstrates a failure to see shared obligations, or solidarity, in truly non-racialized ways (Hooker 2009).

It is also undeniable that attempting to understand the Parish Federation requires addressing these claims and the Parish Federation's incessant denials that it was racist. We agree with Seymour Lipset and Earl Rabb's notion that calling people stupid or racist does not solve problems (Lipset and Rabb 1970). We want to understand the actions of whites in the context of social change and how whites made sense of the complexities of racial change. While the common understanding of racism suggests that it is rooted in prejudice and psychological predispositions, we argue that racism extends beyond mere prejudice and involves a defense of privilege and power. Wellman (1993: 29) argues that rather than seeing the racial consciousness of whites as the product of ill will or the aberrant or hostile expressions of "intolerant, unsocialized bigots," we need to understand race as a structural and cultural construction. Thus, it is valuable to understand racist beliefs as "culturally sanctioned, rational responses to struggles over scarce resources" and to understand that regardless of the intentions, they protect "the advantages that whites gain from the presence of blacks in America." The racist actions of whites are not simply about the hearts and minds of men and women but are structural in nature, best understood as whites defending their group position.

Finally, in many ways, the communities that the Parish Federation and other groups were attempting to stabilize were indeed vanishing. They were fading away not simply because of racial change, but also because of larger demographic, social, and economic trends. Certainly, race and class were the building blocks on which whites understood their social bonds, neighborhoods, and, ultimately, themselves. Thus, as they struggled to stabilize their communities, racial boundaries were central to this process. And while only a handful of our respondents had parents who were active in the Parish Federation or other organizations, it is important to understand the neighborhood context in which they were growing up. In many ways, examining the Parish Federation's organizing and discourse reveals some of the principal themes of color-blind discourse that emerged in the decades after the passage of national civil rights legislation. In fact, as we shall see in the next several chapters, elements of the white reaction from the 1970s and 1980s—for example, aggrieved status, powerlessness, and efforts to maintain racial boundaries—are found in the memories and reactions that our respondents shared with us of growing up in neighborhoods threatened by racial change.

3

On the Borders

WITH NANCY MICHAELS

In response to the urban riots of 1967, President Lyndon Johnson formed a commission headed by the well-connected Otto Kerner, who was born and bred in Chicago. The Kerner Commission's report concluded, "Our nation is moving toward two societies, one black, one white—separate and unequal" (Kerner 1968). The commission identified institutional racism and pervasive racist behavior of whites as the underlying causes of urban riots, arguing that racial unrest would be repeated unless racial inequality and racist behavior were changed. On the night of Thursday, April 4, 1968, one month after the report was released, Dr. Martin Luther King Jr. was assassinated in Memphis. It should not have been a surprise, thus, that the next morning in major urban areas throughout the country black communities exploded in anger. Friday morning on Chicago's West and Southwest sides, blacks took to the streets to protest. High school students were first, departing school by midmorning. By the late afternoon, the first fire alarm was sounded, and crowds had formed along Madison Street, breaking windows, looting stores, and setting buildings on fire (Rivlin 1988). Firefighters rushed to the scene as thirty-six major fires were reported and more than six hundred alarms were tripped. As firefighters flooded the area, rioters pelted them with rocks and bottles (Rivlin 1988; Groves 2006). By the end of Friday, the first of three thousand Illinois National Guard troops had arrived to back up police. On Sunday, the National Guard troops were joined by several thousand U.S. Army troops, and soon Army vehicles outfitted with machine guns were seen along the main thoroughfares of Lawndale and Austin on the West Side and Woodlawn on the South Side. When it was all over, eleven people were dead, 170 buildings had been destroyed, 350 had been arrested for looting, and thousands of people were left homeless (Coates 1968).

For whites living on the West Side, that day and the weekend that followed left an indelible impression. Until that point, the racial border had provided whites with a sense of safety and security. Barb, a middle-age woman who grew up on the West Side, had a vivid memory of that Friday, when she was pulled out of school and sent home:

> It was when Martin Luther King [died], and they rioted that night. I was at school, and there was a group of maybe twelve of us, and we were the troublemakers. It was morning, and they started calling all of our names down to the office and, we're all like, "What did we do? What did we do?" All of us, you know. When we got down there, they said, "Your parents have called. You are to get your coats and your things, and you are to take your Pulaski bus and get off at Armitage. You are not to go any farther south." Well, there was still Fullerton [Avenue, to the north], but they weren't taking any chances, and they said, "You will be met by family." And we're like, "What's going on?" And they said, "There's rioting going on, and there is looting, and they're burning everything down." So we had to get off [the bus], and all of our parents were there. The fathers came home from work, because it was that bad.

The flames and smoke rising over Madison were visible from some respondents' front porches. Others recalled events being canceled or their parents' wanting to keep them at home and restrict their movement or, in some cases, seeking out their teenage children and bringing them home, in fear for their safety. Almost all, similar to the emotions surrounding details of the day Barb expressed, recalled the confusion, fear, and intensity of the events.

In contrast to the recommendations of the Kerner Commission that the nation address pervasive racism, many whites living in segregated white neighborhoods felt anger toward and fear of blacks. Neighborhood networks and the growing popularity of television (offered in color for the first time in 1968) created an imagery of blacks and blackness as the root cause of the riots and violence. Like many kids at the time who were raised in segregated communities, Gil was socialized to believe blacks were violent and a threat to white people. He had little contact with black people and, as many other whites did, learned about race in isolation. He asked, "How could I deny what I was seeing? Everywhere blacks went, violence followed. We watched it on our television." Similarly, Vince, a child on the West Side at the time, reflected on how the riots affected his life:

> I think a lot of the feelings, fears and prejudices were a byproduct of watching the news. A very important event in our history took place in 1968 while we were living there: Martin Luther King was killed. My dad was a cop, so we saw my dad go into work every day with his riot gear on, and we couldn't wait to hear the key in the door in the evening, knowing that he came back safely. We saw the smoke on Madison Avenue (on the West Side) being burned [and] the National Guard right on our front porch.

For Vince and others, the borders between white and black neighborhoods provided a sense of protection. The riots and racial change not only made the racial borders more visible; the riots and racial change also threatened whites' sense of safety.

Certainly, the West Side and South Side riots had multifaceted effects. Beginning in the late 1950s, whites across the city had been fleeing to other western neighborhoods or suburbs. The riots and media reports of the events exacerbated underlying racialized anxieties. On the day the rioting began, according to Gary Rivlin (1988), city switchboards were jammed; workers were sent home early; people rushed stores to stockpile goods; and some bars and restaurants closed early. The border between black and white, previously held in place through legal and extralegal means to a white advantage, was ever more threatened. As if to punctuate the border breach in the minds of whites, one week after King's assassination, with the rioting still going on, Johnson signed into law the Fair Housing Act of 1968, making it illegal to discriminate based on race or color.

While the riots provide a clear lens into the depth and intensity of racism, conflict around racial borders was long-standing. Moreover, throughout the 1960s and 1970s, many whites, fearful that their lives, lifestyles, and property values were threatened, chose to flee, while others stayed with a renewed sense of the need to maintain neighborhood racial borders. As they engaged in the struggle to reinforce racial borders, many whites initiated or were tolerant—and even supportive—of and engaged in violent and explicitly racist tactics. Isolation and violence were the hallmarks of the active individual and organized white response. To make sense of the white response to perceived racialized "threat," we examine institutional protections in housing, policing, education, and the economy. These institutions that had previously supported white privilege were challenged under the bright light of the Civil Rights Movement. In other words, institutionalized white racism was in the process of transformation (Omi and Winant 1994). Whites reacted to these changes in various ways. As outlined in Chapter 2, many whites felt abandoned when these social institutions shifted and defined themselves as victims of both "dangerous" blackness and the political apparatus. At the neighborhood level, those whites who chose to stay took it upon themselves to uphold racial borders. For those whites, isolation and violence were the hallmarks of the active individual and organized white response.

In this chapter, we explore the racial borders that demarcated segregated white communities, focusing on how respondents understood their community boundaries. We address how children within these borders were racialized (or socialized into particular racial ways of being) and how they internalized racial borders. We show throughout this chapter that racial identities are shaped by family, community, media, and other social institutions and are inextricably tied to place—in this case, the demarcated and bounded neighborhood. As Brian Osbourne (2001: 12) has noted, "The abstraction of space is transformed into a social and psychic geography. Both a cognitively derived knowing about place and an intuitive sense of place are profoundly integrated into peoples' identity." Understanding this interplay among identity, race, and neighborhood highlights how borders are (re)created, ideologically and institutionally, through the complex processes of "doing" race. We begin with an overview of the racial borders, then explore how racialized divisions are maintained physically, ideologically, and institutionally.

Racial Borders

Borders—physical, ideological, and institutional constructions—give form to our reality. They define and shape where we belong, our status, whom we view as our people; they also define the context of our opportunities, goals, and dreams. Historical creations, borders have become institutionalized and internalized. Borders exist in how society is structured, as well as in how individuals learn to think and act (Dalmage 2000). Borders protect power and privilege and are thus reflected in the structure of society and in our relationships. While borders are upheld in an effort to protect privilege, they also are upheld to protect solidarity in order to struggle against inequality. In other words, the borders become a central organizer of society as differently located groups work to uphold or challenge the very existence of borders. We are assigned, at birth, to various locations and then name and claim our place in society. Some individuals accept their assigned role as "natural," while others struggle to name and claim their place. Many borders exist that frame social locations, including gender, ability, religion, class, citizenship, sexuality, and language. *Racial* borders are the contested, patrolled, and often hostile spaces near the color line. Borders are seen most clearly in religious gatherings on

Sunday mornings; at hair salons; and in public education, housing, and other locations in which segregation, racial inequality, and historical patterns separate human beings. When white privilege and resources are at risk, borders serve as barriers or dams protecting those with resources from those without. At stake is both a way of life and path to whiteness and property values and identities (Dalmage 2000; Ballard 2004; Low 2007).

In Chicago, borders are often stark because of a city layout that has been referred to as "Balkanized," in which adjacent neighborhoods are demarcated by specific streets, and each community is defined by race, class, or sexuality. "Don't cross Western Avenue," "Stay away from Chicago Avenue," and "Stay on this end of Garfield Park" were a few of the ways our white respondents remembered the starkness of the border between "us" and "them" during their youth. Delivered in myriad ways, the message about where whites and blacks belonged was clear. For whites, the borders were symbolic of achievement, success, community, goodness, and earned privilege on the white side and symbolic of failure, undeserving-ness, and lawlessness on the black side.

Within the boundaries of these segregated neighborhoods, whites created and policed one another around acceptable and appropriate ways of being. These ways of being were displayed through particular types of cultural capital, including lawn care, clothing styles, child rearing, and religion. Those who were able to display such appropriate cultural capital were rewarded socially and economically. Moreover, the collective ways of being were mobilized to maintain the borders of community. The labor whites expended to distinguish themselves from "others" is captured in Maria Kefalas's in-depth analysis of a working-class Southwest Side neighborhood, just west of Midway Airport in Chicago. Kefalas (2003) argues that boundaries or borders were strengthened through "place-bound moral distinctions" between good and bad neighbors around issues of cleanliness, lawn maintenance, homeownership (versus renting), and absence of graffiti. In these ways, whites fortified "the cultural and moral boundaries between themselves and more stigmatized groups" (Kefalas 2003: 155). The process of differentiation was a key element in creating and maintaining racial borders. For whites in the urban North, the work of protecting those borders became clearer as the Civil Rights Movement forced a legal, if not a de facto, opening in the housing market and blacks began buying homes in formerly all-white areas. The borders, in fact, became the battleground as panic peddlers, unscrupulous realtors, bankers, lenders, and insurers exploited and exacerbated racism to create profit. The borders that whites believed were natural, worthy, and governmentally protected (and thus taken for granted) were now weakened and raw.

In the United States, various institutions function in ways that maintain racial borders to white advantage. As discussed in Chapter 1, legislation allowed and even encouraged racial discrimination, while institutional actors in various sectors of the housing industry engaged in explicit practices that created and maintained the strength of borders. Whether through denial of loans, racial steering, or broadly practiced redlining, the borders were held in place. Due to these complex practices that allowed whites to avoid and maintain borders, they lived with a sense that their security and protection came from living in segregated white communities. Once racial borders were challenged in the housing market, many whites who believed that any breach of the borders would create an unstoppable flow of destruction chose to flee to other white neighborhoods or to the growing homogenously white suburbs. Those who believed the borders could be reinforced and strengthened through individual and community effort stayed and fought; some fought to maintain the borders, and others fought for peaceful integration. Whites who worked toward integration banded together to form more than two hundred different neighborhood coalitions across the country between 1960 and 1980 (Saltman 1990). Many pro-integration organizations encountered insurmountable difficulties in challenging racial borders. For example, one neighborhood with particular support for integration was the St. Sabina community. The parish had a large fund to promote integration (nearly $800,000) and a sizable group of advocates, backed by some of the church's clergy. Attempts to create integration, while hopeful, proved unachievable against the larger institutional and ideological forces. As was the case for many coalitions, a high-profile racialized violent incident ended hope for integration of the community. In this case, a black youth allegedly shot a white youth. Paul was in elementary school at the time. He recalled, "When that happened, . . . that whole parish wanted out. That's when that whole parish changed over." Once the borders appeared to be breached, whites began to flee. Those living in the neighborhood remember that the next day, "For Sale" signs popped up all over and became the outward symbol of flight.

Physical Borders

Physical borders, generally streets or avenues, frame the "safe" and "good" boundaries of a neighborhood from the undesirable and dangerous parts. The value of property can differ dramatically from one side of the border to the other. Borders often reflect economic differences so that one side will receive better city services. As Rich Ballard (2010) has noted, spatial and social distance are closely aligned. Physical borders clarify and define "us" and "them," the in-group and the out-group, and are constructed as natural. Parents allowed their children to play unsupervised in "safe" spaces. Most whites consciously avoided the physical border while living daily life with a belief that segregation was a reflection of a natural order. The closer families lived to the borders, the more they exercised control and consciously negotiated the border (Dalmage 2000).

In neighborhoods of the West and Southwest sides of Chicago, whites were very aware of the borders. Until it appeared that a breach of the racial border was imminent, most whites were mindful of but did not engage in active and public forms of patrolling or policing the racial borders. Randy, who grew up in Chicago Lawn, noted, "Western was always the dividing line; like, you wouldn't go east, you know? That's what always stands out in my mind. There always seemed to be a dividing line, you know. Well, first, like, my parents didn't really say, 'Well, don't cross Western' or anything, but it was just in everybody's mind that [the blacks] were on the other side of Western, [and] we're over here." The idea that Western Avenue was "always" the dividing line constructs and assigns naturalness to the border. If the border was natural, it would not need to be so actively upheld and fought over. The fact that the battles were intense reflects the precariousness of the border. While reflecting on what life was like on the West Side in the days after Martin Luther King Jr. was assassinated, Bill explained the process of border patrolling:

> I do remember something else from that day. It got bad. It got real bad. You didn't want to be white and be on the other side of Chicago Avenue. And you didn't want to be black and be on this side of Chicago Avenue. There was that problem. There were rocks. . . . I remember being on Hamlin and Chicago Avenue . . . on the white side . . . and there were rocks being thrown and people getting hit. I remember there was this one kid—unfortunate black kid who was running and everything . . . but fortunately there was a black guy going by in a car who opened the door. The kid ran right in, and they took off and saved his ass. This was during King Day. It was either that day or the next, but it was during the conflict. The guys from the other side were coming back and forth. If you were on the South Side [of Chicago Avenue], you were in big trouble.

Bill describes a naturalizing of the racial borders. The borders were static spaces that defined interaction and safety. He refers to one side as the "white side," and it is likely that this is how neighborhood kids conceptualized the space. Yet while these borders were "naturalized," he also speaks to the work (i.e., the violence) used to maintain them.

The physical borders did not just appear, however; they required effort to maintain and patrol. Jeanine, who grew up on the West Side, reflected on the "watching" of the border between whites and blacks:

I never spoke to [blacks]. We used to go shopping at Pulaski and Madison. If you look it up . . . there was a huge shopping area especially for Italians that lived on Chicago Avenue. . . . [E]very year it was getting a little worse and a little worse and a little worse, you know. They [blacks] looked different. They were not groomed. They looked poorer than us. And so that was the boundary. We couldn't go anywhere south. It was different because they were a different color, and I had never had any interaction with these people.

Here Jeanine speaks of her awareness that the borders were porous. Her use of the phrase "getting worse" to describe the entrance of blacks into a shopping district speaks to the imagery in the minds of whites. Blackness and integration signify a worsening of life conditions, with the visible race and class differences being read with her "trained, discerning eye" (Rothman 2001: 54). While Jeanine had not interacted with blacks, she was able to read the social distance and claim her sense of superior status. Indeed, from this perspective, interacting with blacks created in Jeanine what Barbara Ehrenreich refers to as a "fear of falling" (Ehrenreich 1990). Jeanine's construction of the integrated shopping area (what Jane Jacobs referred to as a "social seam") could have provided a space for whites and blacks to become more comfortable and thus accepting. In fact, all physical borders had the potential to serve as such seams, creating spaces of cross-racial interaction. However, as we can see from Jeanine's comments, the sense of fear and danger whites experienced at the racial borders was the foundation of whites' distancing and isolation rather than interaction. The strength of the sense of danger was especially pronounced among whites who lived or moved near a physical racial border.

As a result, white kids growing up on the Southwest and West sides were racially insulated and isolated. The border, supported by an established social order along with deep fear, was clear and stark. Joseph depicted both the clear, unambiguous borders he negotiated as a kid on the West Side and the fear involved when he crossed the border: "Well, yeah, you had to avoid [Le Moyne Street] . . . you know? I would cut from Latrobe to North Avenue and avoided that. You didn't go south of North Avenue—no way. It was like Le Moyne, one street south—forget about it, you don't go there. Don't even think about going to LaFollette Park to play basketball. . . . [T]hat ain't happening! I did that once by mistake, went upstairs, walked in, said, 'Oh my God!' and ran down the stairs and left. You know, I was the only white kid there." Paralleling the sentiment expressed about Western Avenue on the Southwest Side, West Siders were very clear about North Avenue as the border. These borders clearly limited what many whites imagined as possible in terms of whom they should or could interact with and where they felt safe.

Even in the school systems, following the U.S. Supreme Court's decision on desegregation in *Brown v. Board of Education*, white youth remained isolated from blacks either directly through continued school segregation (Orfield 1978) or through internal tracking mechanisms within the schools that kept whites in college-bound tracks and held blacks out of those tracks (Kao and Thompson 2003). In the spaces where white youth could have interacted with blacks, institutional racism ensured separation and a racial border that funneled white children to upper tracks and black children to the lower tracks. This separate and unequal arrangement had a remarkable impact on the children. For instance, Rhonda talked about her experiences at a Southwest Side school in developing a viewpoint steeped in a sense of "natural" white superiority:

> I mean . . . any dealings we had with the black kids was, you know, mainly in school. I actually wasn't in classes with a lot of them. I was always in calculus, and to be very honest, in honors and [advanced placement]. There were a couple of really brainy black kids that would do homework. You know, Mae Jemison came from Morgan Park, the astronaut. . . . Yeah, I remember her being there, and she was, you know, head of student council and all that kind of stuff. Very out there and, you know, super-smart. There were a bunch of really smart ones.

Rhonda not only carries the memory of racial isolation but also believes, as her explanation highlights, that racial borders are natural reflections of essential racial difference. Her statement that there were a few "brainy black kids that would do homework" implies that most black youth were not smart or committed enough to be in the upper tracks—the system itself is not unjust or racist. In this telling, the borders are thus a natural reflection of human talent, skill, and work ethic; whites have earned their privileged position because they possess admirable qualities. In this way, racial borders function in a way that confirms whites' sense of superiority.

Whites feared that a porous border would lead to a watershed "invasion." They were very aware of the differences in social status between themselves and blacks living on the other side of Western or Chicago Avenue. Barry, like many other whites, expressed his overriding sense of fear concerning different parts of the neighborhood: "LaFollette Park was on Laramie. I went there a couple times, but because Division Street back then—and we're talkin' from, like, '73 to '81—Division Street was a huge divider as far as the neighborhood went. A lot of the blacks would come in, and LaFollette Park was taken over almost immediately, so it was, like, really dangerous to go there." The underlying sense of fear was the foundation on which white children were socialized. For the children, blackness was taught as dangerous before interaction had taken place. Similarly, Pete recalled, "[I] didn't know one [black person]. There wasn't one in our grammar school. Not one. Not one on our block." Unlike contemporary research showing that white youth live racially isolated lives and make claims to color-blindness (see Bonilla-Silva, Goar, and Embrick 2006), the individuals in our study lived through racial change and near racial borders. Premised on an underlying sense of fear and danger, their negotiation of race produced a drive to either avoid the borders or engage in conflict to "protect" their community.

When a dual housing market is present, physical borders protect privilege and exaggerate difference. As long as borders are in place, whites are not conscious of their racial animosity. For many whites, their racial identity is invisible, and race becomes visible only when interacting with nonwhites. The closer a family lived to the border, the more race was visible. When asked why her good friend left the neighborhood before she did, Betsy recalled:

> Because [the perceived danger] was closer to Western. She was on Rockwell, which was only a couple blocks from Western, and she was probably in eighth grade, freshman year, and by that time the other side of Western was probably turning almost all black. So there was—well, 'Don't go walking on Western anymore.' Even though we would go to the Sears, but we wouldn't tell [our parents] we were there. So I think that's probably, you know, why . . . because we were closer to Kedzie. . . . [W]e were on Whipple, Albany, Troy, so I think that there were probably stages, and because the majority of us were on the other side of California, we didn't have to move again, and we finished high school and graduated from there.

Like Vince, Betsy is suggesting that once the borders were breached and their own resources challenged, racial animosity was introduced. Thus, many whites believe that racial hatred develops at the point of contact. In fact, while it may stir explicit emotions within whites, our data in this chapter—and in Chapter 4—show that whites are willing to accept the outcomes of institutional practices that enacted bias toward blacks. Inverting reality, blacks were seen as the cause of the conflict, white loss, and suffering. As a consequence, whites felt a legitimate—perhaps even prudent—justification for patrolling and maintaining racial borders.

The connection between physical borders and the construction of identity is tightly intertwined. In discussing the housing market in South Africa, Ballard (2004: 54) suggests that, when it comes to physical and spatial borders, "People attempt to control those things that threaten their identity" and "the boundaries around one's sense of oneself are matched and managed through spatial boundaries." Indeed, when discussing their neighborhoods, respondents were clear about how the physical borders framed their sense of neighborhood and community. Thus, both the physical and the social boundaries give those with privilege a sense of safety and comfort and a way to protect their "nice" community from invading outsiders (Low 2007).

Racial Socialization and Racial Borders

Physical borders often can be named and identified in reference to particular streets, schools, or shopping areas. Internalized racial borders do not have the same level of tangible expression. The internalization of racial boundaries is a matter of socialization. Like all socialization, racial socialization is a process in which values and beliefs are transmitted in specific and general ways, at the micro and macro levels, through language and action. Racialization happens in particular sociohistorical contexts and is "developed and modified over the life course" (Carter, Picca, and Murray 2012: 133). As Shannon Carter and his colleagues illustrate, racialization happens in a dialectic fashion between a child's private space (home, family and community ties) and public spaces (schools, media and other institutions). At this intersection, however, most white children are living in racially isolated private spaces. Thus, they learn about race in isolation and carry that socialization with them as they begin to interact (if they do) in spaces with nonwhites.

White youth saw blacks from a distance and drew conclusions based on inferences and imagination, fed by a steady reinforcement from television, neighbors, police, and the caring adults in their lives. As we will see, this imagination, based on fear and isolation, became a driving force in the ongoing creation of ideological borders and bounded empathy. Whites who had not interacted with blacks were raised to believe that racial borders were necessary for their very survival. Without social interaction with blacks, the youth had little chance to challenge racist ideologies. The racial borders were naturalized and stark; crossing them was not tolerated. Dominic Griffiths and Maria Prozesky (2010: 31) write, "The way we imagine ourselves at the most profound level, the values and judgments are so deeply ingrained in us, both individually and as a society, that we do not even know we have them and cannot consciously articulate them." The process of internalizing and naturalizing the borders in racial isolation was central to how white children imagined themselves and the boundaries of their communities.

Research on racial socialization in an era of color-blindness shows that for whites, racial socialization is a low priority (Hamm 2000). In fact, color-blind discourses prevail, and the racial socialization of white children happens "indirectly, unintentionally, and subtly within white families" (Lesane-Brown et al. 2010: 461). Since segregation and isolation remain a central aspect of the U.S. racial landscape, it should not be surprising that whites do not see segregation as a problem or even as a race-based phenomenon. As Eduardo Bonilla-Silva and David Embrick (2006: 340) note, whites "either do not see any need to explain these things at all or explain them away through phrases such as, 'Race has nothing to do with it' or 'That's the way things are.'" In a society in which rewarded values and norms are those most aligned with white cultural capital, Jill Hamm found that white parents believe black youth should "conform to standards in terms of behaviors and values of mainstream middle class society rather than for white youth to develop expertise with members of a different culture" (Hamm 2000: 89). This, of course, puts blacks in an untenable position of being required to conform before being accepted, but acceptance is not granted to those whose features do not match the dominant group (see Ballard 2004; Low 2007).

The contemporary research on racial socialization helps us to understand how racialization happens and racism is reproduced, even as white parents believe that they are color-blind and raise their children to be color-blind. However, research shows that race matters to children. Based on yearlong participant observation of a preschool classroom, Debra Van Ausdale and Joe Feagin (2001) show that children as young as three years old have internalized dominant racial beliefs, language, and practices. Without critical awareness and the necessary language tools and experience of close interactions with racialized others as the basis for analyzing race, children default into dominant racial beliefs in which across institutions whites have unearned privilege and power. When parents socialize their children in ways that match dominant racial ideologies and children do not have interactions with black children, white children are most likely to maintain racist ideologies that uphold racial borders (Carter, Picca, and Murray 2012).

In her book *Raising Racists* (2011), Kristina DuRocher shows how white southern parents worked to ensure that their children internalized white-supremacist beliefs and actions. For parents, the goal of this instruction was to lay the foundation that would prepare their children to combat black opposition to segregation. Consequently, they taught their children that they, as whites, bore the burden of their race in keeping blacks subordinate to whites (DuRocher 2011: 17–18). The process of racialization happened in the context of families and communities that shared a class, race, and religious understanding of the world. In the Jim Crow South, "white culture desensitized children to racial violence so they could perpetuate it themselves one day" (DuRocher 2011: 94). In the process of socialization, then, white children learned that whites are uniquely worthy of their empathy and understanding, and to protect those considered kin and community, they were socialized to lack empathy for blacks.

Our research captures a unique time in history, and thus offers a unique lens into both passive and active racialization of white children. The individuals we interviewed lived in racially segregated communities with clear racial borders. The borders were institutionally protected and allowed whites a sense of safety, a protection of property values and the path to upward mobility (see Low 2007). As the Civil Rights Movement gained momentum and achieved success in housing and employment rights, whites began to feel threatened by larger cultural, political, and economic shifts that threatened physical borders (Omi and Winant 1994; Diamond 2009). As local borders were threatened, white children were given explicit and active lessons about race from their parents and others. These lessons instilled fear and an understanding of difference among children on the Southwest and West Side neighborhoods of Chicago.

A discussion of the process of racial socialization has to be understood in the context of the way whites had "taken for granted" the borders when they were protected by institutions. Once those protections shifted, whites needed to respond. It is the ways individuals made sense of their own socialization that helps us to understand how racism is transmitted in families, communities, and society while ensuring that whites continue to think of themselves as good, morally upstanding people. The physical borders wrap a community, a space that creates an internalized racial border through the process of socialization. Specifically, a sense of community and empathy across racial borders was absent from the white imagination. Instead, the border was seen as a specific, static, and naturally derived physical space. Whites believed the physical borders and segregated racial social structures that privilege whites were a reflection of a natural order and, as we heard from many individuals, "just the way it was." The border separated safety and danger, us and them, deserving and undeserving, human and less than human. We see this socialization through families, the community, and larger institutions.

Learning Race through Families and Communities

White imaginations and understandings of the world are reinforced through physical separation, which ensures the racial isolation in which the socialization and imagination develop (see Ballard 2007). For example, when asked about the extent of his interaction with blacks, Vince responded: "None. The one kid we had in school, his name was Freddy Jones. He was not what I'd call my running-around buddies, but . . . I can't ever remember him ever being shunned by people, but look at it from my perspective. He was one of eight hundred kids in the school." Other respondents shared similar experiences, with some parents going to considerable lengths to avoid sending their children to integrated schools. Margo shared the following story of her parents having her lie so she could go to a less integrated school:

When I was in eighth grade, they were moving boundaries for high school. I went to a public high school, and my parents couldn't afford to send me to private school or a Catholic high school. So initially my high school was supposed to be Lindbloom, because people that lived a house or two away, their kids all went to Lindbloom. Lindbloom at that point was pretty heavily integrated. It had a larger black population, and my mother almost had heart failure. It really was farther than Gage Park [High School], and they just couldn't see me going there. They had a friend who had a daughter a year older than I was, so they came up with this plan that we were going to register, and I was going to go with their friends. . . . I mean, I still remember memorizing the address and then memorizing the phone number so that when I went, I could just rattle it off. We sat down, and we registered and everything, and I had all my transfers. . . . [O]ne of the counselors, Mr. Vavegas, he sat there and he looked at her and he looked at me and he said, "I know you don't live here" . . . and we were, like, dumfounded—like, what do we do now? But he said, "Don't worry." He said, "They're talking about changing boundaries again." Fortunately, they did, and I ended up at Gage Park, but that was a big concern.

Like Vince and Margo, most of our respondents reported little interaction with blacks in school.[1] The lack of interaction is important, given that whites develop a sense of themselves, humanity, and community through racial borders. Gunnar Myrdal (1944) wrote that while segregation had a range of deleterious outcomes for blacks, whites did not escape unscathed. In fact, he argued not only that whites lost access to many areas of the city because of segregation and racial borders but also that these self-imposed limits stunted their humanity.

A lack of interaction with blacks resulted in a perception by whites, like Jeanine, that blackness was a sign of a worsening neighborhood condition. In fact, most whites lived with racial borders "on their minds," but not consciously or explicitly articulating how they built their lives around not getting too close to the border. Dean remembered about growing up on the West Side that "there were no blacks around us. There was no reason for them to come in our neighborhood. There was no reason for us to go in their neighborhoods. So because of that issue, it wasn't—up until that point, there was no hate. I didn't know a black guy, so how can I hate you? You know what I mean? And even our parents, there was none of that, until the neighborhood started changing. That's when race came in. Until that point, race was never an issue." For many whites, their own racial identity is invisible. Race becomes visible only when they interact with nonwhites. When whiteness is invisible, whites can innocently believe that race, with all that it encompasses—hatred, violence, and degradation—arrived when the border was breached. Thus, racial problems arrive when blacks do, not as the result of the behavior of whites or larger institutions. Yet most of our respondents did not arrive at such notions by themselves. Messages from their families were key.

Families serve a function of caring, nurturing, and socializing the young. The family is often considered a primary socialization force, given the intensity of parental and sibling connections. Our respondents remembered their socialization experiences in a variety of ways. For some, the experience of living in a racially changing and charged space involved a slow realization of their race and ultimately the power of whiteness. For example, Tim recalled:

> Maybe because you were just younger and you're blind to a lot of that stuff [and] all of a sudden you reach an age where you're aware of what's going on. You know, when you're seven years old . . . you're just going outside to play, and you do this and you do that, you know, and now all of a sudden as you're getting older, you're able to venture farther away. . . . [A]nd then you got your mother and father [saying], "Don't go too far because . . . we want you in front of the house." "Why?" You don't understand, and then all of a sudden you become aware. . . . I don't think it's a matter of one specific incident. I don't remember it just being like, "Wow, a black person just did this." You become aware of this.

For Tim and others, racialization involved both messages from parents and a broader recognition from others on where they should be and with whom they should interact. For others, more direct messages came from parents. Tammy, who grew up on the West Side recalls clear statements from her parents: "We had been taught that [blacks] did bad things and that they would do bad things to us—that they didn't like us." These socializing experiences around racial differences are then transformed into a more polarizing sense of "us" versus "them" (Steyn 2001: 51).

The way socialization transforms people around race is intimately connected to the types of racialized language heard in one's home, among friends, and in institutions like school. Language is quite powerful, moving beyond individual conversations to shape both how we think and, ultimately, how we act toward others (Myers 2005). In this way, racial discourse is the "collective text and talk of society with respect to issues of race. If racial ideologies can be viewed as global systems of thought, then racial discourse is the arena in which political/ideological struggle occurs" (Doane 2006: 256). The words we select have the power to influence both the opportunities and constraints that different groups face (Habermas 1984). In this way, racial discourse frames our common-sense ideas of the world and is used to support group interests (Fields 1990). While often dismissed as merely words, the way we talk about race is always a "political choice" (Collins 1998: xxi) in the sense that it is often used to empower some groups at the expense of others (Myers 2005).

A shared story among the individuals we interviewed was the process of racialization through dialogue in isolation. Vince remembered dialogue he heard in his home as a child growing up on the West Side: "I will say that if you were to take the dialogue that took place in homes back then, it wasn't very kind toward black people. You know, the words that people used and, yeah, I don't know what happened in black families' homes. I just know what happened in ours, and it was a culture and an environment that probably bred hate." The racist language and negative inferences that Vince recognized in his home were influential in shaping his worldview. Similarly, Betsy from the Southwest Side recalled the warnings of her parents relating to the borders in her neighborhood (in isolation):

> We [Betsy and her friends] always felt like we were secure and part of a group, part of the neighborhood. It was great. Parents, like I said, didn't really see it that way. . . . [W]hen we would get to go to our friends' houses and hear things around their table, their moms, because they were home, were definitely more, "You know, you really should not be going out at night; we hear that there's, you know, black people here and . . ." And even when some of the black families were moving in around Western Avenue, it was like, "Did you hear? Did you hear? There's black people living there." They were just all freaked out, and they would talk to the police . . . to us, because we didn't know any better, for good or for bad. We were kids. We were isolated from it.

Although they were distanced from their parents' and other adults' anxiety, our respondents were influenced by how adults framed the world.

In some instances, even if a child's parents did not speak about blacks and racial integration in derogatory ways, the child heard it at friends' houses. Tina, from the Southwest Side, remembered: "I think, probably, my feeling about it is it's the way, what your parents taught you. If your parents said things like that, then you probably. . . . I think it's hard to overcome; it's hard to admit a belief that is different from your parents'. My parents never . . . said anything derogatory about anybody, but, you know, my friends' parents, I would say, were not like that. You know, 'The blacks are coming.' The word [that they used] would not have been 'blacks.'" A few respondents were able to come to terms with the prevailing norms around racial discourse in their neighborhoods. In a moment of self-reflection, Tanya talked about how she and her parents, neighbors, and peers used racist language:

> I know the neighbors two doors down were very racist and very open about it. You know . . . just derogatory terms, and especially when the neighborhood looked like it was going to change. "Oh, no. Here comes the [n-word]," and just, you know, really, really bad stuff. That word was thrown around a lot more than it is now. . . . I'm sure I uttered it in my young-hood, and I don't think it was considered quite as hideous—well, it probably was to African Americans, but that word I didn't discuss with them. My parents were probably a little less racist than many. . . . [T]he general feeling was we're probably a little more tolerant than, I would say, the average person. You know . . . jokes flying around; you heard a lot of black jokes, and people didn't hesitate to tell them and, you know, now that I think about it, those jokes are terrible.

The racist discourse these children heard at home and on the streets of their racially segregated neighborhoods became part of their social consciousness. For some, this language had an impact well into their adult lives. Tommy reflected on his childhood in the following manner:

> I don't . . . I'm not . . . it makes me sad. It makes me sad because when you're young and you hear older people talking and they talk in a bigoted way—and let's make one thing clear . . . I'm no angel. I mean, there's things I choose to do in my life, and there's things I don't choose to do in my life, but I believe that some of the bad vibes and some of the bad feelings, um, people may have had for other people . . . and this is probably more racial than anything else, is a byproduct of what you heard in your house. I mean, there's no denying it.

In all cases, through various forms of interpersonal conversation, our respondents were receiving and constructing knowledge about the world, regardless of whether it was true, mythical, rational, or irrational (Doane 2006). The process of passing on information, particularly when it occurs in isolation, shapes larger social structures.

Even when direct dialogue about race was rare within a child's home, the neighborhood and community were infused with messages about racial borders and how accepted community members should act. Crossing racial borders was unthinkable and unacceptable. John explained this in direct language.

> We used to own a hotdog stand on Chicago Avenue, [and] there used to be a school bus, two school buses. . . . [O]ne was from a school . . . Ashland Avenue. If you were bad when you were younger, they would send you to school over there. Montefiore, it was called. Well, they used to come with a busload, and they were all blacks, and these [older white teenagers] used to wait for them every day on the corner. They'd bomb the bus; they'd scream, scream back and forth, throwing things at the buses. I mean, I seen guys, you've seen a lot of things happen in that neighborhood there. All racial. Nobody knew nobody; nobody befriended nobody. It was a black and white issue strictly . . . because it just kept progressing, the movement kept progressing northward, and people . . . just kept getting more bitter.

In such an environment, there was little space for integration. For whites, the norms of the community dictated remaining segregated and opposed to blacks. Such separation and border maintenance were a collective accomplishment (Steyn 2001) that involved social labor and a commitment to the interests of the group (Spelman 2007).

In addition, whites, throughout history and across geography, have socialized their children to defend themselves and their community from outside "threats." For instance, DuRocher (2011) shows how white families in the Jim Crow South encouraged their children to participate in the lynching spectacles to learn the importance of defending a way of life from threatening outsiders. Before Homeland Security and Stand Your Ground laws, we found, Chicago police were encouraging whites to arm themselves and "defend" their families and communities through violence. In short, borders served to preserve a sense of safety and a way of life. Kids heard this not just from their parents but also from other, "trusted" community members. For instance, Jean learned about the need for racial borders from the police: "The police that were there said, "Get a gun." And they said, "Somebody breaks in your house, the next time, shoot them." [They also said,] "If you shoot them and they're running through your yard, pick them up and drag them in the house before you call the police." This is what the police said. And that was the mentality—like, protect yourself. My father came home from work that day and had a handful of big nails and nailed shut every window in that house."

In fact, the police were actively involved in maintaining and patrolling the racial borders. Steve, who grew up near St. Sabina on the Southwest Side, remembered: "We had a group of policeman from Gresham, [a] very well-known police district. When they were off-duty, a bunch of white officers would drive around in one of their cars, and they would take the kids in the neighborhood . . . my friends who were black, and they would beat them up.

They would put them in the car, take [them] to the alley, and beat them up, [then] let them go." Here we see an example of institutions (i.e., law enforcement) prescribing racial boundaries and reinforcing the physical boundaries of the Southwest and West sides. Given the strength of the message by some and tacit approval by others, white teens who might have been viewed as a nuisance in the neighborhood at another time were embraced and encouraged to turn their efforts toward patrolling the streets against blacks. Given adult indoctrination and support, white youth felt justified in, and responsible for, maintaining racial borders. They were encouraged to maintain the borders, even if that meant engaging in violence.

As the adults were fielding panic-peddling realtors, joining together informally and formally or developing a plan to leave, the youth were given a clear message that they were also mandated to protect the family and community from invading outsiders. The messages were strong enough to create a sense that it was young people's job to protect the older generation from blacks, particularly on the West Side, where the racial borders were particularly contested. Dominick recalled, "You had too much respect for the people, and the people respected us, so we were sort of like the protectors . . . inside our own neighborhood. They were safe around us; their children were safe around us." Many youths embraced the protector role. Paul, for example, said:

We used to hang out in front of [a certain] building, and there were other buildings at all four corners. When we were smaller, we'd be playing hockey, making all this noise, and the people in the buildings and the neighbors were always complaining because we were pain-in-the-ass kids. "Don't you guys ever go home?" or "Shut up. It's 10:00 P.M., and my kids want to go to bed." Well, as the years went on, now we're eighteen, nineteen years old; we're still on the corners. Now these people are coming up to us and telling us, "We're glad you're here because when we come home at night, we feel safe." So . . . it was a circle. . . . [N]ow when they came home, they felt safe because they knew we were there. We were their protectors. We weren't bad kids . . . taking advantage of people. But, you know, when we were younger, we were pests to them, and now as we're teenagers . . . and young men, they felt safe coming home because they knew we were out there. They would look out there, and if we weren't out there, they would feel . . . threatened.

Historians note the crucial role of neighborhood youth as the most "visibly active participants" when conflict arose around racial boundaries (Hirsch 1983: 74). In his study of youth in Chicago during from the 1950s through the 1970s, Andrew Diamond (2009: 5) notes that white youth in Chicago neighborhoods played essential roles in "constructing and maintaining cultures of hostility at the boundaries of their communities before and after the major outbreaks of group violence that made the papers." As we see in the next chapter, the role of protector led white youth to engage in violence against blacks to protect the borders. In this sense, white youth had picked up on the lessons from adults that racial change meant the deterioration of their communities and organized to defend whiteness against integration.

For whites growing up in these neighborhoods, the socializing influences came from a variety of sources, including family, peers, community, and institutional actors. Racialization delineated the contours of their social worlds, framing the borders and limiting their interactions across racial lines. As blacks started to cross the racial borders and as racial change appeared more likely, the context in which white children were being socialized shifted from one in which the community had a vague but looming sense of danger that was held at bay by racial borders to a specific and explicit fear—and hatred—of blacks. Such fear was most evident among those close to the borders. Through interview data we were able to capture the central contribution of the fear to the process of racialization of white children.

Fear as the Foundation of Racialization and Borders

The construction of racialized fear has been reflected in our nation's historical dehumanization of blacks, which created a foundation for the acceptance of a slave system and its legacies. Today, media images intensify a broad fear of and disdain for blacks—images that have been insidiously constructed into the fabric of American society (Street 2007). The evening news in most major metropolitan areas covers numerous stories of crime and violence. As Mary Patillo notes, for most middle-class white Americans the reporting of such incidents in distant and troubled inner cities is typically viewed as a symbolic threat rather than as reality. She notes, "Newspapers fill in the gaps of the more sensational tragedies about which the television could provide only a few sound bites; rounding out the flow of urban Armageddon stories are the gossip and hearsay passed informally between neighbors, church friends, and drinking buddies" (Patillo-McCoy 1999: 5). The steady stream of media messages produces fear and reinforces an imagined reality, nourishing one's racial identity and sense of place.

Fear of blacks was central to the socializing of white children in segregated white communities. Ron, who grew up on the Southwest Side, succinctly named the feeling he carried as white child: "Fear. The whole thing was fear. A huge amount of fear." Various adults taught white kids to be fearful of blacks and thus uphold the racial borders. The children lacked interaction with blacks and received messages from secondary sources that blacks hated them and wanted to do harm to them. We heard this sentiment in the course of many of our interviews. For example, Fran, who grew up on the West Side, remembered the messages she received about how blacks felt toward whites: "You knew you were hated. That's what scared me the most. We were . . . I was hated. I grew up believing my parents [who said] that I was hated by these people, and they would kill me just for being white; [that] they hated the white people."

For our respondents, then, the implicit lesson was that the only way to stay safe was to avoid and, if necessary, contain blackness. The fear instilled in children aided in the process of dehumanizing blacks and set the stage for white children and others to accept violence against blacks. For some respondents, blacks were believed to harbor an intrinsic racial hatred and the power to do harm. Thus, whites had to live in fear. Children were socialized to believe that a sense of safety is achieved by maintaining strict borders in which whites hold power and privilege. The clear message was that if they interacted with blacks, they would be victims. Thus, as children they were not given the necessary tools to see the institutional inequalities and how their lives benefited from various structural arrangements and whiteness. They believed they were innocent, and thus victims, not beneficiaries or enactors of an unjust racial order. Consider the story told by two sisters who grew up in West Englewood:

> We were playing in the schoolyard. . . . [W]e were playing softball, and it was all girls. We were different ages, and we were little kids. . . . I was probably, like, thirteen or something, and a group of boys came in. They were African American boys on bikes, and they surrounded us. We never had boys that did that to us, and, you know, and if the boys were going to be teasing us like that, we would say something to them. But we were afraid. So it was a whole change in the atmosphere of . . . I mean we were . . . whatever the parents did or didn't do or however they acted, kids were innocent of it. I mean, we were kids. We can't say anything. We can't do anything. So we were somewhat afraid. We weren't somewhat afraid. We were afraid.

In the absence of intervention by parents and other adults, many of our respondents were left without the skills needed to interpret the events in any other way than to fear or blame blacks.

The sense of being hated was anchored for many of the youths through one or two high-profile incidents that caught the attention of both whites and blacks. Although whites made efforts to protect physical and social borders, fear ran high, and these high-profile events tipped the balance for many neighborhood residents. On the West Side, a white girl was thrown off a moving bus by a group of black girls and died. Sal remembered and vividly recalled the incident:

> There was one big event. I was a freshman. A girl that I was friends with, that was in my grade, we graduated grammar school together, got pushed off a bus and was killed by a group of black girls. She was on the way home from high school. She went to a Catholic girls' high school. . . . [W]e all went to Catholic schools. She was pushed off the back, and in the old days they had these stairs, and when you step on up on the stairs at the back of the bus, you open the doors. When they pushed her off with her weight on there, her skirt got caught on the stairs; she flipped over and got run over by the back tire. . . . [T]hat threw everybody up in arms.

On the South Side, the fear of violence was provoked by a killing outside St. Sabina parish (see Chapter 1). Paul told the story of the shooting of a white teenager by a black teenager:

> A boy [Frank Kelly] was playing in a St. Sabina lot on Seventy-Eighth Street. . . . He was shot by a black guy, but I don't remember the circumstances. That would have been in, like, '63 or '64. When that happened, then that whole parish wanted out. That's when that whole parish changed over. So that might have been, like, '63 through '65. It happened when I was in grammar school. . . . He was shot by a black guy, but I'm not sure if [Frank] had a gun. I don't remember the circumstances. He was always made out to be as innocent on his part as possible, but I'm not really sure if that was true. And as soon as that happened . . . [W]e didn't have guns, and the neighborhood was 100 percent safe when I lived there. You could be out at midnight. There was no crime. So something like that scared everybody.

These events, which represented the culmination of an ongoing buildup of white anxiety, were interpreted as evidence of "naturally" destructive blackness and led to white flight.

The bus tragedy and the Kelly murder became turning points in each neighborhood because the events were so horrific. But they also provided an opportunity for whites to anchor, justify, fuel, and act on their racial fear. Fleeing or fighting made sense when it became clear, through these high-profile incidents, that whites were hated by blacks and under attack. Moreover, the pervasiveness of the fear and hatred that created the border violence became the lens through which the incidents were understood. Memories and stories of specific events punctuated more generalized fear and confirmed the messages that whites were hated and blacks wanted to do violence against them. As Margo, who grew up in Gage Park on the Southwest Side, recalled: "It wasn't one specific thing that turned you against them. It was just in the air. If you'd see them walking down the street and you were with your mother and father, then they'd [say], "Nigger," or something like that. That was just the way you were brought up. That was just the way of life." Specific incidents, such as the bus incident, and the community response anchored the fear, yet fear was already "in the air" before any particular incident took place. The fear and hatred were transmitted to the youth through general and specific socialization. The socialization and awareness of the borders happened over time with a series of small incidents, rumors, and background conversation, primarily in isolation from blacks.

While children were getting direct messages about hate, fear, and their own superiority, acceptable practices were defined and policed across the community more broadly. Central to securing one's place in the community was to avoid blackness or showing any empathy or appreciation for blackness. Betsy stated, "People didn't want to express contrary opinions as being non-racist because everyone else had this hatred for blacks, and they didn't want to be heard saying, you know, 'They are not bad people; they wouldn't be a problem. What are you talking about?' They didn't want to be singled out." Likewise, Tina talked about how this played out on the West Side:

Well, we used to go . . . you either went to Chicago Avenue or you went to Madison Street. So Madison Street at this point was already changing. . . . When we were twelve, fourteen, it was already turning black. So your trips to Madison Street were becoming less and less, because they [older whites] were scared to death. That's what it was. They were scared. They were frightened; they didn't know what to do. They were like, "Where are we going? The black people are taking over. What are we going to do?" . . . [S]omething new was happening that had never happened before, and now what are we going to do? Then you're seeing all these things escalate. You're seeing riots, you're seeing. . . . These people never dealt with this in their life. They left their doors open.

Similarly, respondents from the Southwest Side were aware of the racial borders and began to internalize where they should not go. Tommy talked about the freedom he had as a teen and how he and his friends altered their behavior based on fears of blacks and learning from adults how to be safe: "We had the freedom that if you wanted to go to the swimming pool—the Gage Park pool—you would go, and you were safe because nobody bothered with you. Nobody messed with you . . . but it was always spelled out. If you go past Ashland Avenue, you know, you're risking your life and that's how it was." Fear led youth to adopt practices that were similar to those of their parents, although they drew on the resources they had as children. Some youth worked to avoid the borders, fleeing inward to the white community and home. Others, as indicated above, saw themselves as community protectors and defenders and employed violence to hold the border. Research has shown that the greater the race and class differences across the borders, the higher the fear level (Covington and Taylor 1991). While other, intersecting variables could help to explain the fear (e.g., the withdrawal of social services and policing and greater housing turnover with the entry of "strangers"), in fact, fear is the foundation on which white racialization is built. And that fear preceded particular incidents and spurred the formation of borders that became sites of violent interaction.

In this chapter, we have focused on how the socialization experiences of our respondents mediate how they have defined themselves and their communities in the world. The vast majority of our respondents experienced racially segregated schools and home environments that were not racially progressive. We did, however, observe some minor differences in terms of what respondents heard in their homes, schools, and neighborhoods. These differences largely centered on how racially explicit their families were in talking about race. However, we encountered only a few examples of respondents who had radically different socialization experiences, both at home and school. In the end, these appeared as outliers among the majority of the interviews.[2]

Writing about modern gated communities, Setha Low (2007) argues that a central aspect of whiteness is the desire to live in a "nice" area. Here, "nice" is defined as clean and orderly and includes a house that is a positive financial investment. Since white children were raised to see blacks as the antithesis of this niceness, the protection of community, or keeping blacks out, became directly about protecting whiteness and white privilege. Whether the border we are discussing was a street or a wall with a gate, whites actively worked to maintain those spaces based on a desire for protected, safe, and nice spaces. Unlike the gated communities set up as protected white spaces with written rules, regulations, walls, and gates (see Low 2007), the segregated communities of the Southwest and West sides of Chicago were held together through informal control and the grassroots efforts of parishes and other local networks, as well as a shared racial and class position. The goal of segregated white communities during the 1960s, 1970s, and early 1980s was the same as that of the gated white communities that followed: protect white privilege by protecting a way of life, cultural capital, and housing values.

From the 1960s forward, as better employment and housing opportunities opened up, blacks were able to afford housing in working-class and lower middle-class areas. Whites in segregated neighborhoods where the housing stock was affordable looked at upwardly mobile blacks with hostility and disdain. Since whites had moved into protected all-white spaces and did not actively organize to create those segregated spaces, working together to protect those spaces was a new idea. Many whites saw the border as a dam that was about to burst, and many began to work in earnest for the first time to protect their privilege and power. As individual whites took on the work of border maintenance, they needed to be clear about what they were willing to sacrifice and what goals they hoped to achieve. Whiteness and racism were now consciously "anchored in real practices," and some whites were willing to accept and even initiate violence as means to achieve their goal (Bonilla-Silva and Foreman 2000). The goal was to protect a way of life, a community, their families, and, ultimately, their opportunity to rise in society as full members of the white middle class. As discussed in the previous chapter, this was a status that, for members of the third wave of immigration—that is, those from southern and southeastern Europe—was not necessarily secure. Clearly defined borders assisted in the achievement of firmly rooted middle-class status and the American Dream. This meant distancing oneself from blacks, and in the case of many people whose American identity was vulnerable, this meant becoming "more white."

Given that racial borders were lived at the ideological, institutional, and physical levels, many whites believed that segregation was "just the way it is." The borders were often understood as existing in a world beyond the control of whites. However, what we learned through our interviews is that whites put a great deal of work into maintaining borders. The ways in which white children were racialized, directly and indirectly, shows the involvement of adults across the community in cultivating a fear of blackness and the recognition of a distinct border separating white from black. Youth recalled receiving racial lessons from trusted adults, and in the process they began to develop identities oriented around a clear border between "us" and "them," safe and dangerous, "nice" and "ghetto," valuable and degraded, loved and disdained. These lessons, translated into racial identities, shaped lives in numerous ways, including, as we show in the next chapter, how these Chicagoans commemorate the past through storytelling.

4

The End of an Idyllic World

Frank Clement grew up in the 1950s and 1960s in West Humboldt Park, on Chicago's West Side and remembers his neighborhood as an idyllic, tight-knit place. The heavily Italian and Polish neighborhood centered on the Catholic parish known as Our Lady of Angels. Frank's father, a Chicago police officer, made just enough money so that his mother could stay at home with Frank and his three siblings. The house the family lived in held a lot of meaning. Frank's grandparents had bought it in the 1940s from another family member who had owned it since the 1920s. The small house was now home not only to Frank and his family but also to his grandmother. Other family was not far away, either: Frank could visit three sets of aunts and uncles, not to mention almost ten cousins, within seven blocks. Neighbors knew one another well, creating a strong sense of community. A commercial district along Chicago Avenue strengthened the neighborhood feel. A movie theater, a grocery store, and a pizzeria were regular haunts for Frank and his buddies, making it unnecessary to leave the neighborhood.

For kids growing up in West Humboldt Park, life involved few adult-controlled activities. For Frank and other like-minded boys, most days not spent in school centered on playing sports with the guys in the neighborhood. While formal baseball games were often played at Kells Park, kids mostly played in the alley or in the street, using the sewer covers on the corners as bases. When it got too cold, Frank and his friends turned to hockey. For Frank, this was a simpler time, when his parents rarely drove him to lessons, sport practice, or little league games. For kids Frank's age, activities were initiated and controlled by kids, with occasional check-ins for lunch and dinner. Curfew was when the streetlights went on. The dynamic led to strong friendships that lasted year-round. Frank walked to the Our Lady of Angels grammar school every day, which was rebuilt after the original building was the scene of a horrific fire in 1958 that killed ninety-five people, all but three of whom were kids (Cowan and Kuenster 1998).[1]

The idyllic period of Frank's childhood began to change in the late 1960s. In April 1968, blacks on the West Side reacted violently the day after Martin Luther King Jr. was assassinated, looting white-owned business and setting fires on nearby Madison Avenue (Coates 1968). Like other kids, Frank witnessed the smoke rising above Madison Avenue and members of the National Guard filtering into the neighborhood. Unlike other kids in the neighborhood, however, Frank watched his father leave the house for work in riot gear, creating a sense of unease until he came home from his shift. Other changes were also happening. Later that year, many of the surrounding neighborhoods went through racial transition. The schools were the first to integrate. Frank's sister, Connie, went to a school that was integrating, and there was a lot of racial tension. Connie had a number of run-ins with black students, Frank said, and once was physically attacked. Frank's younger brother was also harassed, in this case when a group of black kids allegedly tried to take his bike. In 1970, after a long year of such events, Frank's father decided the family had had enough of integration and moved them six miles north, to the Portage Park neighborhood. Many neighbors followed suit, and in the span of two or three years West Humboldt Park's racial mix changed dramatically.

After moving, Frank often returned to the neighborhood to be near his friends. When school started in the fall, however, his visits became few and far between. Today, nearly forty years later, his powerful memories of this idyllic time are so strong that he often finds himself thinking of the neighborhood. In recent years, Frank has parked his car in front of the old house more than once, usually in the winter when few people are out, trying to scare up the courage to knock and ask to tour the old place. The train Frank takes to his job in downtown Chicago offers him a view of the block he grew up on and his grammar school. He admits wistfully that he often dreams of buying a house on the old block. And like many adults who visit their childhood homes, Frank was surprised by how small everything looked. Yet size is only part of the issue. Things are not OK in West Humboldt Park today. Many of the houses in Frank's old neighborhood are boarded up or are vacant lots. The area is very low income, and there is little vitality. The owner of the hotdog stand near Frank's old house carries a semiautomatic gun. The nostalgia and melancholy in Frank's voice were clear as he described a place that is a far cry from the neighborhood he remembers, where communal ties were strong, men meticulously maintained their lawns, and kids ran around without a care in the world.

It is not difficult to sympathize with Frank's sense of loss for his old neighborhood. Undoubtedly, Frank's departure from the neighborhood—a decision made by parents—upset his world. Mindy Fullilove (2005: 14) refers to such loss as "root shock," a "profound emotional upheaval that destroys the working model of the world that existed in the individual's head."[2] The root shock Frank and other respondents felt was indeed shared by many people who had grown up in neighborhoods in northern cities beginning in the 1950s.[3] Making sense of such stories is not easy. "Everybody's got a story. Some are bathed in sepia. . . . [W]here does the folktale stop and reality begin?" as the journalist Ray Suarez (1999: 3) has asked. The line between reality and folktale is made murkier by a steady drumbeat coming from authors lamenting the loss of community and related declines in participation in voluntary associations and the values that supported strong neighborhood associations (Sampson 2012; Putnam 2000; Etzioni 1993). For example, Alan Ehrenhalt extends the folktale in *The Lost City* (1996), his exploration of the rootedness of neighborhood life in several Chicago neighborhoods in the 1950s. Ehrenhalt's depiction of neighborhoods like the one Frank grew up in romanticizes the *Gemeinschaft* or community elements, decrying their decline in the face of emergent hyper-individualism and the accompanying cultural obsession with personal choice, rather than on the workings of race or structural causes. Nonetheless, it is important to pay attention to these stories as they carry memories and connect us to a larger community. How can we understand these stories of such tight-knit communities without lapsing into nostalgia or romanticizing the past?

In this chapter, we explore the stories white residents tell about the periods prior to and just after racial change occurred in their neighborhoods. Racial change did unravel the knit-together nature of the community in that close bonds of friendship were broken when people scattered to other neighborhoods and even suburbs. Like Frank, other respondents told stories that were tinged with nostalgia for their lost neighborhoods. Clearly, racial transition generated varied emotions, with fear and anxiety about declines in property values, anger against blacks, and a sense of loss prominent among them. Indeed, the construction of attachments to place is important to an individual's well-being and sense of social connectedness. According to Yi-Fu Tuan, what starts as undifferentiated "space" becomes "place" through the "steady accretion of sentiment" (Tuan 1974: 33, 1977). This affective bond between people and places (usually residences and neighborhoods) is best known as "place attachment" (Altman and Low 1992; Manzo 2003). Place attachment can take on social, material, and ideological aspects as individuals develop kinship and community ties, own or rent property, and get involved in public life (Altman and Low 1992; Manzo and Perkins 2006). The importance of place meaning to people becomes quite clear when one examines disruptions of place attachments. Studies of families forced to relocate by urban renewal projects demonstrate a profound sense of grief and mourning for places that no longer physically exist, as the physical and social fabric of their communities was destroyed (Fried 1963; Gans 1982; Marris 1986; Fullilove 2005). Studies of environmental disasters also illustrate how disruptions of place attachment can disturb a sense of continuity (Belgrave and Smith 1994; Brown and Perkins 1992; Erikson 1976; Katovich and Hintz 1997; Smith and Belgrave 1995) and cause feelings of loss and alienation (Hummon 1992). Finally, and most applicable to our research, Scott Cummings's research on the effects of racial change on whites illustrates that such change can generate similar emotions of loss for their neighborhood and the emotional security it provided, particularly for those who are unable (or unwilling) to leave as the neighborhood shifts (Cummings 1998). In each case, change in the physical world, and thus to one's place attachments, leads to feelings of loss of what was taken for granted and identities that were constructed.

Nostalgia is an important way individuals react to such a disruption (Milligan 2003).[4] Nostalgic memory shapes memory to particular effect, however, and thus is a function of present fear and anxiety, involving an active choice of what to remember and how to remember it (Wilson 2005). In this way, nostalgia narratives serve as a tool we use in the continuous process of building, maintaining, and reconstructing our identities (F. Davis 1979). Nostalgia narratives, then, are imagined stories of the past that select positive elements from one's personal history while scrubbing away stories that are unpleasant or even shameful. Individuals compose nostalgia narratives when they feel their identities, status, or attachments to a place are threatened, and these narratives provide a means for constructing or framing group identities that are positive (Schwalbe and Mason-Schrock 1996). Like other tools (e.g., dress, talk, deviant acts), nostalgic narratives serve as a method of group-level identity work, are often used to defend territory, and create a sense of authenticity and legitimacy (Kasinitz and Hillyard 1995). Narrative construction is particularly important for reinforcing racial identities, establishing and reproducing an understanding of what "characteristics and values" make one a member of a group (Boyd 2010: 95).

In cities, nostalgia narratives have emerged in struggles over redevelopment and threats of social and cultural displacement. In their research on Brooklyn, Philip Kasinitz and David Hillyard (1995) explored how old-timers use nostalgic storytelling to highlight how their self-sufficient, morally decent, and authentic communities were destroyed and, in contrasting the area's golden age with the present era of decline, to assert ownership of the neighborhood. Mary Patillo's study of a gentrifying black neighborhood in Chicago highlights how existing residents, threatened by residential, social, and cultural displacement, use nostalgia tales of community, shopping, and entertainment prior to gentrification in an effort to stake their claim for the future (Patillo 2007). Similarly, Michelle Boyd's study of the same area demonstrates how leaders used nostalgic renderings of history to make claims about the future of the neighborhood—in particular, the political goals surrounding redevelopment projects (Boyd 2010). Finally, Richard Ocejo's study of Manhattan's Lower East Side examines how early gentrifiers use a nostalgia narrative to combat the social and cultural change brought on by commercial gentrification, as highlighted by the increased presence of bars and nightlife (Ocejo 2011). As early gentrifiers faced being displaced as social authorities in the neighborhood, nostalgia narratives gave them a way to claim an identity as the area's authentic and symbolic owners. Together, these studies share a focus on battles over physical space, highlighting the power of nostalgia to construct new identities that confront, redefine, and challenge change in the present and, in doing so, serve as a basis for political action.

Examining the use of nostalgia narratives is an important element in grasping why and how people construct communities and identities. While memory is indeed personal, remembering is also a communal and historic act (Johnson and Dawson 1982; Bellah et al. 1985; Lowenthal 1985; Ferrarotti 1990; Schwartz 1996). Through storytelling we construct communities and our notions of ourselves. Thus, the collective memory process helps us reaffirm identity, define in-groups and out-groups, and guide how we think about ourselves and orient or situate a sense of identity (Hobsbawm 1972; Irwin-Zarecka 1994; Schwartz 1996; Zerubavel 1996; Hooker 2009). Yet memory is not fixed. It has to be continually created and maintained, a process that is accomplished in a group context and that reflects the concerns and anxieties of the present (Halbwachs 1992; Schwartz 1997). Recognizing that both identity and memory are ongoing processes rather than static properties, scholars have explored the various ways in which identities are fashioned and sustained. The most basic method of realizing this socialization is through talk, particularly in small groups, where we ground and substantiate our reevaluations of our personal recollections and thus do the work of constructing identity (Casey 1987; Revill 1993; Fivush 1994).

We know less about how memory is used in the construction of racial identities. Two notable exceptions are Ruben May's study of how collective memory is created through face-to-face interactions and Boyd's study of how black leaders reinvent neighborhood history to achieve certain political goals (May 2000; Boyd 2010). May's study, which centers on a racially homogenous neighborhood tavern, explores how African American men use race talk to give individuals "an opportunity to re-create themselves with positive racial self-identity" (May 2000: 202). He reveals how individual young and older patrons construct memories through storytelling that reveal the past and present state of race relations. Given that most Americans live in highly seg-regated neighborhoods and socialize in race-segregated groups, race talk in these settings is restricted and offers a limited vision of race relations. As others have pointed out, this limited vision is not specific to blacks (Bonilla-Silva, Goar, and Embrick 2004). In her study, Boyd examines how leaders and residents use nostalgia narratives in a black middle-class community in Chicago to frame neighborhood development and racial identity (Boyd 2010). Focusing on how community leaders reinvent residents who once lived in the community, she uncovers the ways in which political elites use this reconstruction to define the preferences that are worthy of group support and, in the process, increase the neighborhood's appeal to outside investors.

The construction of racial identity through memory-making projects is certainly tied to how race is understood and discussed. In a color-blind era, two trends have emerged in how whiteness is supported. One involves stories whites tell about themselves that extol "non-racial" virtues of white residents and neighborhoods, with little acknowledgment of how institu-tions have supported whites, while ignoring or discriminating against others (Feagin 2010). The other related trend involves whites' articulating and con-structing themselves as victims of institutions, laws, and an overly powerful government that created an unfair playing field for them (Formisano 1991; Gallagher 1993; Bonilla-Silva 2009; Hooker 2009). Whites have articulated the latter notion in a variety of ways. For example, whites often rely on a naturalization frame when interpreting racial segregation, racial isolation, and racial change, failing to see these issues as a problem or, importantly, as something over which whites have control or can change (Bonilla-Silva, Goar, and Embrick 2006; Sokol 2007). Yet while whites may profess to be powerless, they do act in ways to protect white privilege. Scholars have dem-onstrated the numerous conscious and deliberate actions that have institu-tionalized white group identity in the United States to create a "possessive investment in whiteness" (Lipsitz 2006). These efforts have included policies sanctioned by the state but also involve cultural stories. Stories of powerless-ness and white valor allow whites to not implicate themselves in a system of racial inequality and still maintain white privilege. Nostalgia narratives are quite similar in this regard and represent culturally legitimate responses that defend the advantages that whites gain due to the presence of blacks in America (Wellman 1993).

For residents of Chicago's Southwest and West sides, racial change resulted in an "involuntary disruption of place attachment" (Milligan 2003:

385). Frank Clement and others felt this loss and displacement as their parents fled the neighborhood, and because of their age at the time, it was a formative experience. However, this displacement occurred as the Civil Rights Movement altered racial discourse in the United States, leaving whites with a different context in which to understand race and racial identity. As we shall see, through nostalgia narratives and race talk whites construct, maintain, and repair a positive white racial identity by calling on color-blind discourse, even as this discourse is undermined by actual social conditions. Recalling racial change through a nostalgic lens and calling on color-blind language, whites frame white racial identity in terms of innocence, virtuousness, and powerlessness, making claims of being victims of overwhelming circumstances (state-based changes) or of "others" (unruly blacks), and are rarely able to see other alternatives (e.g., integration). In the process, nostalgia narratives of the old neighborhood prove a useful and culturally sanctioned strategy to regain white ownership and provide a common-sense understanding of how to achieve a good life and validate a social hierarchy of white as good and justifiably dominant.

Nostalgia Narratives around Racial Change

Frank Clement was not alone in his dreams of the old neighborhood; other respondents voiced similar romanticized feelings about their houses and neighborhoods. A relative of one respondent, now a Chicago police officer, went as far as to knock on the door of his old house and inform the occupants that the police had received a report of suspected child abuse. His place attachment was so strong that he created a ruse to once again walk through the house. While no one else went to such lengths, the majority of our respondents repeatedly spoke nostalgically of the old neighborhood and a time that life seemed good—that is, orderly, friendly, safe, and homogeneously white. The good life, couched in the specific geography and history of segregated white neighborhoods in Chicago during the 1960s–1980s, is viewed as having been disrupted, destroyed, and rendered unrecoverable because of unavoidable racial change. Sometimes through racially explicit language but most often through racially coded language of crime, housing upkeep, religion, and culture, nostalgia narratives are consistently built around a segregated white world. Blame for destruction of their special neighborhoods is generally placed on individuals, particularly those blacks who moved into the neighborhood. The memories of the loss of the old white neighborhood converge with nostalgia for a time that white culture was unquestioningly synonymous with American culture. In the shared storytelling of this nostalgic past, whites construct a present that plays by color-blind rules while reproducing, reiterating, and strengthening whiteness by making explicit claims about what it means to be a good American and human being. Since nostalgia is never simply about the past, analyzing the stories whites tell of this time offers an opportunity to examine not only how they understand themselves but also how they construct their racial identities. In relation to such identities, we start with the assumption that racial politics are not simply the result of preexisting identities. Rather, the construction of identity is a form of political behavior (Boyd 2010).

As noted in the Methodological Appendix, our interviews began without asking about race at all. Instead, we asked general and generic questions about the respondents' childhoods, homes, and neighborhoods. Out of these general questions emerged several story lines regarding race and space. Here we explore three narratives that whites used to reposition whiteness in a color-blind era in which many whites felt they were losing institutional support for their tight-knit communities. The first, a nostalgia narrative, depicts the idyllic world as homogeneous, caring, and tight-knit. The stories begin with a portrayal of an idyllic time when the world was white and homogeneous and protected by institutional practices that created and allowed segregation to exist. In this space, whiteness is expressed as virtuous and naturally good through the construction of integration as naturally destructive to communities and property. In other words, the tight-knit community and white goodness are possible only in the absence of integration with blacks. The second narrative builds on the nostalgia of the first narrative. Once integration and blackness are constructed as naturally destructive forces, whites then position themselves as powerless victims of this natural disaster over which they had no control. This part of the narrative turns on an "until" moment in which their idyllic worlds were lost due to blacks' moving into the area. Finally, several cracks in the nostalgia narrative emerge, particularly when whites attempt to reconcile nostalgic renderings not only with the racial isolation and racism in their homes and neighborhoods but also with the present. Here we examine the complexity of how whites reconcile their experiences of living through a racially explicit period with the color-blind rules of the present. In the end, our analysis makes sense of how whites use nostalgia narratives and storytelling to construct positive white racial identities, as well as to normalize racial segregation as many continue to live it today.

Narratives of Eden: White Is Natural, and Good Communities Are Homogenous

The power that memories of the time before racial change hold is the core of the nostalgia narrative and the basis for white racial identity. Whites on the Southwest and West sides constructed place attachments amid the city's tight-knit, largely Catholic neighborhoods. The connections between neighbors and friends were tight. In the storytelling of that time, life was magical. Phillip, who was from the Southwest Side, remembered the magic:

> You could stand out on the front porch and just yell, "Baseball!" and, boom, you had a baseball game. We used to play baseball in the streets. If I remember correctly, my mom used to say we had eighty-some kids on our block, because we had a double block. Everybody knew everybody, you know? Someone would call up my mom and say, "Could you watch the baby for a couple hours?" "Oh yeah, just bring him over." She'd put the baby out in the backyard to sleep, and our boxer would just lay at the foot of the crib. . . . [I]t was just a fun place to grow up.

Fun, goodwill, and a sense of shared obligation defined this tight-knit community. Barb, who grew up on the West Side, conveyed a sense of excitement and safety that came with being surrounded by friends and family: "It was, like, because you had this close family, there was always something going on. Somebody was always visiting. You had, like, three mothers. If you left the house and went down Chicago Avenue, you were just always going to run into people you knew . . . someone at the bakery, or friends, or your aunt and uncle. There was always something going on. It was that type of community, where you didn't worry about anything happening to you, because you knew someone on every block or several people on every block." The neighborhood's "parochial autonomy," where everyone knew everyone else, created a strong sense of community and is central to the narrative (Kasinitz and Hillyard 1995).

Related to a characterization of strong communal ties are the repeated assertions that residents grew up almost in a "small town" within Chicago and in a "different time." For working-class and young whites growing up in these neighborhoods in the late 1950s through the late 1970s, life began and ended in the neighborhood (Ehrenhalt 1996; Kefalas 2003). John, from the Southwest Side near Marquette Park, noted: "Living here was like living in a small town. When you were a little kid, you didn't need to be driven to any parks. You didn't have to be involved in organized sports. It was always neighborhood kids. Everybody was the same age. . . . [Y]ou had the benefits of living in the big city but the small-town benefits of living in the neighborhoods. Everyone thought this was the best of small-town life living in the neighborhoods." For residents in these neighborhoods, everything that mattered—education, church, socializing, and shopping—happened in the neighborhood. Noting that this was an era before malls, Donna, who grew up on the Southwest Side, observed, "Every neighborhood had its own little grocery store and a drugstore. We had one, and they had a fountain service there. You'd get a Coke or a cherry Coke or whatever." The localness of such neighborhoods made it likely that few traveled far outside the neighborhood. As one respondent described the area he grew up in: "Our whole life was there—our family, friends, everything we knew. All our safeguards were in that neighborhood."

The small-town feel of the neighborhood was also tied to what our respondents referred to as a "different time," a time that kids were given a lot more freedom to explore; they walked with friends or played sports with little fear of crime. A strong community spirit strengthened this feeling of safety. Kenny, one of the last to move out his West Side neighborhood, noted: "There was no doors. There was no locks. People were outside. . . . I mean, you would come home at night, and there would be thirty-five people having iced tea, laughing, sitting . . . outside—all the parents, all the kids. So it was a different world; it was a different life. . . . [T]he majority of people that you talk to, they'll all say the same, they'll tell you the exact same thing. I would think every one of them has the same story." Jenny, who grew up on the Southwest Side, echoed this sentiment: "We didn't have to have our parents driving us all over. You just walked. You know, you called somebody up on the phone or you walked over to their house and yelled outside the door." Indeed, most respondents shared this characterization of their childhood neighborhoods as being a different or simpler time. Articulated through this part of the nostalgia narrative is a wider insecurity about contemporary urban life and an implication that this time was indeed a better one.

A second and interrelated theme of this part of the nostalgia narrative centers on the notion of shared parenting and close peer networks. Respondents recalled having their grandparents, uncles, and aunts living within a three- to five-block radius of where they grew up. On the West Side, it was not uncommon for multiple generations to live in the same modest home. This family-oriented and close-knit life fostered the image of a cheerful and congenial community. Pete, who grew up on the West Side, said: "Not only did my grandparents have four children. All of their children's spouses' relatives lived within twelve houses. So every night was just my aunts, my uncles—you were in and out of any house on the block. It was all family. It was the greatest, greatest thing you can ever imagine." Many other respondents shared this experience of having extended family within a few blocks of their home. Such friendship and extended familial bonds led to feelings of social solidarity, where people looked out for one another. Lee, a former West Side resident, reinforced this sense of community cohesiveness:

[We] stayed by each other. It didn't matter where you were. You know what I mean? You go by anybody's house—wow, a call from your mom: "Are you coming home?" Everybody knew everybody, and they'd watch no matter where you went. I used to do things five blocks from my house. By the time I got home, my old man would be waiting on the porch. And I'd say, "So what's up?" He'd say, "You don't think I know people in this neighborhood?!" You know what I mean? He'd get a phone call that would beat me home.

The sense of knowing people on the block and having other people act like their parents created a strong sense of unity for kids. Reflecting on his Southwest Side neighborhood, Keith stated: "You knew everybody on your block. Everybody got along. It was just a great place to live."

Strong peer networks deepened feelings of solidarity and a sense of the "specialness" of this idyllic time and place. Residential blocks, usually with dozens of children, enhanced this sense of a serene childhood by offering camaraderie, social cohesion, and safety. Respondents remember a wide-open childhood in which kids navigated the community with their friends, often with few adult-controlled activities. Children knew one another quite well from playing on the block, going to common schools, and attending church. Joe recalled that "there were a lot of kids around" on his West Side block. "All my friends were on the block, and a lot of us went to the same high school together." Shelia, who grew up on the Southwest Side, had a similar memory: "We would gather at Sixty-Third and Richmond at a place called Kings. It was, like, a hotdog stand. All the different age groups from the neighborhood would hang out there, and you would stand in your little packs. It's almost like a '50s movie, you know? We always viewed it as very, very safe, and we didn't really think too much about what was going on in the outside world." Similar to accounts of working-class neighborhoods across the United States and in Britain, this narrative is punctuated with themes of family, loyalty, and social cohesion, emphasizing residents' and neighborhoods' respectability (see Young and Willmott 1957; Gans 1982; Kasinitz and Hillyard 1995).

A third theme of the nostalgia narrative involves a tale of prosperity, particularly for those living in less well-off sections of these neighborhoods. This tale highlights the virtues of hard work and well-kept houses and gardens. Many respondents recall parents working multiple jobs to keep the family on the rungs of the middle class. Also, although the houses were quite modest, the neighborhood before racial change is recalled as attractive and the kind of place one might still want to live. Pete, from the West Side, recalled: "Not knowing much when I was growing up, I thought Trumbull Avenue was the greatest street ever. The houses were immaculate. . . . [W]e are talking 1960, [and] every man was out there with his hose watering the lawn . . . and every lawn was perfect." Here the theme includes idealized memories of neighborhoods marked by beautiful streets, safety, close family and friends, strong commercial districts, and solid values, all built through the hard work and thrift of their parents.

The final theme of this aspect of nostalgia narrative centers on the proprietorship of neighborhood life, where feelings of loss and displacement are attached to places and time periods, highlighting favorable memories while ignoring painful ones (Wernick 1997; Boym 2001). While most of respondents stayed true to the mythical tale of the old neighborhood, elements of struggle would leak out. Respondents remember the strain of doubling up with extended family in relatively small houses. Others talked about parents' working multiple jobs to make ends meet and rarely taking vacations. Residents rarely strayed from the neighborhood partly because they did not have the money, not only because of the completeness of the community. Finally, others talked about the insular nature of the neighborhood, particularly when it came to meeting members of different racial groups. Marty, from the West Side, noted: "There was no opportunity to speak to blacks. . . . I mean, the first time I really had interaction with them was when I went to work. I became a fireman. . . . [Y]ou know, you're older, you're somewhat wiser, and then you're in a fire and a man reaches out to save your life, [and] you're not going to say, . . . 'It's a black hand. I ain't taking it.' You know what I mean?" The mythical tale of the old neighborhood dominated most memories, rarely divulging hard times, lack of freedom, and diminished opportunities to experience diverse groups and ideas. It is through nostalgia that the positive aspects of our respondents' tight-knit communities are highlighted and the less comfortable aspects are avoided.

Our interpretation of this part of the nostalgia narrative might suggest that we are questioning whether the respondents' childhoods and neighborhoods were indeed idyllic or the simple result of the virtuousness and hard work of the residents. The accuracy or significance of the memory is less important than the deeper sociological meaning of memory making. The construction of collective memories establishes racial identities, a process that is almost always tied to the pursuit of particular ideas about how to protect advantages (Boyd 2010). Thus, it is reasonable to assume that respondents are not simply recalling their neighborhoods and childhoods; they are selecting certain memories to identify and create boundaries around what makes up a good neighborhood, community, and world. In a purportedly color-blind era in which white privilege remains visible, whites use narratives to explain their reaction to racial change and hostility toward blacks while casting themselves as innocent, good, and ultimately morally superior. Examining the nostalgia narrative here helps us uncover how whites construct a virtuous white racial identity in a way that makes sense of the past and explains the continuation of segregation and whiteness today.

And importantly, some elements of their childhoods are indeed left out. In particular, the nostalgia narrative omits explicit appreciation that these bounded communities were possible because of institutional mechanisms that served to protect segregation and the value of whites' property (Massey and Denton 1993; Diamond 2009). While all of our respondents were children growing up in these neighborhoods and thus were not aware of the larger social forces, almost all acknowledged as adults that they later realized that institutional forces were involved. Such acknowledgments for the most part were afterthoughts. Thus, the nostalgia narrative presents the idyllic world as the result of tight-knit, strong, and good families and communities (i.e., virtuous whiteness) rather than of a racially skewed social order. In fact, most respondents did not see their neighborhoods or childhoods as racialized—they saw them just as normal, great, and ideal. Neighborhoods became racialized only when their borders were threatened. The idyllic period ended once blacks moved in. In other words, things were great *until* blacks crossed the border and breached the idyllic world. In short, this narrative presents "evidence" of the idyllic world that is possible when whites are protected through institutional segregation.

Narratives of Losing Eden: Constructing Positive Racial Identities during Racialized Housing Battles

Along with the stories of the neighborhoods' "glory days," former residents incorporate the impact of racial change in their nostalgia narrative. In our interviews, the nostalgia narrative turned on an *until* moment—that is, everything was glorious and beautiful *until* blacks edged closer and moved into the neighborhood. Donna, who grew up on the West Side, captured this moment when asked what she most remembered about her childhood: "The good—until that happened. Until it happened, and then they just kept coming." The nostalgia narrative turned when discussing when racial change began to really affect their lives. The nature of the discussion depended on the age of the respondent when racial change began, how close her or his family was to the borders, and whether her or his family had fled. For example, respondents who lived close to the borders of racial change and were just starting high school when racial change began expressed stronger emotions of loss and anger. In the end, however, the narrative was consistent. In recalling the experience of racial change and white flight, individuals construct themselves both as pawns and agents, as innocents and aggressors, while trying to maintain their decent way of life. As they weave stories of personal experiences with racial change—what was taken away, and who was to blame—we get a glimpse of how they made sense of race and, ultimately, how they understand themselves racially. In this part of the nostalgia narrative, various contradictions emerge.

As individuals spoke about their lives, two interrelated but contradictory expressions arose. First, while most respondents saw themselves as victims of racial change—and, in particular, of the blacks who moved into their communities—they also articulated their own and others' individual and organized violence against blacks. Moreover, they were able to articulate the workings of institutions to destabilize their community, yet they reserved the biggest share of blame for their loss for the incoming blacks. Second, while they saw themselves as powerless against racial change and the resulting demise of their way of life, they remembered myriad individual and organized "fight or flight" responses that both addressed and anticipated racial change.[5] The nostalgia narrative gave them a way to manage these contradictions by softening those elements that implicate them (or their parents) while highlighting those that implicate others. In a color-blind era, the nostalgia narrative provides a way to discuss race in less overt ways while bolstering white racial identity.

A central theme of this part of the nostalgia narrative is loss and regret, particularly for those who lived very close to racial borders. As children or adolescents, the respondents were not part of the decision-making process. However, as Gary, who grew up on the West Side, explained, "These people were scared to death, our parents. They didn't know where to go. 'What do we do? This is our neighborhood. Where do we go?' They were freaked out, and because they were freaked out, it just automatically rubbed off on the children. Whether you realize it or not, you hear the talk, . . . you see things going on, you realize your neighborhood is starting to go away, and nobody wanted it to go away. *People still wish they lived there*."[6] Regardless of their position in the process, the respondents' regret over losing their special world remains strong. The language used is important. Gary states specifically that the "neighborhood [was] starting to go away" and that folks "still wish[ed] they lived there." In other words, the respondents remember themselves as victims in a process they could not stop. Connie reflected on her experience before her family left the neighborhood for the (white) suburbs: "When it came time to leave the neighborhood, I knew it would never be the same. I remember sitting on the grass in front of the house and just scanning. I can remember just saying, 'Everyone's gone. It's over. It's over.' We might as well have moved to another state." The strength of the emotion expressed here has to be understood in the context of how racial change is explained. Regret and loss, while palpable, hinge on feelings of anger, blame, and victimhood. The respondents felt powerless over the forces that were altering their community. Given their parents' understanding of tight-knit community as dependent on the absence of blacks, integration was never viewed as an option.

Regret often turns into anger, and blacks received most of the blame in the respondents' narratives. Pete, who grew up on the West Side, recalled thinking, "Why did they have to come here? We didn't want their neighborhoods." Respondents felt resentful of racial change, particularly at blacks for invading their communities. Vince, from the West Side, explained: "That was my neighborhood. It was, like, not a betrayal, but you felt like you were being invaded. I mean, I moved to that neighborhood when I was five years old. I learned how to walk to school, which was a mile away. I spent my whole grammar school, my whole high school years there. Now all of a sudden, you're chased away." Charlene also recalled her feelings of anger during this time: "It was like I couldn't go out at night. A lot of my friends had left. Stores closed. There wasn't the same group of people hanging out at the church and the school. It was different. And it just . . . it killed me, it just killed me to see these other people living in these houses, and I was mad, and I hated those people for doing, causing that. . . . [L]ook at what you took away from us." The rage expressed in this recollection is quite stunning. Clearly, with their place attachments taken away from them, residents, particularly young people, felt that the incoming residents were taking what was once theirs.

The anger felt by residents whose parents fled the neighborhood due to racial change lingered some forty years later. Lee, from the West Side, captured this sentiment: "[I'm] still mad about it, so I still say, 'If that never happened, my kids might . . . we might still be living on Trumbull Avenue, down the block from all their cousins and everything else. So it's very unfair. On a personal level, which is where I live, it is a very unfair. [I feel] very cheated." Donald, who was also from the West Side, articulated similar ideas when he said, "I mean, there's still some bitter people [who] lost their homes. They lost money, but, you know, you're going back forty years. Either you make the change and join the human race and what's happening or you get left behind. Some of these people are still bitter." Donald thus acknowledges that, while a set of institutional forces (and, thus, white human agency) was involved, a lot of former residents of the community had a hard time not remaining angry. Indeed, many residents, particularly those whose parents had fled the neighborhood, felt re-victimized, first by the "black invasion," and then by the broken solidarity with their white neighbors and friends whom they had considered part of the fabric of their interwoven good community. Embedded in the nostalgia narrative is a sense that whites had little choice. Integration was never considered an option. These expressions of powerlessness, as articulated by whites, help us make sense of the loss and anger over what was viewed as a very special place in terms of family and friends, a special place lost because of blacks.

Woven into the narrative is a disjointed recognition of the institutions that supported the respondents' idyllic worlds before racial change. The narrative contains detailed stories of the various external forces in place that were undermining the community. Scholarly literature is clear that in segregated white neighborhoods, city services, such as police, street and sanitation workers, park clean-up, and construction of libraries and other municipal buildings, had been delivered in a timely and efficient manner. In the nostalgia narrative, integration and the withdrawal of institutional support happened simultaneously. Prior to this time, institutions, including business, real estate, police, and politics, worked to support segregated white neighborhoods. As blacks began to move into white neighborhoods near theirs, whites began to see that the government or businesses would no longer protect their neighborhoods. Instead, their communities would be viewed as sites for predatory real estate practices. These predatory practices required, and ultimately thrived in, the context of whites' fear of racial integration.

Before racial change, whites in these neighborhoods viewed racial segregation as the natural order of things and expected that institutions would maintain racial boundaries. By the late 1960s, whites were beginning to see that the institutions were no longer working to maintain racial boundaries in the city neighborhoods. The concerns of our respondents' parents became centered on property values, a particularly important issue, given their class location. Dave, a longtime resident on the West Side, described the scene:

> We had the one real estate guy [who would] come. He'd knock on the door. Now, my grandmother lived next door, and he told us, "I hate to be a burden or bring bad news, but [did] you know that the woman next door just sold to blacks?" My mom was looking [at us]. He didn't know that our grandmother [was the woman next door], and she said, "Really?" You know, and then it started from there. It was a company . . . that did a lot of block busting. They did a lot of panic selling, and people started departing. You know, people started moving . . . but at that time, too, our houses were in it for a long time. This was [my parents] neighborhood. They got married in the neighborhood. Their [wedding] reception was in the neighborhood. And as the blacks [were] buying . . . property values [were] declining. People were frightened. They were scared . . . , and the neighborhood went fast when it went.

Various institutional actors, with realtors prominently represented, are viewed as instigators who used the problem of race to make money and drive whites from their idyllic worlds. Moreover, these actors were often white. Jimmy, from the West Side, recalled: "Our parents were influenced by people who had other motives, the business motive. Yeah . . . we want you to move out of here and sell your property. And their intent was only to make a buck on the transaction . . . and they could give a shit about the fact that they were disrupting the community we lived in." Candice, from the Southwest Side, echoed Jimmy's sentiment: "We were a product of the white flight period and may as well be honest about that, because we moved, and a lot of that was fear generated by banks and real estate both in areas that were selling in the neighborhoods that we lived in and surrounding areas, so they encouraged this fear. You know, as kids we just kind of had to go along with it." Our respondents' memories of innocence, safety, and social solidarity were interrupted either subtly or overtly as racial change edged closer to their neighborhoods. Their reflections center on anger, regret, loss, and a recognition that their parents' tenuous grasp on the lower rungs of the middle class were threatened. Here one contradiction emerges: although the respondents demonstrated that they could see institutions, such as banks, as having influenced the changes in their neighborhoods, they generally did not identify those institutions as the central figures in what occurred. A sense of white ethnic identity stopped whites from seeing blacks also as victims of these institutions' actions; instead, the institutions were seen as taking advantage of a form of natural destruction that came about when the neighborhood was breached by blacks.

A similar contradiction emerged when respondents asserted their powerlessness to stop racial change even as they revealed the efforts they made to prevent integration or deal with racial change. For those residents who lived near the shifting borders of racial change, violence between white and black youth was a regular occurrence. As Tommy noted, "At the beginning, it was brutal. . . . I mean, there was a lot of fights. There was a lot of, uh, black. . . . It was just a black-white thing." Several respondents recalled getting into fights with blacks along the borders of the community to protect their neighborhood from integration. For example, Pete explained: "There was a lot of violence for people our age. [I don't remember] the adults . . . being upset, but we sort of felt like it was our neighborhood to protect. There was a lot of [fistfights]. 'Don't come on our side, or there will be a price to pay.' That went on for several years." The violence in which some whites engaged was also explicit. One respondent reported that whites burned crosses in the yards of houses sold to blacks. Another stated that some whites engaged in acts that were so violent that people began to stay away from the neighborhood. Researchers have documented the role of youth as the vanguard, protectors, or defenders against racial integration in their neighborhoods (Levin and McDevitt 2001; Diamond 2009).[7] Violence occurred so regularly that most viewed it as a normal component of life, although it occasionally went too far. As Mike, from the West Side, remembered:

The only thing that stuck to this day was that when things started
to get a little bit crazy, we would get into fights with black kids. That
bothered me . . . not so much that we got into fights with them; it
was what we would do. In some cases . . . we had this one guy . . .
he had a baseball bat and he cracked this guy right across his back.
You know, that wasn't right. To me, I don't care, black or white or
whatever. It started with this kid who was on the wrong side of the
tracks, if you want to call it that. We saw him in the neighborhood,
and he shouldn't have been there. We took it upon ourselves to police
the area as kids. And he cracked him. . . . I don't know if you saw that
[talking to a second respondent], but I felt really sorry for that kid.

In these moments, whiteness was not invisible: whites acted to defend
what they perceived as their turf and, ultimately, their sense of white racial
identity. Recalling these moments was not always comfortable for some
respondents, although their regret concerned specific individuals who were
physically attacked rather than how blacks were treated overall.

Thus, even as they expressed their powerlessness, our respondents
revealed a deeper story of racial solidarity. Whites living in racially segregated neighborhoods learned that they needed to stick together. Solidarity was
how to "save" the neighborhood from "invaders." Whether it was through
formal organizing, informal roving gangs, or, as one respondent reported,
carrying a baseball bat as a threat to those who dared to cross the line, stick-
ing together was a form of power exercised to maintain segregation. Whites
were learning the lessons long understood by blacks: when institutions do
not support a group's ability to survive and thrive, the group must work
together to do so. Through social networks, parishes, and outside community organizers, whites began to band together to "save our neighborhood."
Informal and extralegal forms of white organizing also continued. Although
former residents of the Southwest Side derided the Nazis during our interviews, a broader sense of "white power" was embraced in the neighborhood.
As Andrew Diamond (2009: 302) recounts, "Some fifteen hundred mostly
young men gathered for a lively American Nazi Party rally in Marquette
Park, Chicago [following a civil rights march on the Southwest Side], got
a glimpse of what white working-class subcultures oriented around racial
exclusion had produced. . . . [T]he actions of these youths must of course be
understood both in the context of community-wide mobilizations as well as
in the broader context of the anti-integration movement that took shape in
the urban North." The demand for racial solidarity in white communities
was so strong that families who decided to sell their homes needed to do so
in the middle of the night for fear of their neighbors' responses. As Phil, who
grew up near St. Sabina on the Southwest Side in the mid-1960s, recalled:

> I remember how the block—you know, the block one day is totally white, and then, because nobody could tell that they were moving.... You know, you always kept it to yourself. Then somebody would move, and the people on either side of them.... [W]ell, now [that] there's a black person on the block, the people on either side would not want to live there because their property values went down, and just the prejudice of that time, and so they would sell then. The people next to them had to sell then. There goes the neighborhood. Everybody's selling.

This is the response of people who feel they are left without options and who have lost white institutional protection. They are not "fighting" in a progressive way; instead, they are moving toward reductionist self-protectionism.

While the nostalgia narrative helps maintain a racially virtuous identity, the choices whites made in response to feelings of powerlessness steeped in white racism worked to increase hostility and undermine the possibility for stable and integrated communities. Consider the following remarkable story retold in a Southwest Side focus group. When asked how the church approached integration and the parishioners' response, Don recalled: "[The priests] would say, 'Be more tolerant,' and then they'd say, 'We're going to help poor parishes in other parts of the city.' And then people would say, 'Wait a minute: we're giving money to black communities?' So [the residents would] color their money [in the donation basket] with black shoe polish." Kristin added: "Most of those people that went to those parishes were not Catholic. [Blacks] were sending their kids to get a Catholic education because they didn't want to send them to public schools, so most of these kids . . . were Baptist. That's what the resentment was, 'Why are we paying for Baptist kids to go to a Catholic school when we have families here that have six, seven, eight kids and are struggling? Why aren't we helping them?' That's what the resentment was." Just as whites initiated stories of violence, whites also maintained feelings of powerlessness, and yet they reacted by rising up against the church hierarchy. It is important to note the discursive tactic used in the retelling of the story. Don noted that parishioners painted pennies they put in the church donation basket black. But instead of directly saying that the white parishioners did not want their money to go to blacks, Kristin switched the complaint to reflect a religious, not a racial, difference.

In constructing such narratives, whites reveal the impact of racial ideologies, which prevent them from responding progressively to the institutional threat to the neighborhood and considering the possibility of integration. As such, the neighborhood was lost due to the entry of blacks. Whites thus are able to construct themselves as powerless victims, despite the evidence of their role as active victimizers. While our research shows that whites blame blacks for destroying their idyllic worlds, in specific instances whites also recognize that they played an active part in destroying their own communities. Whites use the nostalgia narrative to recall the wonderful times and places while blaming blacks and avoiding the racial complexity of what happened to their communities. They continue to ask themselves, "What happened to our idyllic world?" Once they have constructed themselves as innocent victims, they are relieved of social responsibility and "allowed" the space to reconstruct an idyllic world of their childhood—a world that was segregated and homogeneous.

Narratives of Reconciliation: Understanding Race and Racial Change

The nostalgia narrative that respondents used was not always seamless. After telling the tale of their idyllic neighborhood and the time after racial change, many of our respondents attempted to reconcile the idyllic period with their anger over racial change. In these moments, attempting to explain white flight, they acknowledged that their childhoods were not entirely idyllic. As respondents made sense of themselves and race as part of this time period, some recognized that race and racism were key elements in their memories. Yet moving from a discussion of a racially explicit past to a present that purports to play by color-blind rules involves a delicate shift for most individuals. Often whites expressed themselves in ways that maintained their racial innocence and virtuousness. By failing to see themselves in racialized ways and underplaying the continued significance of race, whites avoided associating themselves as "complicators" in a system of racial inequality (Wellman 1993: 60). In other moments, some respondents were clearly seeking ways to reconcile this time with the present. In the end, most lacked a language to understand themselves as racialized and their whiteness as a problematic fact.

The first crack in the nostalgia narrative centers on recognition by our respondents that they had limited interactions with nonwhites, particularly blacks. This fact must be understood in the context of this point in Chicago's history, when racial segregation and isolation were at its highest levels. Dean, from the Southwest Side, depicted this reality by saying, "The biggest issue was the unfamiliarity with the people. You know, they weren't Catholic, so you didn't know how they raised their kids, you know, because they were different. And they were no different from us, but they were different in that they didn't go to our school." Echoing a very similar idea, Don, from the West Side, recalled meeting a black person for the first time when he was thirteen:

That was the first black person that we really ever talked to. There were no blacks. We never went to school with a black. We never went

to high school with a black. We never . . . It was a unique experience.
It was something new to everybody. Nobody ever dealt with that
before—nobody, ever. I mean, you might have did it at your job . . .
but still, when you come back to the neighborhood, there wasn't,
there was not color change. Everybody was the same color. Everybody had the same mentality. Everybody was the same. They were
all the same people.

Finally, Ginny, who grew up on the West Side, said, "It was a way of life. You
had nothing to do with them. Nothing." As we noted in the previous chapter,
some respondents did acknowledge how racially separate their childhoods
were. Yet whites tend to naturalize this racial isolation, often not acknowledging the role both individuals and institutions played in this reality. Nonetheless, the lack of interaction with blacks denied whites an opportunity to
see blacks as anything but the "other"—that is, a group not viewed as equal.

Racial isolation was not a neutral process; it had some long-term effects
for our respondents. In more honest moments, several acknowledged that
their restricted interactions with blacks were socially problematic. Two
extraordinary stories emerged about how a lack of interaction with blacks
negatively affected one respondent's ability to navigate integrated settings.
Donna, who grew up near her cousin Pete on the West Side, told a story
about driving with her husband and children through the old neighborhood
after a trip to the Lincoln Park Zoo:

I had the three [kids] in the back seat, and I said to [my husband],
"Go down my old street." I said, "I want to show them where I grew
up." And [my husband] went down the street, and it was a summer
day, and the guy in front of us was parallel parking or stopping, and
that was it: [blacks] were circling the car. I want you to know that I
was literally, "Oh my god, oh my god, oh my god!" My babies! [My
husband] yelled at me, "Don't show them you're scared. Sit up, and
don't you show them you're scared." And I'm going, "Oh my god, my
babies are in here!" That's the kind of fear I had, and all they were
probably doing . . . he's right . . . was just standing, you know, hanging in the street. That's the fear I had.

The fear and lack of perspective is palpable. Connie provided a similar
account:

When I moved [to the suburbs], I still had no interaction. Then I went
back to [Community College in the neighborhood where I grew up].
I'm ashamed even to say this, but it means something. I went all by

myself, and it must have been registration week, and there were a ton of people there. I parked in the parking lot and remember walking to go into the place I needed to go and get started. Two or three black guys, young kids, were walking toward me, and I kind of froze for a second. . . . I'm sorry to say this. I kept saying, "This is nothing. That's old stuff, this is nothing. Nothing is going to happen." OK, I did scream when they got near me. I ruined those kids' lives . . . and when I screamed, they all went, "What?" And I just walked away. I was afraid. And as I'm walking, I'm thinking, "Why did I scream?" They were such nice boys. Then I went to school and, uh, took computer classes and didn't even know how to turn [the computer] on, and guess who helped me: all the young black boys. They got me through that class, and they became my friends, and I met them for lunch.

These two stories capture an element of the legacy of living through racial change, particularly for those who lived in neighborhoods close to the racial borders. The extreme fear of blacks expressed by Donna and Connie undoubtedly is due to both the lack of interaction with blacks and the racial socialization that occurred in their homes and in the broader community. The racial socialization Donna and Connie received did not prepare them to interact with blacks because it taught them to see blacks only as dangerous and threatening. It is also clear that both respondents felt so ashamed of their reactions that they barely had the language to discuss their feelings.

Another crack in the nostalgia narrative emerged as respondents reflected on the racism that was present in the neighborhood during their childhoods. Almost all of the respondents referenced racist attitudes in their neighborhoods or their homes, and few remembered knowing blacks as neighbors or friends. In fact, most said that one or both of their parents held a negative view of blacks. As a result, many reported being left with problematic views of blacks. Reflecting on living through racial change, white flight, and the West Side's reaction to Martin Luther King's assassination, William noted: "Just think of it. . . . [W]e were tainted. Racism was blatant back then. You heard your parents talk about it. You saw it on television. You see the consequences of the riot. You didn't want that to happen to your neighbors, so you protect your territory." Like William, others easily acknowledged the racism present in their homes and in the larger community. However, explaining such racism often meant calling on color-blind language that reduced its scope or naturalized it by distancing it from extremes. In doing this, whites work toward constructing and maintaining white racial innocence, even in the face of socially unjust beliefs.

A good way to understand this involves looking at how respondents made sense of what they heard while growing up. One way respondents explained how race was discussed and lived in their neighborhoods was to designate the time period as a "different time" or "a way of life." Ron captured this well by describing his racial socialization as natural:

> I mean, I was small—twelve or thirteen years old—but you see it on the news. You hear it at school. You hear your parents talking about it. It's just in the air. It wasn't one specific thing that turned you against them. It was just in the air. If you'd see them walking down the street and you were with your mother and father . . . , they told you "nigger" or something like that. That was just the way you were brought up. That was just the way of life. Then when you went to school, you had to deal with them and your coming from different neighborhoods.

John, like several other respondents, explained racism as the result of economics: "My dad was racist. He was real bad. . . . The way he looked at [it] was the money. He was getting beat up . . . financially and everything. And he was too old to go out and get another job." The common thread in each of these responses is an effort to minimize the racism that they all knew was there. Similar to the nostalgic renderings of the idyllic period were the references respondents made to this different time period to lessen the impact of what can really be described only as racism. In other cases, respondents avoid or underplay the reality of race in their lives either by saying their parents were not as bad as extremist groups or by referencing socioeconomic status. For this group of whites, one's whiteness is not a problematic fact; it is just the natural way things are, or in moments in which racism became obvious, it was in the hands of people other than themselves (Frankenberg 1993; Steyn 2001). In this way, whites work to keep their virtue and innocence intact.

Finally, white racial identity is not monolithic. Indeed, racial identities, like other dominant group identities, are fluid and can change (McDermott and Samson 2005). In their attempts to explain white flight and the racism present in the neighborhood, a few respondents sought a way to reconcile the past with the present without neutralizing the role that race played in the neighborhood. Some were able to see it and regretted the outcome but in the end lacked a language to critically reflect on their white racial identity. Articulating a sense of regret over the feelings that came with racial change, these individuals expressed remorse over the role of racism in their lives. For example, Joan talked about the election of President Barack Obama in 2008 and a desire to come to terms with racism:

> You know, terrible things were going on, and that's why today it . . . I can't tell you . . . living in that era and experiencing those things,

and I personally had no friends that were black or other races at all. I mean, we were just all Italians, and we weren't exposed to anything else. We really weren't, and that's why when Obama was elected president . . . I felt like it was over. I felt like I could breathe. It felt so good that we . . . got to this point in this country because that was all so terrible, and to see white and black and everybody—the mixed races out there—just so exuberant over him being elected, it felt wonderful. I know that there's still a lot of prejudice, of course . . . but I felt like, OK, this is huge. This is so good, because there was nothing good about any of that that I lived with.

Acknowledging the mistrust generated during racial change, Joan and others seek a way to reconcile the mistrust of blacks generated during racial change. Others extended these ideas as they attempted to change things through their housing choices. Karen, who grew up in Marquette Park, explained her decision to move to an integrated neighborhood:

I didn't want to be part of white flight or anything like that ever again, so I moved into an integrated neighborhood. When I moved . . . , I made a choice that East Beverly is already integrated. They've already gone through this; they're stronger than this. They know about the whole white flight thing. This is where I wanted to put down my roots. My parents didn't agree with this because having to move tainted how they felt about it . . . and I just said, "Look, I want to know who my neighbors are. I don't want that tension with everyone else with not knowing or not understanding or having the unknown about who's moving in next door, and I want to get beyond it because in my mind . . . you know what, it's people, they're people, just people, you know. I don't care. They can be jerks no matter what nationality or what the color of their skin."

Both Joan and Karen made honest statements about the role of racism in their lives and sought a way to resolve the past. The similarities, however, end there. For Joan, the racism of the past was reconciled by the election of Barack Obama, with little effort from whites, whereas Karen was actually doing something to distinguish the present from the past, although she expected to pay a price. Yet in the end, neither respondent speaks to a deeper understanding of the power and complexity of white racial identity and racial privilege.

By examining some of the cracks in the nostalgia narrative, we get a nuanced understanding of how whites understand race and the role it played in their homes and neighborhoods. Here we see how respondents generally struggled in their attempts to reconcile their formative racial experiences with the present. Minimizing or neutralizing race while maintaining innocence was a common strategy. In general, the narrative provided strategies for respondents to put distance between themselves and blacks; they considered themselves fair-minded, a product of their upbringing, and misunderstood. While a few respondents were able to recognize race as a key factor in their lives and their neighborhoods, these efforts fell short of critical reflection on their white racial identity and attendant white privilege. Here the stories they tell offer a way to frame themselves as virtuous even as they talk about a period that was racially charged. Their responses can best be interpreted by focusing less on their personal prejudices, as few would oppose civil rights or demands for racial equality. Instead, they are employing strategies that defend their group advantage and refusing to challenge "a system from which advantage is derived on the basis of race" (Wellman 1993: 210).

Critically interpreting the narratives of whites who lived through racial change does not mean that we should discount their experiences or the place attachment that they hold. For Frank Clement and people like him, the neighborhood remains a powerful force, imbued with a set of emotions that are likely strengthened by its loss. Yet our research suggests that these narratives need closer examination. Closer scrutiny indicates the importance of looking at racialized nostalgia narratives that do the work of maintaining racial boundaries in an era of color-blindness while allowing whites to speak about their own role in the racially explicit housing battles of the past. Through the specific historically and geographically bounded time of racial change in Chicago's segregated neighborhoods, we are able to better understand how whites manage the duality of living racialized realities and yet declare themselves color-blind. By examining nostalgia narratives that whites use, we can illustrate how racialized communities take shape. This is a racial legacy that ties racially explicit experiences to color-blind discourse in ways that maintain boundaries of white advantage.

Nostalgia narratives are imbued with ideology and thus give us insight into how domination and subordination are rationalized and justified (Brantlinger 2003). Importantly, through these narratives contradictions that question whiteness as "goodness" or "virtue" are neutralized, and whites are able to create and maintain a positive identity. As we have shown, the narratives neutralize contradictions in three primary ways: (1) whites portray themselves as innocent victims even as they remember their own violence and aggression, (2) whites blame blacks for upheaval even as they remember institutional discrimination, and (3) whites maintain that their lost neighborhoods were perfect worlds even as they acknowledge that their perfection resulted partly from racial exclusion. The ability to manage the contradictions, as we have shown, is a central piece of hegemonic whiteness (Nakayama and Krizek 1995).

Collective memories and collective forgetting at the intersection of racialized experiences are part of the process of maintaining boundaries around racialized communities (Hooker 2009). The maintaining of boundaries is of central importance to the value of whiteness itself. That is to say, as long as whiteness holds value tied to housing, education, and income (Lipsitz 2006), whites have reasons to work to maintain the boundaries of whiteness. Whites involve themselves in such boundary work because they benefit from an unjust system that continues to reward whiteness as "property"—that is, a system in which white racial identities are inextricably tied to property ownership (Harris 1993). The investment in whiteness is so strong, in fact, that contemporary research in places such as South Africa, where whiteness does not provide the kinds of returns it did under apartheid, shows that whites are willing to leave their country in search of better returns on their whiteness in white-dominated countries (Dolby 2001; Steyn 2001; Griffiths and Prozesky 2010). In both the United States and South Africa, color-blind discourses give whites a means to specify their individuality, freed from racial legacies that continue to privilege their lives (Dolby 2001; Steyn 2001; Dalmage 2004; Lipsitz 2006). Moving forward, it is important to build on these studies by examining how whites maintain racial boundaries in other spaces and places in an era of color-blindness. In other words, as the settings shift, what other strategies might whites employ? Also, it will be important to develop an understanding of how we can challenge contemporary collective memory constructions that (re)produce hegemony across various communities of difference.

5

Racial Ignorance, Bounded Empathy, and the Construction of Racial Solidarity

66 "Trauma," "sadness," "abandonment," "loss," and "violence" are all words whites used to describe how they and those around them experienced racial change in their neighborhoods. Even these many decades later, our respondents lamented about the time in which their worlds were being turned upside down. Rarely were they given an opportunity to talk about their experiences and the accompanying emotions and memories they have carried all these years in a constructive, open, and empathetic manner. Clearly, understanding race and racism in the United States is not an easy task for whites, particularly in an era of ideological color-blindness, segregation, and limited cross-racial interaction. In fact, rather than having spaces in society for individuals to think about race, the United States has been on a path of color-blindness since the 1980s in which whites have been taught that talking about race is impolite and, in effect, racist. Thus, at exactly the point of trauma and pain, whites also lost a language with which to process what happened and move forward in a more open, antiracist way. The result has meant that for many whites, their sense of community is racially bounded.

In our interviews, specific discussions of respondents' neighborhoods and the impact of racial change included their attempts to understand race and how race plays out in their lives. While it was clear that racial change generated different emotions (from anger to loss and regret), many respondents reported knowing people who had never "gotten over" racial change. Instead, they remain angry and blame blacks for ruining their neighborhoods. The process of understanding (and accepting) this reaction by whites to racial change involves particular forms of insight and knowledge as the basis for accepting family and friends who continue to blame blacks. Most of us accept family and friends with a variety of flaws, big and small: poor table manners, talking too much, drinking too much alcohol, and even, at times, heterosexism and racial and ethnic bigotry. In this chapter, we explore how whites come to frame racism as a reaction to a history of white suffering. Analyzing how whites who self-identify as "not racist" come to accept family and friends whom they identify as racist gives us insight into the production of white racialized solidarity. The process of acceptance of racist family members and friends (the foundation of racialized solidarity) includes the moral elevation of the "accepter" and a judgment about and empathy for the ignorance of a "racist." A racist is judged as lacking exposure and education, yet acceptance of the white "racist" person is based on an empathetic understanding of the history of suffering. Thus, as we will show, the boundaries of whiteness and white racial solidarity are strengthened through empathy—racially bounded empathy.

Ignorance is part of the human condition. We cannot know everything. How we know, what we know, and how that shapes who we are, what we feel and think, and how we act are of central interest to any critical inquiry into social interaction. In this chapter, we explore the construction of knowledge and ignorance—that is, ways of knowing—as active processes that result in the maintenance of white racial privilege. As we discussed in regard to nostalgia, a central piece of this exploration is understanding how whites are able to accept and enact contradictory positions of racism and view themselves as good, tolerant, and loving, even while expressing intolerance and sometimes hate. The contradictory positions are managed through *racialized* empathy and work to maintain the boundaries of whiteness. Empathy, or the ability to stand in another person's shoes, requires cognitive, emotional, and contextual understanding and awareness. Thus, it is tied to particular ways of knowing and feeling. Indeed, empathy is an important element in the construction of solidarity among humans. White racialized empathy is empathy developed within a particular context, often without an understanding of the historical context of race, and is therefore shaped by white ways of knowing.

Exploring the experiences and insight of whites who lived through racial change gives us a lens into how they make sense of—how they know *and feel*—that history. Given the racial strife and suffering caused by racial change, we have an opportunity to explore whites' ways of knowing history, and how this knowledge either expands or restricts the empathy they feel for their own or other racial groups. Such ways of knowing—that is, how individuals "know" what they know—are used as the basis for action. Interestingly, as we were exploring how whites made sense of race, we discovered that whites were also trying to make sense of how other whites in their lives were making sense of race. An interview with Steve, from the Auburn Gresham neighborhood near St. Sabina parish, captured this idea well. In attempting to understand racist white friends and neighbors, he commented:

> They are angry with themselves. I think people get angry with them-
> selves because . . . I really believe that there is something inside of
> us that knows what is right and knows what is true. That part keeps
> eating at us. With things like racism and anger and hatred and blam-
> ing other people for what you did . . . , it keeps eating at you sub-
> consciously that "oh no, it is your fault." I see that a lot. I have white
> friends where, my god, I have to get up and walk away. The word
> "nigger" runs freely from their lips all the time, but so do all the
> other words . . . racial words. . . . [T]hey are such angry people, and
> they are unhappy with their own lives. Or it is out of ignorance some-
> times. . . . [I]t is almost generational. It is handed down. The hatred
> is taught like anything else is taught. Like the ABCs are taught. It is
> taught from the time you're kid. I heard it in my family. . . . I don't
> know what it is in a person that makes some people accept that as
> part of their lives and make some people say, "Wait a minute."

As Steve notes, racism involves not just certain attitudes and perspectives; it also involves a level of knowledge and ignorance. What we know and do not know are the foundation for framing the world and our actions. It guides whom we accept and reject. And while we often do not think too much about it, ignorance plays a key role in regard to race.

During the interviewing, "ways of knowing" were often told to us in the form of wisdom—as in, "I understand this; my kids don't" or "We lived through racial change; suburbanites didn't." Wisdom is the knowledge and insight grounded in self-reflection on lived experience that works to inform how people act in the world. When our respondents spoke about their race-based decision making and analysis of their friends and family, they framed it in terms of the knowledge they had acquired as a result of living through racial change. Yet it was clear that a great deal of knowledge was being inten-tionally ignored or forgotten as our respondents reflected on and accepted continued racism in society.

Individuals who grew up during racial change experienced concurrent emotional, physical, and financial upheaval; some experienced trauma. The experiences that caused them pain and suffering provided lessons for how to live in the world. Many individuals learned to create and maintain white networks as a way to feel safe and protected. Others to varying degrees have struggled and made efforts to cross the racial borders. We explore the ways of knowing, both cognitive and affective, that are the basis for negotiating racialized solidarity in attempts to strengthen and to undermine it. As defined by Juliet Hooker (2009: 40), racialized solidarity is "racial seeing and thinking [that] trains whites not to see the pain and suffering of nonwhites and to be less concerned about it when they do see it."[1] As discussed in Chapter 3, such racialized training is often indirect, occurring through a web of social institutions in which white lives are presented as complex and valuable, while black and brown lives are presented as dysfunctional and violent. In this pervasive public (and private) telling, whites learn to fear the "other" in the process of developing their own sense of community and humanity. Isolation and fear drive many of the ways whites frame their lived experience, serving as a filter through which they evaluate the best ways to act in the world. This filtering process is shaped by whiteness—that is, a "systemic production of misrepresentations, evasion, and self-deception in relation to race" (Swan 2010: 478). Racialized solidarity is strengthened as whites use racial ignorance in strategic ways. As a result, as our interviews revealed, acceptance and tolerance of racism and empathy for racist family and friends are prioritized over racial justice.

Knowledge and empathy are inextricably linked. To walk in another person's shoes, we must have knowledge of their experiences, emotions, and expectations. If our knowledge is limited through racialization, so, too, will be our ability to empathize. In the discussion that follows, we begin with an overview of racialized knowledge and illustrate how such knowledge is connected to empathy and the boundaries of empathy. We then examine the role of exposure and education in building relationships across racial boundaries. While whites may not always be stretching across race lines based on empathy for nonwhites, they are searching for ways of being that can undermine racial hostility and help them make sense of the racialized trauma of the past. As we note, education and exposure are not sufficient to generate empathy across racial boundaries. We agree with Zeus Leonardo's assessment that "a critical reading of whiteness means that white ignorance must be problematized, not in order to expose whites as simply racist, but to increase knowledge about their full participation in race relations" (Leonardo 2009: 107). After critically exploring our respondents' racial knowledge, we end the chapter with a discussion of possible paths forward that must involve empathy, education, and exposure to build a sense of community across racial lines.

On Racialized Knowledge

If we are to fully understand the complex practices of knowledge production and the variety of factors that account for why something is known, we must also understand the practices that account for not knowing, that is, for our lack of knowledge about a phenomenon or, in some cases, an account of the practices that resulted in a group unlearning what was once a realm of knowledge (Tuana 2006: 2).

Ignorance has been discussed by countless philosophers, political scientists, and feminist theorists. Ignorance is not just the absence of particular knowledge; rather, it has many faces and can be both passive and active. In some instances, individuals are ignorant because of a lack of exposure and education. In other instances, individuals choose to ignore information. Knowing and not knowing is complex, tied to forms of hegemony, privilege, power, and (un)conscious needs for safety and connectedness. In addition, ignorance has strategic uses. In a positive sense, ignorance can be used strategically by whites who are willing to acknowledge their ignorance and to listen to and trust blacks and other people of color to provide knowledge (Townley 2006; Bailey 2007; Steyn 2012; Olson and Gillman 2013). In this way, ignorance helps to create the foundation on which empathy can develop across racial boundaries.

Various scholars have also noted that forms of ignorance serve to protect white racial privilege. For example, Philip Olson and Laura Gilman (2013: 62) argue, "Whites are *positively motivated* to remain ignorant of the injustices of social realities that invent and nourish white privilege." In his noted *The Racial Contract* (1997), Charles Mills argues that white racial ignorance develops from a system of white supremacy in which whites, as a group, have privilege and develop particular "handicaps" about seeing the context of their own lives and the lives of others:

> In all societies, especially those structured by domination, the socially recollecting "we" will be divided, and the selection will be guided by different identities, with one group suppressing precisely what another wishes to commemorate. Thus there will be both official and counter-memory, with conflicting judgments about what is important in the past and what is unimportant, what happened and does matter, what happened and does not matter, and what did not happen at all. So applying this to race, there will obviously be an intimate relationship between white identity, white memory, and white amnesia, especially about nonwhite victims. (Mills 2007: 25)

Here Mills is arguing that white supremacy is the context that shrouds white racial ignorance and the ignoring of contexts that have caused pain and hardship for blacks. Such ignorance allows whites to empathize with the context of white racism and thus accept racism.

A recurring theme within whiteness studies is that race is often invisible to whites because of their privileged position in the racial order, allowing whites to make color-blind claims. Color-blindness is the dominant discourse that "frames or *set paths for interpreting information*" (Bonilla-Silva 2009: 26). As Mills (2007: 23) writes, "'Color-blind' ideology plays an important role in the maintenance of white hegemony. . . . [B]ecause whites tend not to see themselves in racial terms and not to recognize the existence of the advantages that whites enjoy in American society, this promotes a worldview that emphasizes *individualistic* explanations for social and economic achievement, as if the individualism of white privilege was a universal attribute." Similarly, Alison Bailey (2007: 77) speaks of "blank spots that make privileged knowers oblivious to systemic injustices." In other words, through color-blind discourses, race and racism are viewed as individual pathology, and whites continue to miss the institutional context of racial injustice. The outcomes of this way of knowing allow whites to dismiss racism as an incidental "flaw" and thus not so harmful. Moreover, without "knowing" the context, they are able to construct blackness as the context that has caused whites' fear and pain. As we discuss below, whites are actively involved in ignorance even as they show that they "know" the context of white pain and suffering.

Scholars have emphasized the role of agency in racial ignorance, identifying some forms of ignorance as willful (i.e., not knowing and not wanting to know) or strategic (Tuana 2006; Bailey 2007). For instance, Peter Vitebsky has argued that ignorance is not just about having or not having particular knowledge. Rather, it is about making choices and focusing on some knowledge while willfully denying other knowledge. He states, "Ignorance is knowledge denied or denigrated, and its apparent 'growth' is really a growth in the knowing party's power to denigrate other knowledges and to refuse to engage in dialogue with their knowers" (Vitebsky 1993: 114). Similarly, Melissa Steyn (2012: 8) explains white racial ignorance as a "social achievement with strategic value." By examining whiteness through recollections of "apartheid childhoods," she illustrates how white youth were socialized to ignore the indignities of apartheid and social exclusion, thus enabling them to not understand social injustice and the "other." Steyn argues that ignorance is structural, exercised through human thought and interaction. In this way, racial ignorance is both the outcome and the cause of white supremacy.

In this chapter, we show that silence is a primary way whites are able to avoid engaging in dialogue and challenging ignorance, both their own and that of others, while simultaneously maintaining closeness and solidarity. Silence represents (and can be read as) tacit approval and acceptance of racism, a shared understanding of the world. As such, the boundaries of whiteness are strengthened. When confronted with white racism, most of our respondents spoke about consciously remaining silent so they would not appear to be judging other whites. Furthermore, they explain their silence as an outcome of knowledge of an era of racial change and empathy for the pain and suffering whites had endured during racial change. In other words, racism and racist comments are deemed understandable, given the shared knowledge of the historical context. Tolerance and acceptance of racism thus become qualities of good empathetic human beings. Inverting calls for tolerance across race lines, these folks are "tolerating" racism with an outcome of strengthening racialized boundaries and communities.

To understand how racial ignorance is central to creating racialized solidarity, it is important to explore how ignorance, knowledge, and empathy for others are connected. There are other, more progressive and antiracist ways of knowing, but this involves whites' moving beyond interpreting "social life through white racial knowledge" (Leonardo 2009: 109). Typically, whites use some knowledge while ignoring other knowledge. Our interviews with whites who grew up in an era of racial explicitness show that race is central to white action and choices and is anything but invisible. In fact, racialized knowledge is the basis for racially bounded empathy. In other words, empathy is expressed and context matters for whites, yet this matters almost not at all for blacks. White pain and fear are legitimated through an understanding of a historical context in which whites suffered; thus, that pain and fear are to be accepted and understood. The pain and suffering of blacks, however, are ignored, and black life is framed as ahistorical, static, and naturally bad. As a result, white racism is tolerated, and boundaries of white racialized solidarity are strengthened.

The Boundaries of Racialized Empathy

Research clearly demonstrates that whites tend to have less empathy for blacks than for other whites. For example, when African Americans consult with white physicians regarding physical pain, they can expect that their pain will be taken less seriously than if they were whites with the same complaints (Drwecki et al. 2011). When African Americans face the trauma of a child lost to violence, they can expect less concern for their emotional pain from whites and the media (Chiao and Mathur 2010; Silverstein 2013). A black defendant can expect less empathy from jurors in capital cases (Edelman 2006). In fact, in most daily experiences, black people's physical and emotional pain will be taken less seriously than white people's. The reason for this racial empathy gap (Silverstein 2013) has been explored in the helping professions and more broadly by social scientists. Understanding the empathy gap is central to making sense of racialized solidarity as the means for creating and maintaining white racial privilege and power.

Various disciplines have searched for answers to why such a disparity in empathy exists, although the goals of or reasons for reducing it vary. For example, neuroscientists are currently locating the ability to empathize in "mirror neurons," neural networks they have located via brain imagining (Decety and Moriguchi 2007; Ramachandran 2010). The excitement surrounding the discovery of mirror neurons rests in the knowledge that humans are physically *capable* of developing empathy. If we learn from others to empathize, then, it stands to reason, we could also learn within differing contexts ways of knowing that lead to bounded empathy, non-empathy, or even hatred for those who are not deemed worthy of empathy. This seems to be the case when it comes to race. Recent research by Joan Chiao and Vani Mathur (2010) using functional magnetic resonance imaging of the brain indicates that, for blacks and whites, empathy for other humans varies along racial borders. Thus, all people have the potential for developing empathy, but socialization and larger social forces tend to lead to the development of the idea of "us" and "them." This binary is what underlies the boundaries of our empathy. Below we explore the context in which empathy develops, particularly in the manner in which whites manage certain kinds of experiential contradiction. As we discussed in previous chapters, we began our research curious about how whites made sense of living through racial change and how they learned to love their families and communities at the same time they learned to dehumanize and disdain blacks. Bounded empathy gives us a way to understand these contradictory positions.

Given the importance of empathy to human communication and connection, developing empathy has become an important part of developing "professional competence" in a variety of fields, particularly for therapists, medical doctors, and social workers (Townley 2006: 44). Important research and insight about the need for and development of empathy comes from these disciplines. Various studies have looked at how to build empathy, including how to help the helpers "walk in the shoes of another" in an effort to best help the client (Ryback 2001; Freedberg 2007). Karen Gerdes and her colleagues (2011: 129) explore the importance of working "at the 'gut' level of shared experience." This implies that to really feel for another person, we must imagine what the other is feeling. The imagination is, of course, bounded by knowledge. To imagine what another person is feeling, we need to understand the nuanced context that has shaped their experiences. When we do not have knowledge of the context, we must trust the other person's telling of that context. In the therapeutic setting, the overriding goal of developing and using empathy is to help the client, across a range of differences, in the process of self-discovery toward a more engaged life (Freedberg 2007). This research helps us to understand the importance of knowledge and ignorance in the use of "imagining" another's pain and suffering. If our knowledge and imagination are bounded racially, our empathy will also be bounded. Thus, it is important to continue to explore the role of social context and "knowing."

Within the fields of sociology and political science, empathy is discussed as "ways of knowing" or as the "politics of recognition," contextualized within unjust and unequal social relations. In *Multiculturalism: Examining the Politics of Recognition,* Amy Gutmann (1994: 7) asks, "What does it mean for citizens with different cultural identities, often based on ethnicity, race, gender, or religion, to recognize ourselves as equals in the way we are treated in politics?" Clearly, misrecognition can create false, distorted, and reduced images of groups, effectively inflicting harm on certain groups—for example, blacks and women (Taylor 1994). It is also certain that the question of seeing someone as equal is about seeing the other as human, being able to recognize and be empathetic with feelings and emotions across difference. A lack of awareness and concern for another person's feelings and emotions and a lack of trust in another person's telling of her or his lived experiences are central to the process of dehumanization.

Most human beings have the capacity to develop empathy within particular social contexts. In a racially unjust system, in which inequality is built into institutional and ideological practices, stories are used to convey the boundaries of empathy. As humans grow into and through social categories, they begin to name, claim, assign, and reject particular ways of knowing and being. At the heart of this activity is understanding and developing empathy toward others, as well as the extent to which empathy extends and the boundaries that inhibit it. Empathizing across racial boundaries is a complex process and requires individuals to develop certain understandings, including awareness that a boundary is in place; awareness that racialized ignorance exists; motivation for change that will lead to a reworking of historical understanding and social networks; a leap of faith that the imagining of the "other's" context is accurate (Nussbaum 2007); and trust that what another person tells us is his or her reality (Townley 2006). Trusting means believing another human being in the face of ignorance. However, admitting ignorance makes one vulnerable, and vulnerability flies in the face of a sense of superiority and "knowing" that is central to whiteness and white racial identity. Unfortunately, then, the development of empathy across racial difference is quite difficult when the motivation to make the first move to reach across race lines is not strong. To change the context and the structurally produced inequality, it is necessary for individuals in privileged positions to be motivated to understand others as "equals" with a shared humanity (Taylor 1994; Halpern and Weinstein 2004; Hooker 2009).

Accepting Racism through Bounded Empathy

On the level of human interaction, people with whom we interact may say things that hurt our feelings, run counter to our sense of humanity, or be outright insulting. When this happens, we must decide how to respond: we may "educate," berate, ignore, or make light of it (Dalmage 2000). In each case, our relationship to and knowledge of the other person and our understanding of the world and who we are in the world matter. In our interviews, for example, we heard responses similar to Darlene's when individuals hear friends or family making racist remarks: "I just let some people say it. . . . I feel bad that I don't correct them when they do that, but, like, I just don't, you know? I don't go along with it, but I don't say, 'I wouldn't say that' or anything." Similarly, we also heard expressions of understanding and empathy in the ways people explained their parents' racist views and actions. Dana captured this notion when she said, "You know, these people were scared to death, our parents. They didn't know where to go now. 'What do we do? This is our neighborhood. Where do we go?' They were freaked out, [and] because they were freaked out, it just automatically rubbed off on the children. Whether you realized it or not, you'd hear the talk, you see things going on, you realize your neighborhood is starting to go away and nobody wanted it to go away." Such expressions of understanding demonstrate empathy, but they also perpetuate racial ignorance by failing to acknowledge the pain that racist actions caused for blacks. Stating that "nobody wanted [the neighborhood] to go away" is a strong nod to the marked boundaries of who is included as a "somebody" or a person.

These ways of knowing and being are learned over a lifetime and inform our responses. As we saw in previous chapters, these ways of knowing are very much tied to socialization. Consider Deborah's reflection of growing up on the West Side: "That's the way it was! You may have wanted to, and we may have talked to a black person; however, it was the overall consensus of the neighborhood: don't deal with them. Maybe we can save this part [of the neighborhood] from here, because it just kept progressing, the movement kept progressing northward, and people were just getting more bitter. You come in; you're just destroying our neighborhood. That's it. Period." The context in which Deborah was learning about humanity was explicitly, deeply, and pervasively racialized and racist. Similarly, Betsy spoke about how the family and intimate relationships held racial boundaries or borders in place through a shared pressure toward conformity (Steyn 2012). In the context of love, Betsy and others were learning to hate and to determine the boundaries of empathy: Think back to Betsy's words presented in Chapter 4: "People didn't want to express contrary opinions as being non-racist because everyone else had this hatred for blacks, and they didn't want to be heard saying, you know, 'They're not bad people; they wouldn't be a problem.' . . . They [the people who objected to racism] didn't want to be singled out." Being able to empathize, to walk in another person's shoes, then, is dependent not only on neurons but also on socialization and larger social relations that place human bodies into differently valued categories and establish boundaries between these categories.

One element of social relations is how we understand racism in society. A prominent value guiding responses to racism in an era of color-blindness is that the individual speaking or acting in a racist manner has a personal problem. In other words, institutional racism is ignored and reduced to an individual pathology or flaw. Leonard expressed an example of this logic when he explained that blacks and whites were equally uncomfortable with each other: "I don't bla[me]. I mean, I didn't bla[me]. I could see . . . both sides of it, because [whites] came from other neighborhoods and those had changed, and they felt pushed out. That's a big thing. They always say, like, you know, the whites always . . . The blacks say they . . . don't feel comfortable in white neighborhoods, and it's like we're both the same. Whoever's in the majority is looking down. And whites feel they've been pushed. I live in Mt. Greenwood now, and it's sort of the same there now." Leonard quickly dismissed the larger social inequality between whites and blacks by stating, "It's like we're both the same." In a version of history that explains housing segregation as the equally shared responsibility of blacks and whites, white racism is not viewed as institutional, powerful, or hurtful. As a result, white racism is viewed as the outcome of pain and suffering and thus should be understood and accepted. Eduardo Bonilla-Silva (2009: 124) refers to this as a "free market logic on human relationships," a logic that reduces racism to equally situated individuals. Adages such as "To each his own" are mobilized to express this logic and justify silence in response to racism. Silence in this regard is most often read as tacit acceptance. As we heard from our respondents, the silence is about a desire not to outwardly judge and an expression of empathy for the pain and suffering that underlies white racism. The enactment of empathy (through silent acceptance) was tragically discussed as evidence of goodness and humanity—that is, as the acceptance of another human being, despite his or her flaws. In other words, racism is viewed as an individual human failing based in histories of pain and suffering.

According to this logic, empathy, developed through an understanding of the past, is needed to accept flawed humans. The person who accepts racist talk and action can then construct a self that is both knowledgeable and good. In other words, the acceptance of and empathy for the flawed person shows goodness. In talking about a cousin who makes racist comments, Darlene stated: "You're . . . gonna hear from everybody how they feel. I don't need to know how she feels. *I love her either way.* And as long as no one is mean to anyone, it's her right. For me, I truly believe everyone is equal. I truly believe everyone deserves the same chances." Darlene constructs herself here as someone who believes in equality and in an individual's right to "feel" racist. In explaining that it is fine as long as no one gets hurt, she is constructing racism as an individual pathology, disregarding the destructive and pervasive ways institutional racism has controlled, contained, and destroyed the lives of so many African Americans. Moreover, Darlene explains that she doesn't "need to know how [her cousin] feels"—that is, to accept her cousin, she chooses to remain ignorant, a strategic choice so that she can maintain racialized ties.

In his work on color-blindness, Bonilla-Silva (2009: 31) has shown that whites "ignored the effects of past and contemporary discrimination on the social, economic, and educational status of minorities." Darlene's acceptance of her cousin "either way" justifies her silence about racism and the daily "meanness" of individual and institutional racism. This is one of the places that white racial ignorance develops from color-blind discourse and in the process sustains white racialized solidarity. In the end, Darlene has constructed herself as loving and a fair human being who simultaneously tolerates racism. In a similar way, Jerry talked about spending time with friends: "It's funny because I actually still pal around with some guys that I became friends with in the '70s. [W]e play softball, . . . and if you listen to the language that goes on, *I'm not going to tell them . . . that they're racist or anything like that, because these are my buddies.* But . . . it continues to this day. I'm not the ethics police. We've come a long way."[2] Jerry's acceptance of his friends: and their racist words depends on his sense of empathy for the individuals who are being racist. Empathy requires understanding and knowledge. Of course, the knowledge develops within a context of whiteness and color-blindness. It is through his "knowledge" that Jerry is able to make a claim to being above racism himself and choosing to accept his friends regardless of their objectionable language or other character flaws. In short, by accepting his racist friends, Jerry believes he is displaying wisdom, empathy, and that he is a good person.

Throughout our interviewing we heard stories explaining how whites had been victimized in the process of racial transition. The contextualizing and development of empathy extended only to whites, however. Leonardo (2009: 14) argues that knowing how to act in racially "acceptable ways is a form of knowledge that whites develop in their everyday life." Thought, emotion, and action are grounded in ways of being racially appropriate. For whites, this means that they learned love and empathy within a clear racial boundary defined through a particular understanding of history in which whites are viewed as victims. Tommy captured this notion when he talked about the pain of leaving the neighborhood:

My father worked two jobs; Grandpa worked his whole life. They paid for what they had. They took care of their stuff. *And then when they see people come that don't and then just destroyed things, I think, you know, that hurt them.*[3] You know, because Grandpa . . . wanted to work, whatever he had to do—dig ditches, he didn't care, but he was coming home with something in his pocket to take care of his family. You know, it was just the pride they had in themselves. . . . That had a big effect on them also, when they see their neighborhood being given up. And they worked their whole lives to have a house.

In this telling, the pain was caused by blacks. Thus, the knowledge on which Tommy has developed empathy is racially bounded. In fact, his empathy for his father's and grandfather's disdain of blacks rests on his understanding of blacks as the destructive context that caused his family's pain and loss. In a similar way, Paul, who grew up on the West Side until his family fled to the suburbs during racial change, noted:

We spoke like that for twenty-five years. That's why sometimes when we're driving down the street, I [might] say, "Oh, look at that nigger over there." I know . . . you have to be politically correct now, you have to say the right things. I don't say it out of—to be hateful or mean. I mean, I grew up saying that word; there was nothing ever wrong with it. And now, all of sudden, well, [people tell me] "You can't say that word." And then your kids will hear and say, "Oh Dad, why do you say that? You're so old-fashioned. You shouldn't be saying that word." Again, nobody lived through the times that we lived through—at least, our kids didn't.

Paul's racial knowledge and ignorance, like Tommy's, limit his ability to empathize across racial boundaries. In fact, in the face of being corrected by his children, Paul justifies his racist language by citing the "times [h]e lived through," something he feels his children do not understand.

Whites' stories also explained the perceived source of white victimization. In the course of our interviews, we heard several examples of whites constructing blacks as naturally destructive and as the reason for white suffering. Blacks are thereby dehumanized and thus less worthy of care or concern. In this double step (constructing blackness as destructive and blacks as less human), the boundaries of empathy are tightened in a process that allows whites to believe in their own fairness and goodness. For example, looking back at the neighborhood after racial change occurred and his parents' decision to move, Greg noted: "The one thing I'll say is that no one felt guilty afterward because of all the things that we saw. . . . All the bad things [our parents] were afraid were going to happen did happen. Crime went up. Property values dropped. Neighborhoods looked much worse. They would say, 'Good thing we got out of there.' We were right. We were justified. Nobody felt like we should try and live together. It was a good thing we got out." Here, Greg is naturalizing blacks as inferior, criminal, and incapable of maintaining their property; in the process, he is elevating whites as superior. Here we see again that the context of black people's pain and struggle is not important, just as the workings of institutions in the process of racial change are ignored. Instead, whites like Greg use strategic ignorance and wisdom to position themselves as powerless against "nature" and against social structures. Once blackness is the context of white victimization, then whites are able to empathize with other whites and their expression of pain and suffering rather than with the "other."

In another instance, Don, a middle-aged white man from the Southwest Side, articulated that the issue was structural, but the outcome was inevitable. Therefore, while the pain and loss may not be directly the fault of blacks, it *is* (in this telling) understandable that whites with less education and exposure (less insight and knowledge) would be racist. In this framing, Don positioned himself as more intelligent than racist whites, and like Darlene and Tommy, he accepted his family because he understood the context of their racism: "I see the stupidity of the attitude, but I can appreciate the people that have the attitude. You know, I don't want to say that the attitude is justified, but going back to Mt. Greenwood . . . if you have to live in the city and you . . . you're afraid of black people or you have an opinion of black people that you don't want them living there, I guess you can understand the fear you have when [a black person] moves in. Now you might have to sell, and [then] what? Will your property values go down? You know, I don't know about property values, if that does cause it to go down. So I can understand the fear, but it's just not realistic. It's not well thought out." Such empathy allows whites to accept racist family and friends while positioning themselves as having unique insight or wisdom. In other words, the knowledge that whites construct suggests that whites were victims of a racialized structure and it is therefore only "human" to feel for and accept friends and family members who express racism. In short, fear and pain are the foundation on which racism rests. Many of our respondents contextualized, understood, and accepted white racialized fear and pain while defining blackness as the context for that pain. The result was that black fear and pain were ignored or discussed only to show how whites were victims. Such understandings require willful or strategic ignorance on the part of whites, who chose to ignore particular contexts, emotions, and experiences and highlight others (Hooker 2009).

A good example of whites choosing to ignore the experiences of blacks is apparent in a story that Julie and Jim, a married couple, shared with us concerning the white neighborhood in which they now live. Julie recounted the story of a garage sale that they once held:

> Do you want to hear a classic story? This was just two summers ago. . . . [We were] having a garage sale or whatever. This [black] guy comes. . . . He's in his twenties, early twenties. He's with his buddies. He says, "Hey, I want this bike, I want this bike." Jim says, "I'm selling it for . . . 80 bucks." [The young man says,] "I only got $40. Can I have it?" [Jim says,] "No, come back with the money."
>
> The [black] guy comes back with the money at like six, seven o'clock. Jim's sale was just getting done, [and Jim sold the bike to the young man]. Larry, our neighbor, is sitting in his yard and he sees two black guys walking down the alley with a bike. . . . [R]ight away people's radar goes off. . . . So Larry gets up—he's a cop—he goes in the alley, "Hey, wait!" Tackles them, face down, calls the cops. [Larry says,] "What are you doing with this bike?" And the [black] guys are like, "Wait, wait." [One of them] pulls a note out of his pocket that Jim wrote: "I, Jim R., sold him this bike."

While telling the story, Julie and Jim are laughing about the scene. Julie then explains what Jim had told the black men when he sold the bike to them: "The [black] guy was telling him, 'I'm not gonna make it out of here, man.' Jim goes, 'Don't go in the alley.' [The young man says,] 'I'm not riding down the streets.' It's a funny story! Jim goes, 'All right. If a cop shows up, show him this note.'" After Larry tackled the men and the cops arrived, Jim cleared things up. "The cops knew Jim because he was also a cop," Julie explained. "Jim is like, 'Guys, you're not going to believe this. I'm embarrassed.' They're like, 'Are you serious?' He goes, 'No, he did not steal the bike.' They were crying laughing." Shockingly, rather than seeing the injustice of the events, these whites were "crying laughing." Any concern or empathy for the black man who bought the bike and feared riding down the street in this white neighborhood is replaced with mirth. The fear and pain experienced by the young black man are entirely ignored. The physical pain and emotional hurt and terror this man would have felt being tackled by whites—one of whom was a cop—in a white neighborhood are completely dismissed with the laughter and explicit expression, "It's a funny story!" The shared laughter during the storytelling reflected the bond, shared understanding, and acceptance of the racial order that disregards the humanity of blacks. In this way, through ignorance and lack of empathy, white racialized solidarity is strengthened.

Given this insight into how bounded empathy develops and becomes the basis for racialized solidarity, we want to explore what must happen to unbind empathy. Our respondents reported that while they accepted family and friends who were racist, they were not racist themselves. While disavowing one's own racism is a common color-blind strategy, we can learn from the ways in which respondents talked about the differences between themselves (as self-identified non-racists) and others (racists). For example, we repeatedly heard about the importance of exposure and education in giving these whites greater racial awareness and interaction. We now explore these issues as potential keys to generating empathy across racial lines.

Education and Exposure: The Path Forward?

Parents sign their kids up for sports. Universities send students to faraway lands. Suburban and urban high schools host student exchanges. The goal in each case is "exposure" and education. The basis for questioning, learning about the world beyond our daily life, and growing as humans is exposure to "more." Likewise, as parents of teenagers know, we also attempt to limit the extent of their exposure to those things we deem dangerous or not helpful to their future dreams and goals. For white kids growing up during the 1960s, 1970s, and 1980s in Chicago neighborhoods that went through racial change, parents worked to protect their children from what they believed to be the inherent dangers of blackness. The neighborhoods themselves were segregated through institutional practices, and parents worked to keep the racial boundaries from being breached.

As we saw in previous chapters, most of the white kids living on Chicago's Southwest and West sides grew up with little to no positive interaction with blacks. Respondents in both parts of the city echoed the lack of integration. Jim, who grew up on the West Side, captured what many experienced by simply stating, "There was no opportunity to speak to blacks . . . because there were none around. . . . [T]he first time I really had interaction with them was when I went to work." Asked whether she had had black friends growing up, Maria, who lived on the Southwest Side near Morgan Park High School, where some school integration was occurring, responded "No. . . . [A]ny dealings we had with the black kids was, you know, mainly in school. I actually wasn't in classes with a lot of them. . . . [O]bviously they lived within the school district, but there was a pretty definite dividing line, and it was around the school. If you went east of the school, it was pretty much African American, and if you went west and south, it was all white. . . . [B]ack then, [there] was definitely a dividing line." In short, exposure to and interaction with blacks was limited for whites. When there was exposure and interaction, it took place after racial change had occurred. These interactions, captured in previous chapters, were often adversarial. Without such interaction and exposure, there was little opportunity to challenge racial knowledge and ignorance.

In contrast, the lack of interaction led, for some, to a racial ignorance steeped in a desire to *not* know, a willful ignorance, on the part of adults, of black people and their lives. As blacks began to move into previously white spaces, whites had a developing imagination of blackness that was increasingly informed by reliance on television news, community organizations, and word of mouth. For example, Mary's father, an immigrant from Italy to the West Side of Chicago, held racist understandings of the world. As Mary explained, "The thing I found hard [is that] my parents came from Italy, and think about Italy: there were no blacks in that country. It wasn't a segregated society. They had their culture, and that's it. So how did my father come to be a racist? I think it was because he heard it on television. He heard it from the neighbors." The long history of European immigration and the processes of "becoming white" (a context that both shaped and was shaped by U.S. slavery, colonization, and white supremacy) is the backdrop to Mary's father's experiences. Although she did not cite this history explicitly, she did speak to the importance of the context in which her grandfather lived in the United States. This was a context in which whites lived apart from blacks with a racialized imagination filled with details supplied by other whites, the media, and other dominant group sources.

Parents were not the only ones with distorted images of blackness born out of limited exposure to blacks. In a similar fashion, other whites discussed their lack of exposure to blacks, often revealing their image of blackness. For example, this is how Dana imagined blackness in light of her isolation from blacks:

> You have to remember, it's twenty, thirty, forty years later, fifty years later, and things have evolved. There's a lot of intermarriages, and people look different. But when they were by us, no one looked pretty. That's how terms like, "She's pretty for a black person" came about. They did not . . . their hair . . . they didn't know how to groom themselves, because they didn't have the money. Who was going to take money and go straighten their hair when there was twelve people living with no air-conditioning? And you know how hot and muggy it is in Chicago. There was no interaction; it was never a consideration.

The lack of exposure intersects with a system that upheld white-supremacist ideals and actions that allowed blacks to be dehumanized in the white imagination. While whites had little to no real interaction with blacks, they were getting a steady diet of images through the television, newspapers, neighbors, and panic-peddling realtors. In the absence of interaction and direct knowledge and with a narrow understanding of markers of beauty,

Dana thus makes a judgment about blacks that is grounded in isolation and racism.

Undoubtedly, exposure is an important step in challenging racist imaginings. Yet exposure alone will not lead to "re-humanization" (Halpern and Weinstein 2004) or connections across race lines. Reflecting on his exposure to blackness, Ray spoke about how exposure alone ultimately would not shift racialized boundaries "You know, then you get into the workforce, and you gotta deal with them and work with them. And then they become your friends, and it's not as bad as it was, but, you know, there's still always, not a tension, but there's still always that factor; there really is." A connection across racial lines requires knowledge, trust, and empathy. For some whites, trust and empathy are difficult to come by. For example, as one respondent, a Chicago firefighter, stated, "For me . . . a black person has to prove to me who they are before I will trust them at all." Such barriers make it difficult to build trust, particularly when conformity is demanded before acceptance is granted (Novak 1972). Education is important to broadening whites' understanding of history and thus the context for trust. However, as Alison Bailey (2007: 90) notes, "Whites can 'thumb through volumes of history' to reveal stories that have been kept from us." What is needed is human interaction to develop trust and empathy that will allow the crossing of racialized boundaries. Unfortunately, as Steyn (2012: 21) notes, "White knowledge tends to be expansive, to claim to know all about the other, without recognizing what is not known about other world makings." In other words, a central aspect of white knowledge is a belief that the history told by the dominant group is indeed the only history. As we have shown, knowledge of the racialized other requires an individual to admit he or she does not know all of history and thus is willing to listen to and trust "others" as they talk about their experiences and emotions. Through the process of listening, feeling, and empathizing with the "other," they are able to transform themselves in relation to their past experiences, present identities and emotions, and future action.

As we have discussed, throughout the process of interviewing we heard from respondents that they "understood" why family and friends held racist understandings of the world. In brief, they understood that whites had lost economic value in their homes and had their lives and communities uprooted. We also found that some of these whites distanced themselves from racism by explaining that they had interacted with blacks through work and school. For example, Danny, who grew up on the West Side and now has a professional job downtown, talked about friends who still feel victimized by racial change and hold racist views:

> I think a lot of it is, uh—and I'm not saying I'm better than these
> guys, because I'm not—I think it is just education. . . . I work down-

town . . . with a bunch of smart people. . . . [I]n order to try to grow and excel, you have to do everything you can to get smarter and to be educated and to speak well and to listen and to come up with ideas and be creative and, uh, produce. . . . [L]ots of these guys [who are racist] are laborers and hate their jobs. They hate working when it's cold, and they hate working when it's hot, um, and they may feel that some groups of people get entitled. I don't deal with that here, so maybe I'm insulated.

Here Danny speaks to his exposure (working downtown) and education and is careful to not position himself as different from, apart from, or above other whites. Our respondents and those in their networks shared an ignorance (perhaps willful) of how blacks have suffered. Knowledge of black suffering is not acknowledged. Leonardo (2009: 115) suggests that we need to find "a condition whereby this knowledge is made visible." In fact, as we saw in our interviews, when white racial knowledge and experiences are made visible, whites position themselves not as humble and needing to learn from others but as better situated to empathize and understand racist whites, while claiming insight, wisdom, and experience "above" that of other whites, thus enabling them to "tolerate" and accept them.

A small number of our respondents did convey a desire for things to have been different during their childhoods, particularly when it came to exposure and interaction with blacks. For example, Steve, who grew up in the Auburn Gresham neighborhood on the Southwest Side, talked about the value of whites' being exposed to blacks: "It was the way to grow up, just to be exposed to different cultures and different people. I'm probably more liberal than most, but it would have been an excellent way to grow up. But it obviously was not my choice, and it probably was not doable at that time. But when I see, like, my cousins growing up in [a neighborhood] where their neighbors [on one side] are black and then [on the other side they're] white, I think, 'What a great way to expose your kids to all that, to know that the neighborhood is not unsafe, just because there's . . .' Even more than that, to know your neighbors, even though they are black, you know, you need to be friends with them.'" In a similar fashion, Beverly talked about her choice to live in an integrating neighborhood: "The hatred, suspicion, and anger, I don't want to go through that again. Living here where we are now it isn't happening that way. And, it makes me regret that it couldn't have happened that way then." This desire, however, it only a beginning. The next step involves an attempt to appreciate the larger structural forces that limited exposure and interaction in the first place.

In short, exposure and education alone will not shift the racialized boundaries that encompass a sense of community. Exposure and education will lead to some insight and possibly to a sense of ambivalence about racism, but whites will still be empathizing in a bounded manner. In other words, exposure may help whites see that not all black people are bad, and education can help us understand the world differently, but until whites are able to trust, imagine, and empathize across racial boundaries in a way that compels action, whites will continue to accept white racism because empathy is ensconced in a belief that close proximity to blackness is harmful to whites. Formal education, freed from the moorings of human emotion and the experience of living through that history, can be disregarded or understood simply in the abstract. Education at the intersection of exposure is needed. But those two pieces devoid of empathy will continue to reproduce racialized boundaries. We need all three pieces—education, exposure, and empathy— working together. And, of course, we must mobilize, collectively, our vision, our developing imaginations of a better world, toward creating a more just social context in which human beings truly come together.

In this chapter, we have examined how whites develop empathy for other whites in a way that not only precludes blackness but also requires a further dehumanization of blackness as white racial solidarity is reinforced. At issue are the ways in which the dominant racial group (whites) has constructed history and shaped public or collective memory to foreclose the understanding needed to empathize with the racialized "other." As we saw in previous chapters, the lack of acceptance of blacks was buttressed by racial isolation and segregation. As Hooker (2009: 53) points out, the problem with this is that "as long as the public memory of the political community as a whole reflects only the ethical self-understanding of dominant groups, racialized solidarity will continue to reproduce itself." However, such dehumanization is not inevitable. Jodi Halpern and Harvey Weinstein (2004), concerned with moving society forward after war, genocide, and diasporas, suggest that a process of rehumanization happens through the development of empathy in the context of understanding history through the eyes of the other. For such rehumanization to occur, we have to be able to imagine the context as experienced by others and trust that what they tell us is true. Unfortunately, social distance creates gaps in understanding that the imagination, fed by the media and other racially isolated whites, then rushes in to fill. As Bailey (2007: 90) points out, "Ignorance flourishes when we confine our movements, thoughts, and actions to these worlds, social circles, and logics where we are most comfortable." Continuing to connect with people with whom we feel the most comfortable and not reaching out to hear the effects of racism from those most affected thus leads to bounded empathy.

As has been shown across a variety of disciplines, empathy is expressed for those we deem "our own." In his historical analysis of whites' racial attitudes, Hubert O'Gorman found that if whites think blacks will make other whites uncomfortable, they will work to make spaces comfortable for other whites by excluding blacks. O'Gorman refers to this phenomenon as pluralistic ignorance—that is, the "erroneous cognitive belief shared by two or more people regarding the ideas, sentiments, and action of others" (O'Gorman 1975: 314). In other words, through pluralistic ignorance, whites often believe that other whites are both racist and uncomfortable around blacks and thus act to exclude blacks and include only whites. These assumptions are often based not on conversations but on assumptions—assumptions that obviously further racialize boundaries, including segregated neighborhoods. We see elements of pluralistic ignorance in our study, as whites are attempting to empathize with other whites who express racist views, thereby creating solidarity that is exclusive and the foundation on which systems of whiteness are more easily reproduced. Thus, whether it is through creating segregated neighborhoods, the process of avoiding perceived upsetting of other whites, or maintaining solidarity through empathizing with racist whites, each approach boils down to racial ignorance—that is, knowing and not knowing as the basis for building white racial solidarity.

Building strong ties across difference requires empathy, trust, education, exposure, imagination, and a shared sense of obligation (Waghid 2001; Bentley and Habib 2008; Hooker 2009). Education and exposure to different ways of understanding and knowing history can lead to the development of empathy grounded in the ability to "imagine" the nuanced context of the "other." By contrast, common racialized storytelling words such as "gang-banger," "urban," "juvenile," and "inner city" are dehumanizing, de-historicizing, and lacking in empathy. Changing our ways of knowing through the media, textbooks, popular culture, and personal experience is a process that ultimately requires human interaction across racial boundaries. For the context shift to occur, we need critical dialogue across difference (Waghid 2001; McKinney 2007; Hooker 2009; Leibowitz et al. 2010; Soudien 2010; Leonardo 2011). Rather than isolation, silence, and color-blindness, we need knowledge, as well as acknowledgment of ignorance, for the development of bonds across racial boundaries and among those who currently see themselves as radically different from one another (Waghid 2001). Thus, genuine solidarity between groups requires working to see each other as part of the same community, even when one imagines the other as very different (Hooker 2009). Accomplishing this is difficult work and involves learning to see through the eyes of the "other" and relearning who we are in the context of history.

6

Conclusion

In 1949, Langston Hughes published the poem "Restrictive Covenants." In it, he addressed his experience of living in Chicago, particularly how both native-born and newly arrived European immigrants reacted to the possibility of neighborhood integration:

> *When I move*
> Into a neighborhood
> Folks fly.
> Even every foreigner
> That can move, moves.
> *Why? (Hughes 1994: 451)*

Our project began with a set of similar questions: why did whites leave when blacks moved in? Why did integration not work? How did whites understand themselves in the context of racial change? Few urban scholars have examined these questions by focusing on the processes and politics involved in the defense of segregation or the process of racial change. Even fewer have examined the legacy of racial change and the work of whites in framing racial identities in struggles over housing.[1] Over the course of the project, we have recorded hundreds of hours of interviews in our attempt to explore and uncover answers to these questions. As we talked with whites who grew up in the formerly segregated white neighborhoods of Chicago, we uncovered the

complexity and subtlety of race, whiteness, and the processes of racial segregation. Through our research we identified key factors that help us explain
racialization from the mid-twentieth century to the present, including shifts
in the contours of whiteness and racial discourse. In many respects, the story
we have told applies broadly to relationships between groups with unequal
power in a struggle to shift institutional, ideological, and individual power.

In answering the "why" questions, we sought also to understand how
whites experienced living through racial change. Thus, before we could
understand why racial change occurred, we needed to understand both how
whites experienced racial change and the complexities of how racial transformation occurred over time. Our research explored how whites experienced the loss of institutional backing for their segregated spaces as a result
of the Civil Rights Movement's successes in demanding change. Our exploration led us to look at how whites learned how to think and act on race,
lessons that extend over a lifetime. In the process, we discovered a story that
is about the power of whiteness, an often unrecognized form of social power
that is shrouded in contradictions. For example, we discovered how white
youth who grew up in loving families could still learn, accept, and live with
racialized fear and hate. Our data also revealed how whites claim commit-
ments to racial and democratic equality for all while expressing internalized
notions of white superiority and black inferiority. Finally, we saw how whites
frame racism as a matter of individual pathology while celebrating group
solidarity but ignoring the experiences of nonwhite groups.

Whiteness itself is a process that is woven into the structures of society,
internalized, conflicting, and contradictory. The fairly static and constant
consequences of whiteness can be experienced and measured in larger social
outcomes in the areas of housing, education, media, criminal incarceration,
and employment. Yet at the level of the individual, through day-to-day interactions and ideologies, whiteness is amorphous, shifting from context to
context and across time relative to larger racial formations and understandings. Troy Duster (2001) likens whiteness to water—both are fluid, shifting,
and transformational forms—imagery that sums up our task in this book.
We spoke with adults whom we asked to look back over their lives and recall
specific events, times, places, interactions, stories, and memories from their
childhoods. The way they learned about race was, of course, an organic part
of their lives. We traced that learning and how they understood race in the
context of racial change and over time through larger social changes, from
racial explicitness to color-blindness, from explicit institutional backing for
white privilege to more nuanced, subtle, and covert forms of institutional
discrimination.

Through these changes, the whites with whom we spoke attempted to
make sense of their actions, experiences, and memories in open and honest

ways. Our goal as sociologists was to understand how whites understand racial change and race. As we moved through this project, it became clear that our respondents were engaged in living in ways that they defined as good and in being good people who accepted others (and their flaws). Most of them would consider themselves fair-minded and would not have seen race as important in their daily lives. Yet throughout the interviewing, we saw that race was, in fact, a central organizing principle of their lives (Omi and Winant 1994). Scholars have long noted that racialization affects not only racial minorities but also whites in meaningful ways (Doane 2003). As Amanda Lewis (2004: 641–642) writes, "The seriality of whiteness means that though whites do not necessarily take it up as an active identity, it still fundamentally shapes their lives," including their "feelings, goals, and language." Whites, however, are rarely asked to examine their racial identities and the impact of their actions on the racial structure.[2] In this book, we have taken a close look at whites as racialized subjects, as they overtly and subtly, consciously and unconsciously, bolstered positive white racial identities and white privilege.

We find that whiteness is indeed complex, requires intensive personal and social effort, and is ever shifting. While the ways that whiteness is created and sustained have changed, whiteness as a construct of privilege and power has remained. Our interviews reveal that in shifting racial contexts, whites are repositioning their identities and sense of community relative to the larger context. Such repositioning was visible in a variety of ways, as we show below, but centers on a racial discourse that valorizes white actions and spaces, denigrates blacks and blackness, and redefines whiteness as a liability so whites can be portrayed as "victims" (Doane 2003; Gallagher 2003). The effect of this repositioning is increased racial solidarity. Solidarity is an experience of "willed affiliation," in which individuals have a claim on one another's "energies, compassion, and resources" (Hollinger 2006: 24). Political theorists see this willed affiliation as based on trust and responsibility for others, regardless of differences. However, as Juliet Hooker (2009: 21–22) argues, solidarity in which individuals "engage in relations of trust and obligation with fellow members of a political community whom they may see as inherently 'other' in some fundamental way" is not the norm; instead, we see racialized solidarity. Group solidarity creates a boundary around and an understanding of who is an "us" and defines the qualities of the "them." Group-based solidarity is often founded in contexts with inequality, and the boundaries are reinforced ideologically and institutionally with physical demarcations such as a wall, street, or train tracks (Dalmage 2000). The greater the inequality between groups and the more at stake, the more the borders are patrolled and reinforced. These racial borders create a separation in life so that one group does not interact in meaningful ways with the other group. Thus, whites tend not to know blacks and are less likely to see black people's pain and suffering; consequently, when whites do see pain and suffering, they have less empathy across racial borders. We find that children learn to "be white" and that racial solidarity and whiteness are not a natural part of humanity or society but are created and maintained through many processes, particularly by naturalizing racial boundaries and specific attempts to bolster group position.

A recurring theme in the story of racial change we uncovered centered on the naturalization of race—that is, that racial differences and borders are somehow natural or given. For our respondents, the naturalization of race and racial borders was reinforced through socialization. Within families and communities children are taught a range of social expectations. They are socialized in how to behave "properly" and taught the rules about their appropriate place in the world. Central to this process is learning racial lessons and particular racial ways of being. Examining the process of socialization, as it is remembered by adults who grew up in segregated neighborhoods, sheds a brighter light on the processes of racialization and, thus, the production of whiteness. Against the backdrop of a changing set of racialized institutional practices, parents were raising their children to "be" in the world, and who they wanted them to be was in large part shaped by the borders and boundaries of the communities they claimed. Racial borders protect the power, privilege, and resources of a community—particularly, white privilege and status. Learning about the racial borders was thus a central feature of the socialization process. While the lessons received and the ways in which this socialization process directed the lives of our respondents varied, it is clear that racial isolation, separation, and fear of blackness all served as the context and constraints for our respondents.

For children living in or near neighborhoods that experienced racial change, the borders mattered as a physical location that focused racialized fear and delineated the boundaries of community. In short, our respondents were aware of borders, yet as long as they avoided them, they could go on with their lives, protected and secure. However, once the borders were breached—an outcome of shifts in housing, employment, and education—parents had to make race an explicit feature of their children's socialization. For many of our respondents, race, racial boundaries, and the racial order were largely ignored until blacks began purchasing homes in their neighborhood. At that point, many whites believed that blacks were breaching a natural border. Significantly, while our respondents spoke about a time that they thought the racial order was a reflection of the natural order, they were also able to articulate the social and psychological effort that went into (re)producing the borders. The ability to hold these contradictory ideals is, in fact, an aspect of whiteness.

The naturalization of racial differences and borders is also tied to fear. One often repeated assertion we heard from our respondents was that they thought and acted in the ways they did because they were afraid. While the intensity of fear and the form of fear varied, the most common fear discussed was that integration would signal a decline in property values. Our respondents for the most part were children of first- or second-generation European immigrants, whose arrival in the middle class was quite recent. Moving to the Southwest and West sides signaled success, security, and achievement (Kefalas 2003). Like whites in other working-class to lower middle-class neighborhoods, racial change threatened not only their community networks and their grip on this precarious and "exalted" class position but also their claim as whites (Rieder 1985: 96). For whites, the fear of being "dispossessed" rested in part on some knowledge of what institutional actors were doing, particularly blockbusters and "panic peddlers" (Hirsch 1983: 35). When coupled with the victories of the Civil Rights Movement and the decline of manufacturing jobs, integration then represented a real slippage in both class position and social status. Clearly, race and class intersect here, as institutional racism creates a dual housing market that devalues integrated and black communities. Thus, in a real sense, given the workings of the real estate and lending industries, fear of declining property values was justified. However, blaming blacks for the moral decline of the community and the destruction of property is also a function of racism, even as it serves to protect white privilege and status.

An additional way fear was expressed involved concern over issues of crime and safety—specifically, personal safety and criminal victimization. While this is a complex issue, it is worth noting that we heard few reports of actual victimization of whites by blacks. Yet assertions of fear of black violence and criminality were common. The discrepancy is related largely to socialization, as many of our respondents recalled direct messages from adults that if they interacted with blacks, they would be victimized, thus limiting their ability to develop alternative ways to interpret the world without reference to fear. Clearly, a central element of white racial socialization is a desire for and expectation of racial comfort (Dalmage 2004), and such notions of black criminality frame the problem away from whites. Moreover, as Joe Feagin and his colleagues (2000: 50) suggest, the objects of white fear are often stereotyped images or the unknown, often the result of whites directing their personal or social anxiety onto "society's subordinate racial and ethnic groups" rather than the "actual sources of their discomfort." This language of fear is made pervasive through a color-blind way of implicitly talking about race that nevertheless draws on racial ideology. As Ruth Frankenberg (1993: 61) notes, "White people's fear of people of color is an element of racist discourse crucially linked to essentialist racism, or the idea that people of color are fundamentally Other than white people: different, inferior, less civilized, less human, more animal, than whites." This racial/ ideological line of thinking is visible throughout history, as blacks have been portrayed as naturally violent, dangerous, and sexually aggressive. Importantly, the construction of someone (or a class of people) as an object to be feared results in a process of dehumanization that makes it less likely that one will empathize with those people or consider them part of one's community. Thus, fear is part of a larger process of naturalizing racial difference that again strengthens racial solidarity. As whites feel that they are losing control—when, say, a black family purchases a home on their block—they reassert their power in many ways even as they make claims to powerlessness.

As we discussed early in the book, race is a social construct, but one that has structural causes and consequences. In this sense, the strength and power of whiteness derives from the fact that whites benefit from and actively uphold the system. In fact, as George Lipsitz notes, the unequal distribution of resources and power is not natural; it requires a lot of effort. Lipsitz refers to this effort as a possessive investment in whiteness. He writes, "Conscious and deliberate actions have institutionalized group identity in the United States, not just through the dissemination of cultural stories but also through systematic efforts from colonial times to the present to create a possessive investment in whiteness for European Americans" (Lipsitz 1995: 371). As we have shown, there are numerous conscious and deliberate actions that have institutionalized white group identity in the United States, including Federal Housing Administration/Veterans Administration appraisal and lending practices and urban renewal. These efforts have included both policies sanctioned by the state and involve cultural stories. Whites tell stories that either ignore racial inequality or recount events in ways that do not implicate them in the system of racial inequality. Our study demonstrates the processes of whiteness—that is, how whites invest (intentionally or unintentionally) in a system of racial advantage. In our research, we witnessed the various, sometimes subtle ways in which whites work to bolster white identity by portraying themselves simultaneously as valorous and victims and choosing to highlight differences and the boundaries of race. In this process, we capture the workings of both race and class, emphasizing that while these two factors are held out as separate factors in the struggle for status, they are indeed interlocking and mutually reinforcing aspects of the social world.

The lower middle-class neighborhoods on Chicago's Southwest and West sides are good places to see the workings of whiteness in the post–Civil Rights Movement era. Prior to racial change, whites undoubtedly took racial segregation for granted, making the boundaries between white and black—and thus between good and bad—assumed. Whether residents were aware or not, institutional actors such as banks and real estate agents supported the racial borders and racial segregation. Starting in the 1950s, Chicago began to change from white to people of color, urban to suburban, and industrial to postindustrial. On a larger level, the gains of the Civil Rights Movement were reshaping how institutions acted in terms of race and how individuals talked about race. At the same time, the very institutions (banks and real estate agencies) that had once supported segregation began to turn on white neighborhoods. The totality of these changes meant that whites could no longer take their status or borders for granted. They began to mobilize to protect their status. The case of the Parish Federation illustrates one response by whites to these changes. The particular work by the Parish Federation, which ranged from media campaigns to challenges to panic peddling, blockbusting, and mortgage discrimination and the use of the "white ethnic" descriptor, was based on a rhetoric of class-based complaints. While painting its members as courageous and yet innocent victims, the federation employed a "muted" racial discourse that has the effect, intended or not, of shoring up racial boundaries, particularly given the federation's rejection of integration. Efforts to stabilize the neighborhood, then, reinforced notions of the naturalness of racial boundaries (as opposed to pro-integration communities across the country). Given that racial borders and property values are inextricably linked, anti-integration efforts result in a strengthening of racial inequality in objective forms.

Indeed, the interplay of race and class was quite apparent in this study. In the United States, whites often use race and gender as proxies when thinking and talking about social class. Race and class also are often conflated, with blacks associated with poverty regardless of their background. Discussing Chicago's Southeast Side, Christine Walley (2013: 8) notes that, for working-class and lower middle-class whites, race is often used as "a kind of shorthand for the poverty that they wanted to keep at bay and that seemed all too close both geographically and generationally given many whites' impoverished immigrant forebears." Our respondents came from similar settings and often disavowed race in favor of class. Race and class obviously intersect in ways where one variable does not trump the other. The case of the Parish Federation is an example of the "mutually constitutive" nature of class and race (Walley 2013), as its work centered on maintaining its members' recently achieved status as middle class *and* on constructing positive white racial identities. Thus, while class insecurity or "fear of falling" is a pertinent factor shaping their lives, more is going on. As we have demonstrated, white racial identities are not latent; they are constructed through agents of socialization, conflict, and racial ideology and discourse.

It is also possible to see the investment in whiteness by looking at the memory-making process. Analyzing feelings of nostalgia for the old neighborhood requires unweaving complex issues. As Michelle Boyd (2010: 157) notes, "Nostalgia is not just something that people feel randomly." Rather, it is tied to larger issues in the present, including social change and identity development. Nostalgia for the old neighborhood that our respondents expressed was clearly connected to the loss of the neighborhoods in which they grew up. Some respondents expressed feelings that were quite similar to those of refugees, likely making the memories even more poignant. It is also clear that the social conditions that respondents romanticized are largely obsolete. Small shops were soon replaced by chain stores; women entered or returned to the paid workforce; small shops and small factories left the city; many Catholic schools closed or were consolidated; and even sports activities are increasingly organized by adults. As Sharon Zukin (2010: 227) notes, "The rootedness that connects people to place was made weak by new forms of mobility," including less walking to school and more driving out of neighborhoods. The rise of computers is also relevant, as many of our respondents lamented the proliferation of video games and the Internet as limiting their children's ability to experience the bonds of community they felt as kids. Thus, nostalgia for the old neighborhood reflects the loss of such places and the rootedness that they represented. In this sense, nostalgia reveals discomfort with the changing social conditions of modern society.

Yet race and racial identity construction are also tied to the use of nostalgia. Nostalgia is one way in which whites were able to sidestep race in an explicit form while portraying segregated spaces as having the most humanity, happiness, safety, and empathy. Through the use of nostalgia, then, whites could ignore the history and context of how their neighborhoods emerged and were sustained, instead painting a version of history in which whites are a racialized victim and whiteness is good. Nostalgia is inextricably linked to the use of knowledge, ignorance, and bounded empathy as safeguards on whiteness. On the one hand, nostalgia helps package the stories that portray whites in the most favorable light. As our respondents revealed, nostalgia or the selecting of certain stories from the past allowed whites to bolster their group identity, particularly as virtuous, innocent, and powerless. Such discourse, tied to prevailing color-blind strategies, helps normalize segregation while disparaging blacks as dangerous. Nostalgia narratives also serve to resolve contradictory positions that whites present in their storytelling. By painting the time before blacks moved in as idyllic and the time after as tragic, whites can blame blacks even in the face of evidence showing that fellow whites played the role of active victimizers. Nostalgia then limits the full story of racial complexity and thus allows individuals to evade a sense of social responsibility. Thus, as a discursive strategy, nostalgia helps reproduce what is known and what cannot be recognized, helping solidify racialized communities.

Finally, we also see the work involved in maintaining the boundaries of whiteness through the construction of racial knowledge. Clearly, the histories we know and are able to call on in our attempts to understand others are always incomplete. Given that it is impossible to be all knowing, we all move through the world acting and interacting with others based on incomplete knowledge. Histories are more credible to individuals when they match the experiences of friends and family. Our respondents grew up in segregated—racially isolated—spaces; the histories they learned through storytelling, the media, and other sources served as the knowledge they drew on when empathizing with human suffering. In circularity, this knowledge allowed them, as adults, to empathize with other whites who felt animosity, anger, hostility, and hatred toward blacks. These respondents knew from experience—that is, socialization—that the history of racial change meant "loss" for the whites in their family and community: the loss of property values, community, and a way of life they had held near and dear. Racism could be seen as an expression of the pain whites felt—a pain caused by blacks. Thus, blacks' pain was ignored along with other tellings of history, and the conception of blacks as destroyers was naturalized as either a matter of biology or social structure—in both cases, reduced to "that's just the way it was."

We want to be clear: we are not asking for white individuals to apologize for their childhoods or to feel guilty. We are attempting to explore the veil of whiteness and ask whites to acknowledge the complexity of race and the pain the system has caused blacks, and to see a racialized system that allowed whites to feel safe, secure, and happy at the expense of others. Our research demonstrates that whites often avoid or ignore institutional mechanisms in structuring race while stressing individual animus (when talking about racist whites) or individual pathology (when talking about blacks). The construction of knowledge that stresses individual attitudes and ignorance of a larger racial system keeps whites from seeing how institutions structure inequality, how they themselves benefit from such relationships and their role in protecting privilege. Whites and blacks are not equally situated, and stressing such a myth keeps whites from framing racism as part of a history of pain and suffering. Moving beyond individual experience is even more difficult in the prevailing neoliberal context in which we live (Pedwell 2012). In this context, "personal responsibility," individualism, and choice serve as buzzwords, reflecting an era in which a sense of community has largely vanished (Bellah et al. 1985), and thus racial solidarity is strengthened and reaching across boundaries is more difficult.

Throughout this book we have focused on how whiteness is created in ever shifting contexts. We show how whiteness mediates identities, communities, and resource distribution. Racialized knowledge and ignorance underlay these white identities and communities (Mills 2007; Steyn 2012) and clearly influence the ability of whites to empathize across racial lines (Leonardo 2009). As we have shown, white racialized empathy is developed in a particular context—one of white racial solidarity. We highlight that beyond meeting or getting to know more about blacks (although that is good), we must attempt not only to disrupt white racial ignorance and knowledge but also to develop trust and empathy for nonwhites. Thus, whites need to actively listen to people of color and trust them when they share their experiences and emotions. This is a process of learning to trust, imagine, and empathize across racial boundaries. The connection among knowledge, empathy, and trust is ultimately an issue of cultivating one's humanity. As Martha Nussbaum (1997: 10) notes, "We very easily think of ourselves in group terms—as Americans first and foremost, as human beings second—or, even more narrowly, as Italian-Americans, or heterosexuals, or African-Americans first, Americans second, and human beings third if at all. We neglect needs and capacities that link us to fellow citizens who live at a distance or who look different from ourselves." As a result, whites often miss or avoid chances to interact and become friends with people of color and, importantly, to recognize the responsibility whites have toward all of their fellow humans (see Halpern and Weinstein 2004). As Nussbaum (1997: 10) suggests, the goal should be to cultivate our need for humanity and thus our ability to see ourselves not as members of some group but as "human beings bound to all other human beings by ties of recognition and concern."

Methodological Appendix

Qualitative research is a process of gathering and interpreting stories through a sociological lens. Both the gathering and the interpreting of data require that we be reflective and careful to consider the historical and social context of the stories we hear and the context of the interviews themselves. Qualitative methods require attentiveness to power relations between the researcher and researched (Morris 2007) and to how we name ourselves and others. As researchers, we are part of the context of the interview and thus need to take seriously how our experiences and social locations—for example, race, gender, class, and religion—shape the questions we ask, how we connect and build trust in the interviews, and how we interpret what we are told. We agree with Charles Gallagher when he states that it is centrally important to "critically assess where one's social location, political orientation, religious training, and attitudes on race fit into the research project" (Gallagher 2000: 204). Given our backgrounds and lived experiences, we were keenly aware of and processed together the racial nuances involved in our interviews and social interactions.

Our research questions explored how whites understand themselves, focusing primarily on white racial knowledge and the meanings that whites give to their experiences. Whites as a group are the focus of our project; thus, the social construction of racial categories and internalization of racial identification are central matters for this study. We were explicitly curious about our respondents' experiences as whites in a racially changing world. The dominant racial discourse of the era we were studying and race and racial identities at that time were geographically bounded; therefore, we were careful *not* to have explicit conversations with respondents about their racial identity before the interviews. Instead, we explained that we were interested in talking with people who grew up and lived in neighborhoods on the Southwest and West sides of Chicago during times of racial change. Thus, while we were careful about how we articulated race, we understood that our bodies, language, and other "signifiers" of racialization would be read and interpreted by our respondents. In short, we needed to be mindful of how our bodies signified particular racial assumptions and how we used language to negotiate the process of racial signification. As Judy Scales-Trent (1995: 3) has noted, race is a "demanding verb." It is something that we all "do" in the context of human interaction. We read physical bodies, movements, and expressions to determine our racial location relative to one another. Thus, as researchers we understood that our bodies would be read in ways that would allow us to be "insiders." Whether we would be trusted insiders required careful interaction during the interview process (Acker 2001).

As we entered the field, we drew on a several sources of data. Our central research questions focused on the experiences of individuals who grew up in racially changing neighborhoods; thus, the major source of data for this project was qualitative interviews. These interviews were with former residents of Chicago who grew up in neighborhoods of the Southwest and West sides between 1960 and 1980. We also gathered data from other sources, including interviews with former community organizers who had worked in these neighborhoods, news accounts (both the large metropolitan dailies and the smaller and harder-to-retrieve local newspapers), and the archives of the Parish Federation. The research methodologies we selected were employed to give us both an appreciation of the social context in which our respondents were growing up and insight into the complexities and nuances of racial discourse and racialized identities.

ARCHIVAL DATA

The main source of data for Chapter 2 came from Parish Federation archival data, newspaper archives, and interviews with leaders active in the neighborhoods. Using the Chicago History Museum's Parish Federation papers as the primary data source, we analyzed internal memos, news clippings, letters, meeting agendas and minutes, resident surveys, and a large selection of the organization's publications from 1971 to the late 1980s. This time frame represents the most active period of the organization's history, as well as the period in which it was the most threatened by racial change. While the Parish Federation files are the largest data source for part of the book, we should make it clear that we were careful not to attribute direct intent to members of the Parish Federation. We took such care for several key reasons. First, some of the files reference actions taken by residents of the Southwest Side who may or may not have been affiliated with the Parish Federation. Second, in the early 1980s the Parish Federation formed an alliance with the Northwest Neighbors Federation, named the Save Our Neighborhoods, Save Our City (SON/SOC) coalition. Finally, since most of the principal leaders have either died or moved and the files are not complete, it is difficult to provide a comprehensive examination of the organization. In the end, we were less concerned with the specific actions taken by the Parish Federation than with the racial discourse it employed in how race was framed.

INTERVIEWS

For the main part of our study, we used in-depth, face-to-face interviews with thirty-seven individual participants and sixteen more people convened in four focus groups. The focus groups ranged in size from three to six people. The interviews were conducted using a semi-structured format to allow respondents to give voice to their experiences growing up in an area where racial transition was likely, without our asking them to analyze their experiences specifically through a racial lens. The interview format allowed unplanned discussions to facilitate the unmasking of the subtleties of racialized discourse in the context of their lives. The interviews were loosely structured around two broad areas: (1) a description of the neighborhood in which respondents grew up; and (2) respondents' experiences as the area began to change.

The interviews were one to two hours long, recorded with the participants' permission, and transcribed verbatim. We allowed respondents to choose the location of their interviews. Our goal was to ensure that they felt comfortable and safe in the context of the interview. To this end, we traveled to homes, restaurants, and offices. Three of the focus groups were conducted in homes; one was conducted at a restaurant. To protect the privacy of our participants, all names have been changed to pseudonyms. Among the interviews with former residents, thirty-three were male and twenty-one were female. The respondents ranged from thirty-eight to fifty-eight years old. They had similarities—specifically, they had lived in white, largely lower middle-class Catholic neighborhoods where connections and interactions were circumscribed in a church parish and the communities were bounded by narrow bands of streets. The respondents grew up under the pervasive scrutiny of family, neighbors, and friends. A clear majority of respondents reported coming from working- to lower middle-class backgrounds; thus, our respondents were very aware of their parents' concern about property values. Their parents' class position undoubtedly informed their experiences. However, while all of our respondents grew up in neighborhoods best described as lower middle-class, the majority had earned college degrees and moved into professional careers.

Gender and Class

Gender is a central organizing principle in life. Our earliest experiences with pink or blue blankets set the stage for a lifetime of socialization around gender norms. Throughout life we claim, name, resist, internalize, and use gender as a lens through which to think and act in the world. Thus, we had expectations about how gender would have mattered in the lives of our respondents. Specifically, given the intersection of class, gender, and race in the neighborhoods we explored, we expected gender to shape what our respondents were involved in as kids; the amount of freedom they were given; the emotions they would express about racial change; and, ultimately, their comfort with the interviewers. In a few interviews, conducted together, we learned that respondents made eye contact solely with the same-sex interviewer. With this in mind, we attempted to match interviewers and respondents according to sex, whenever possible, to create a sense of comfort. Moreover, our respondents' experiences growing up were gendered, particularly in terms of action. For example, more male respondents than female respondents recalled being involved in sports. The men recalled being given great freedom, while the women recalled expectations that they would stay closer to home. As the racial border and racial change edged toward their neighborhoods, the boys—teenage boys—were the ones who actively patrolled borders, engaged in violence, and expressed a sense that their role was to protect. There was a clear element of machismo in terms of border patrolling, particularly for teenagers living closest to the border. Conversely, girls were told to "withdraw" or steer clear of borders. However, the expression of emotion was remarkably similar, as both men and women articulated strong feelings of sadness, anger, and regret over the loss of their neighborhoods. Nor was the construction of nostalgia and empathy evidently gendered. Our data do not show clear gender differences in how our respondents organized empathy, nostalgia, and whiteness.

Social class was another central element of this study. Our respondents were people raised in families in the working-class to middle-class communities on the Southwest and West sides of Chicago. Thus, our interviews involved people who were raised in families with the same or very similar social class positions. While there was some variation in the types of jobs our respondents' parents held, that variation overall was minor. Almost all of the respondents grew up in freestanding houses, not apartments, and in most cases their parents owned the home. We saw little variation in terms of ownership versus rental. Thus, given the nature of the communities we studied, our study is class-specific without a comparison group. While our respondents grew up in very similar class locations, the paths they took into adulthood varied substantially, although, as we have noted, a sizable portion attended college and moved on to professional careers. Thus, we are confident that our findings can be generalized to other whites, given that the whites we interviewed are currently situated in differing social classes. We are able to see how constructions of and shifts in whiteness remain fairly stable across class (and class at the intersection of gender and race).

Building Openness and Trust

Given our desire to understand how participants remembered their experiences rather than how they responded to a sequential telling of experiences structured by our questions, each interview began with an open-ended request that interviewees tell us about the neighborhood they grew up in. We intentionally did not begin with questions about race. We wanted to understand how our respondents made sense of the ways race mattered in lives. Through their own storytelling, in every interview, respondents discussed race without prompting from us. We followed up with specific questions about how they felt about certain experiences (e.g., fears they had); descriptions of situations in school and in the neighborhoods (e.g., tension, interactions, and details about moving); how their social networks were shaped; and the messages they received from parents, relatives, friends, and teachers. We ended interviews by asking respondents to reflect on how their experience growing up in these neighborhoods shaped their views of the world and race. Here we explored their views of the negative perceptions of the Southwest or West Sides in regard to race, particularly the sense that these areas are racist and unwelcoming to blacks. The goal of this approach was to understand what was going on in their lives and allow individuals to "remember and retell" (Coffey and Atkinson 1996) in ways that made sense to them rather than relative to an interview schedule. In short, through our careful methodological approach in which we built trust, we were able to discover when, where, and how race entered into the experiences and memories of whites who grew up in neighborhoods before and during racial change.

Researching sensitive topics requires researchers to be particularly vigilant about framing questions and building trust (Charmaz 1991; Booth and Booth 1994). The interviewer must develop rapport and a level of trust as part of creating a space in which participants will be open in their memories and reflections in the interview process. We reflected on each interview and asked ourselves how much we should disclose of our own lives. Our goal was to develop trust as insiders while maintaining our outsider status so that our subjects would articulate their detailed insights and reflections. In most interviews, for instance, respondents spoke about their memories of neighborhoods overflowing with adolescents and teenagers, meeting in the morning and playing until they were called home for dinner. That social milieu, along with the role of Catholic schooling, the parish sensibility, and the similar time period of growing up (i.e., pre-Internet and child-centered), was very familiar to both researchers. To build rapport and trust, we often shared with respondents that we had had similar childhoods and understood the joy in those memories. Neither of us grew up in a major city, although we now both consider ourselves Chicagoans. Because of the archival research, we also knew a great deal about the neighborhoods we included in the study and were aware of the specific contexts our respondents referenced. We were careful to not interject too much, as the goal was to hear from them. In addition, because neither of us maintains ties to the Catholic church, we chose to talk only about being raised Catholic and our connection to childhood memories, not about our contemporary social locations.

Nodding and Passing

One of the most direct ways a researcher can build trust is by responding affirmatively and knowingly to interviewees' statements and insights. This can be done verbally—for instance, by making sounds that indicate agreement, by nodding or smiling, or by making statements such as, "That makes so much sense to me" or "I see what you're saying." Throughout the process of interviewing and transcribing, we reflected on several important conflicts we experienced—specifically, times we responded with a nod or a verbal utterance to indicate that we were listening, understanding, and open to hearing more. While this method works well to build and maintain a connection in the interview process, we were aware that some of our respondents could misconstrue such affirmation as approval of racist statements or insights (see Gallagher 2010). In these moments, our goal of developing trust, gaining insight, and being nonjudgmental was in conflict with our desire to educate and not to condone racism. Given that we were interested in a snowball sample, we were aware that an interview referral would be made if we were seen as agreeable and open. For these reasons, we critically explored our reactions throughout the interviewing process. Two particular themes emerged across the interviewing process: when, why, and how we "pass" by not disclosing parts of our lives and our need to negotiate gender.

Qualitative interviews by their nature require some attention to impression management on the part of the interviewer. In his classic text *The Presentation of Self in Everyday Life* (1959), Erving Goffman noted that impression management refers to a set of intentional presentation strategies that individuals use to enhance their favorable presentation in the eyes of others, including claiming to be what they are not. In later work, Goffman extends his ideas to discuss passing, where individuals mask certain identities by adopting more socially acceptable personas to escape the expectations of others (Goffman 1963). In this sense, passing is the act of impression management so that an audience is either allowed to or led to misconstrue one's social identity (see Renfrow 2004). Passing can be involuntary, as when a person is subject to the incorrect assumptions of others. Or the individual might recognize underlying assumptions and in no manner contradict them. An extreme and life-threatening instance of this is represented by the NAACP activist Walter White's visit to the American South to investigate lynching. Although White was black, he was able to pass as a white man; thus, incorrect assumptions can be said both to have bolstered his knowledge of lynching and, in turn, to have protected him from mob violence (White 1995). After being tipped off that whites suspected he was passing and planned to lynch him, White caught the next train out of town, where, he wrote, a white man said, "But you're leaving, mister, just when the fun is going to start. . . . [T]here's a damned yellow nigger down here passing for white and the boys are going to get him" (White 1995: 51). In White's case, passing was a high-stakes gambit; in everyday life, by contrast, passing does not involve such horrific stakes, and people seek to pass for many reasons.

Passing may also be active, as when a person grows up in a poor family and attempts to "make it" in middle-class networks. The person will need to take on the language, mannerisms, and references—the "distinctions" made by the middle class—to fit in (see Bourdieu 1979). In such cases, the person may allow (and encourage) assumptions about belongingness as an insider. Generally, the goal of active passing is access to resources, safety, or comfort. In choosing to reveal ourselves to our respondents in the ways we did, we were engaging in active and passive passing. That is to say, we were allowing respondents to make assumptions about us while actively choosing not to reveal those parts of our lives that would create distance or distrust. A prime example of this struggle around developing trust, revealing ourselves, and passing happened one August evening when we went to Mt. Greenwood to conduct a three-person focus group interview. As the interview got under way, it became clear that the respondents were active racists, with little tolerance for or insight into black people's pain and suffering. One interviewer (Heather) lived in a multiracial family and chose not to reveal information about herself. She was able to finish the interview, but she experienced a great deal of anxiety from having "passed" throughout the interview. The respondents spoke about justifications for violent action against blacks and the naivety of whites who did not understand the need for a racist approach to the world. As researchers, we continued to nod throughout the focus group to encourage the respondents to keep articulating their reflections and analysis. In the end, we left the site without incident, but we did need to pass to conduct the interview safely.

In less dramatic ways, passing occurred in other interviews, albeit in varied form. We found ourselves removing certain pictures—for instance, family photographs and a picture of Martin Luther King Jr.—from our offices when interviewing respondents. We listened and nodded when respondents stated that race mattered less than issues of class, knowing that race and class are almost impossible to separate in the United States. In a more dramatic fashion, in several interviews we nodded along when respondents said things that were deeply troubling. For example, in several interviews respondents reported visceral fear when encountering black people, including one case in which the respondent reported screaming when a group of young black men and women walked by. To gain greater insight, we remained quiet, debriefing later to make sense of these events. In each case, we engaged in a cultural performance to hide what might be seen as a threatening identity (Renfrow 2004). We continued to discuss the dynamics and our responsibility as researchers concerned with racial justice. We transcribed and read the interviews to explore how we might have interacted so that we did not appear to be complicit with racist statements. Moreover, we were concerned that our nodding and passing were "duping" our respondents in ways that were not ethical. Yet we wanted to understand the depth and complexity of the construction of whiteness and knew this could happen only if we were able to make a connection that allowed our respondents to feel safe as they opened up about their experiences and insights.

Our skin color alone did not allow us to "automatically pass into and have access" to what our respondents thought or to the communities to which they belonged (Gallagher 2000: 205). Thus, passing became a valuable tool for us to develop rapport with respondents and influence how they interpreted our questions. As whites are usually socialized not to see themselves as racial subjects, our perceived shared status likely made respondents feel more comfortable expressing views that they might normally conceal from nonwhites. Such comfort is important in an era of color-blind discourse, in which whites are afraid to speak frankly about race. To that end, we were careful not to bring up race, only asking for elaboration when our respondents raised the issue. We did not "co-interpret" race with them. To bolster the credibility of our interpretation of the data and enhance trustworthiness, every interview was followed with a debriefing. This allowed us to discuss the meaning of the data and emerging theory, as well as to have reflective discussions of our role in the research process (Charmaz 2003).

Finally, each researcher faced a range of responses from whites who were not part of our study when informally discussing this research project. At times, whites responded with suspicion or hostility, questioning our motives and suggesting that our research attempts to blame whites for living "good lives." More often than not, however, our informal discussions were met with genuine curiosity and interest. We found that whites wanted to understand how other whites manage the struggle of being white in a white-supremacist world. For instance, they were interested in hearing how whites manage the contradictions of living simultaneously as loving parents and racists. In other cases, whites who were familiar with the neighborhoods we were studying were curious about the institutions that supported racial division, such as the Catholic church and school systems. The range of responses gave us important feedback about the purposeful framing that was needed in this research to avoid serving as apologists for white supremacy and yet simultaneously to critically analyze the experiences and insights of our respondents without reducing all to racism. In other words, we needed to understand the complexity of whites' lives while recognizing the centrality of race.

In the end, we are all always passing (or managing impressions), and the higher the stakes, the greater the weight to passing. Race is an extremely high-stakes construct—emotionally, ideologically, and materially. To engage in our research, we needed to build trust so that our respondents would be comfortable and open to discussing a potentially difficult topic. We wanted them to speak without having to censor themselves and to "pass" to avoid being judged by the interviewers. As researchers, we understood and repeatedly discussed our need to be sensitive, empathetic, nonjudgmental, and open to our respondents. The unresolved issue with which we leave this study is how we achieve sensitivity and sound research practice without being complicit with racist statements or betraying our respondents' trust.

White Unanimity

We entered the field with a curiosity about the complexities of whiteness. We left the field with a good understanding of the complexities, as well as a story of a fairly stable construction of whiteness across gender, class, and time. Moreover, some aspects of the experience of racial change were shared by all, while other experiences may have been shared but were remembered differently or informed a different outcome. We made note of these nuanced differences throughout the book. Certainly, we found subtle differences in terms of whites' reaction and action, even as they shared a sense that racial change felt traumatic. Most of our respondents shared a strong desire never to go through racial change again. To protect themselves, however, some respondents chose to live "farther out" and find new segregated spaces, while a few of our respondents chose stable racially mixed neighborhoods as a way to avoid the change. In addition, in Chapter 2 our discussion of the racial discourse used by the Parish Federation includes an exploration of how members of that organization understood themselves, including the nuances of these views. It is likely that many in the organization privately held different views. In the end, our analysis of the Parish Federation was not about the beliefs of individuals on the Southwest Side. Instead, it was about the predominant racial discourse of organization and neighborhood. In addition, we attended to the different views (e.g., pro-integration) of whites who belonged to other Southwest Side groups. There was indeed some variation in the reaction to racial change on the Southwest Side.[1] For example, a small number of respondents did have slightly different socialization experiences, including attending integrated schools. In the end, these cases appear as outliers among the majority of the interviews. As another example, in the last section of our discussion of nostalgia (see Chapter 4), we explore the nuanced ways our white respondents framed their memories. We specifically illustrated how some whites recognized that race and racism were key elements of their memories and lives, demonstrating that there is a degree of fluidity to white racial identification. In fact, some respondents attempted to step away from the nostalgia narrative and to understand race in more complex ways (although they lacked language to critically challenge whiteness). Thus, we did find complexity in how whites understood themselves racially and their efforts to maintain or challenge white racial identities.

Throughout the interview process we wanted whites to discuss race in a relatively organic manner. Thus, we neither asked respondents questions concerning their experiences with race in other settings nor engaged them in broader discussion of racial issues (unless they raised those issues, which most did not). We were primarily concerned with their experience growing up in neighborhoods undergoing racial change and did not explore their general or specific racial attitudes. Clearly, there are limitations to such a design, which forgoes seeking a more comprehensive understanding of how race and whiteness play out in the broader context of their lives. However, in the end our findings are consistent with general findings in the whiteness literature concerning racial discourse and how whites frame race in defense of whiteness. Perhaps most interesting, our respondents organized racial knowledge, memory, and empathy in remarkably similar ways, despite the myriad paths they had followed into adulthood.

As with all approaches to understanding our social world, we must consider the context in which we interpret data. Taking a team approach to the research strengthened the interviewing process and the resulting data analysis. We were able to analyze our research critically along the way, making this a reflective project in which we considered our own social locations, as well as the complexities of our experiences, in the process of asking, listening, reading, and analyzing the insights and words of our respondents. We wanted to understand the experiences of our respondents in the context of their lives. We wanted to know more than whether or not they were racist, but, in turn, we were determined not to mount an apology for white supremacy. As with all research, the greater the self-reflection on the part of the researchers in interaction with the respondents and data, the richer the analysis. In the end, we believe our book is a very rich analysis.

Notes

CHAPTER 1

1. "Sickened by Rights Battle," letter to the editor, *Southwest News-Herald*, August 18, 1966.

2. Mike Royko, "White Rights and Wrongs," *Chicago Tribune*, n.d., Southwest Parish and Neighborhood Federation unsorted files, Chicago History Museum.

3. To define the term "whiteness," we use Ruth Frankenberg's notion that whiteness is a "location" of structural advantage; race privilege is a "standpoint" or a place from which whites see themselves and others in a society and a set of "cultural practices" that typically are unmarked and unnamed (Frankenberg 1993: 1).

4. The most disturbing case was Monsignor Patrick Molloy, a priest at St. Leo's on Chicago's South Side. As McGreevy (1996: 121) reports, Molloy occasionally kicked "burr-heads" out of the church, monitored real estate transactions, told blacks who came to register in the parish that the church had no room for "you people," and resisted any integration in the schools.

5. A month after being asked to leave the Chicago area by Cardinal Cody in 1968, Lawlor returned and used this following to create a career in Chicago politics, first as alderman for the city's 15th ward (McGreevy 1996). His successful candidacy is a good example of the growing dissatisfaction with Mayor Daley and ultimately with the Democratic Party, particularly around issues of race (McCourt 1977).

6. The HOLC was created in part to revive financial institutions and the market for homes, as well as to transform the mortgage instrument itself (Freund 2007). The HOLC did several important things, but for our purposes it is important to discuss the development of an appraisal system for making predictions "regarding the useful or productive life of housing" (Jackson 1980: 422).

7. Southwest Parish and Neighborhood Federation files, Chicago History Museum.

8. There are notable exceptions, including Cumming 1998 and Woldoff 2011.

9. For example, *Mean Streets* (Diamond 2009) looks at the role of youth in the main-tenance of neighborhood and racial boundaries. The book, however, is a work of history and as such does not connect how those experiences link to today. Another book is *The South Side* (Rosen 1999), an oral history of growing up in a racially changing neighbor-hood. The book poignantly captures the fear, betrayal, and confusion that white Jewish kids experienced when middle-class blacks moved into their neighborhood. Several studies also focus on the elderly and their experiences as racial change occurs (Cum-mings 1998; Woldoff 2011).

10. Interviews ranged from one to two hours in length, were tape recorded with par-ticipants' permission, and were transcribed verbatim by the authors. To protect privacy, all names of participants have been changed to pseudonyms.

11. When the Southwest Side is described, there is usually a reference to the Nabisco plant, located at Seventy-Third and Kedzie. Nabisco was one of the larger factories in the area and is usually held up as a way to describe the types of jobs that residents had. For many working-class Chicagoans, Alan Ehrenhalt (1996) writes, Nabisco was a good factory job. In the 1950s, the plant operated twenty-four hours a day, in three shifts. Workers were paid a decent wage so that the husband could work and the wife could stay home. No one we interviewed had parents or grandparents who worked at Nabisco.

12. In the early 1950s and 1960s, tuition for Catholic education was relatively inex-pensive, typically $1–$2 per month, making it an attractive option for many (McMahon 1995; Ehrenhalt 1996).

CHAPTER 2

1. "SON/SOC White Ethnic Convention," *Save Our Neighborhoods, Save Our City News* 1, no. 2 (September 1984): 1–4.

2. "The Southwest Federation: The First Ten Years Remembered, 1972–1982," South-west Parish and Neighborhood Federation unsorted files, Chicago History Museum.

3. Mike Royko, "White Rights and Wrongs," *Chicago Tribune*, n.d., in Southwest Parish and Neighborhood Federation unsorted files, Chicago History Museum.

4. "Housing Discrimination" 1980.

5. Ibid., 317.

6. Ibid.

7. "The Southwest Federation."

8. "Talman: The Real Story" and "Will the Real Talman Please Stand Up?" special report prepared by the Southwest Parish and Neighborhood Federation, 1975, Southwest Parish and Neighborhood Federation unsorted files, Chicago History Museum.

9. Personal communication with Chip Berlet, June 3, 2013.

10. This statement is based on the evidence from the Parish Federation files. There was some evidence that privately some residents may have supported the Nazi Party to keep the neighborhood white. For example, a Lithuanian historian we interviewed allud-ed to the fact when talking about his Lithuanian neighbors, "There is for instance the famous incident of the Nazi party over there on Seventy-First Street with Frank Collins . . . and how Lithuanians would try to camouflage themselves by walking through the back door and slipping envelops under the door to support their needs to keep the com-munity a very white community." We could find little evidence to corroborate this claim.

11. "Keynote Address," in "Proceedings of the First Save Our Neighborhoods, Save Our City Convention, April 29, 1984," special supplement to *Save Our Neighborhoods, Save Our City News* 1, no. 2 (September 1984); hereafter, "Proceedings."

12. "Guaranteed Home Equity Slide Show," in "Proceedings."

13. "Our Neighborhoods Are Worth Fighting For," *Southwest Federation News*, September 1984.

14. "1978–79: Guaranteed Home Equity," *Southwest Federation News*, 1983.

15. Scholars have closely examined the role of the house for the aspiring middle class (see Garb 2005; Lewinnek 2014). For example, Elaine Lewinnek's study of early real estate advertisements in Chicago shows housing was presented as a safer investment than bank accounts, particularly in the early parts of the twentieth century (Lewinnek 2006). Her work also reveals the role of homeownership in gaining status and political protection. In a similar way, Eileen McMahon's *What Parish Are You From?* (1995) captures the intersection of homeownership and building the powerful parish of St. Sabina on the Southwest Side.

16. "Proceedings."

17. This presentation goes further to call for an "institute of neighborhood stability that would identify factors that lead to stability and even include an affirmative marketing tool to attract more white ethnics back to the neighborhood. The program would "help our neighborhoods' stability by acquainting young white ethnics with the advantages of our communities: solidly built homes, proximity to shopping and community centers, fine transportation, parks and churches." Like affirmative marketing strategies employed by pro-integration communities, this proposal assumed "white ethnics" would stabilize the community. However, unlike pro-integration communities, no mention of integration is made.

18. "New Mayor Can't Ignore SW Side: No Taxation without Representation," *Southwest Federation News*, April 1983.

19. "Dems: Hear Ethnic Concerns," *Southwest Federation News*, September 1984.

20. "New Mayor Can't Ignore SW Side: No Taxation without Representation," *Southwest Federation News*, April 1983.

21. "The Southwest Federation."

22. "Proceedings."

23. "CHA/Home Equity Committee: Push City to Right Past Wrongs," in "Proceedings."

24. Undated letter to Lithuanian neighborhood group. Southwest Parish Federation files.

25. "Pre-Vote Speech for 63rd Street Redevelopment," in "Proceedings."

26. Parish Federation, "Ethnic Village Plan to be Unveiled: Mayor's Aide Invited to Attend," press release, May 21, 1984.

27. "Pre-Vote Speech."

28. "Ethnic Village Plan to Be Unveiled."

29. "Pre-Vote Speech."

30. "Proceedings."

31. As Thomas Sugrue and John Skrentny (2008) argue, ethnicity became important politically at a time when both the Democratic and Republican parties sought white voters. They show how the GOP drew on the insecurities of whites.

32. "Proceedings."

33. "The Emperor Has No Clothes," editorial, *Southwest Federation News*, 1984.

34. "Pre-Vote Speech."

35. "April 29th Convention Nears," *Save Our Neighborhoods, Save Our City News* 1, no. 1 (April 1984).

36. Jean Mayer, interview by the authors, November 6, 2006.

37. Jim Keck, interview by the authors, July 6, 2007.

38. "The Southwest Federation."

39. "Nazis Stage Neighborhood Rally; Local Residents Stay Home," *Southwest Federation News*, July 1978.

40. Carol Smith, Redevelopment Committee, to Edward Vondrak, publisher of *Southwest News-Herald*, letter, December 26, 1975, Southwest Parish and Neighborhood Federation files, Chicago History Museum.

41. "Set Boycott Today at Gage High over Boundary Dispute," *Southtown Economist*, September 6, 1972, 1.

42. "Gage Park Hi Class Overcrowding Protest Goes to Street," *Southtown Economist*, October 4, 1972, 2c.

43. The news reports on these events are quite interesting, particularly since the case is one of the few where the experience of blacks was reported. One black parent suggested that "one black child at Gage Park would be overcrowding" (Neenan and Masson 1972), while another black parent suggested that the sit-in boycott had the "cooperation, if not the sanction, of school officials" (Neenan 1972). A black alderman, pointing out the hypocrisy involved, noted, "If black students had sit-ins, the entire Chicago Lawn police force would be over at Gage, carting them all to jail" (Neenan 1972).

44. These findings are consistent with other findings at the time. For example, the Southern Policy Law Center reported violence directed toward minorities moving into white neighborhoods was acute in the Midwest. Their report states, "Since 1985 the majority of the 45 arson and cross burnings attempts against move-ins have taken place in the metropolitan areas of the north Midwest" (Southern Policy Law Center 1987: 2).

45. It is important to note that when racial change really began in the greater Chicago Lawn area, it was driven by a Hispanic in-migration. The communities on the Southwest Side today have more Hispanic than black residents. Interestingly, the Parish Federation files have very little to say about incoming Hispanic neighbors. Such a non-reaction is likely due to several factors. First, Hispanics began moving in in the late 1980s and early 1990s and thus at the end of the period of key organizing and after achieving the Home Equity plan. Second, Hispanics, like the white ethnics, were largely Catholic, making their entry and acculturation into the neighborhood a bit more natural than for blacks, who tended not to be Catholic (see McGreevy 1996 ; Klinenberg 2003). Finally, whites historically have been more willing to accept Hispanics as neighbors than blacks (see Charles 2003).

CHAPTER 3

1. There were a handful of exceptions. One of the most notable cases was Terry, a respondent who grew up in Gage Park but attended Quigley Southside Prep, a private Catholic high school. Terry recalled the following experience there, particularly right after Mayor Harold Washington died of a heart attack: "In 1987, Harold Washington died the day before Thanksgiving. We had mass at Quigley, Thanksgiving mass. . . . [A]t the end after communion, the rector goes up and says [Washington] died. It was sort of like when you hear the story about John F. Kennedy. . . . [T]he whole school is [a] shambles right before Thanksgiving. The experience of that in a school that is 40 percent Hispanic and 20 percent black was a lot different than in 1983, with Washington's election. [It was] just very formative, I mean. I think my world opened a lot more at Quigley than if I had gone to other schools. It wasn't like: it's over, and people are cheering. That is the typical Southwest Sider . . . and I am sure that there are some people on the South-

west Side that were happy. But the people in Quigley [weren't]. That idea of . . . respect for diversity and getting along and understanding that it is not easy. . . . There was a recognition of that, but, again, there was a whole rising above it." Overall, however, Terry and others were outliers in our study.

2. Most of our respondents had little interaction with blacks in their neighborhoods and in schools while growing up. In more than fifty interviews, only three or four respondents had experienced integrated settings.

CHAPTER 4

1. It is an understatement to say that the fire at Our Lady of Angels was a pivotal event in the neighborhood. Most respondents from the West Side knew people who had died in the fire, including some cousins. Yet most of the respondents were too young to have been at the school that fateful day. By all accounts, the tragedy led many to leave the neighborhood shortly after 1958.

2. Fullilove's examination of root shock deals with African Americans whose neighborhoods were destroyed via urban renewal in the 1950s and 1960s (Fullilove 2005). While the circumstances are quite different (whites were not forced out), we argue that a somewhat similar psychological process was at work for young whites.

3. Two examples of similar findings include Louis Rosen's *South Side* (1999) and Ray Suarez's *The Old Neighborhood* (1999). Suarez notes that he spoke to hundreds of people who mourn the loss of their block, school, or local church.

4. Scholars have referenced this by noting that loss creates "identity discontinuity" or a "disruption in identity" (Lofland 1982, 1985; Marris 1986). The tendency for identity is continuity over time. Loss interrupts identities, and people attempt to create new ones or find means to preserve their former identities to regain a sense of continuity (Milligan 1998, 2003). Studies that look at identity discontinuity focus on place-based identities (e.g., authentic members of a gentrified community and workers in a coffeehouse). Racial identity seems to be more complex than these identities, as it is reinforced in a variety of spaces. Thus, we avoid the phrase "identity discontinuity," although similar processes are work.

5. The claim of powerlessness is not meant to suggest that whites did not act to stop racial change from affecting their communities. Scholarly literature has documented the efforts of whites to defend their communities from racial change, involving everything from buying out blacks as they moved in (Kruse 2005) to forming property associations to fight racial change (Hirsch 1983; Sugrue 1996; Seligman 2005). In addition, scholars have described the various efforts by community groups to maintain integration in communities experiencing racial change (Saltman 1990; Nyden, Maly, and Lukehart 1997; Maly 2005). Finally, on Chicago's Southwest Side the Organization of Southwest Communities and other groups formed, with significant financial support from Catholic churches such as St. Sabina, to improve neighborhoods, induce whites to stay (McMahon 1995: 149), and stabilize communities as integrated. The role of the Catholic church in laboring to keep whites in their parishes is also well documented (McGreevy 1996).

6. Emphasis added.

7. In his excellent analysis of youth in the early to mid-twentieth century in Chicago, Andrew Diamond shows that much of the violence of the late 1950s was partly built on white anxiety—specifically, anxiety about the proving of white masculinity. For example, Diamond (2009: 195) notes, "A well-known Near West Side gang called the Dukes made the papers for two consecutive days in 1958 after being picked up by police

for carrying around baseball bats and a length of tire chain[. T]he new coverage failed to mention that the gang they were coming after was black and that such racial attacks were business as usual for this group."

CHAPTER 5

1. Hooker (2009: 22) is concerned with the broad concept of political solidarity, a notion meant to refer to the ability of "individuals to engage in relations of trust and obligation with fellow members of a political community whom they may see as inherently 'other' in some fundamental way." This form of solidarity has rarely existed; instead, the tendency is toward racial solidarity, in which racial groups do not see political obligations across racial lines.

2. Emphasis added.

3. Emphasis added.

CHAPTER 6

1. Meghan Burke's *Racial Ambivalence in Diverse Communities* (2012) is a notable exception.

2. It is likely that even if asked, most whites would have difficulty answering or making sense of themselves as racialized subjects (Doane 2003; Lewis 2004).

METHODOLOGICAL APPENDIX

1. For a compelling autobiographical account that captures the subtle variations of views among Southwest Siders, see Jim Capraro's "The Park" (Terkel 1992).

References

Abu-Lughod, Janet. 2000. *New York, Chicago, Los Angeles: America's Global Cities.* Minneapolis: University of Minnesota Press.

Acker, Sandra. 2001. "In/Out/Side: Positioning the Researcher in Feminist Qualitative Research." *Resources for Feminist Research* 28 (3–4): 153–172.

Altman, Irwin, and Setha Low. 1992. "Place Attachment: A Conceptual Inquiry." In *Place Attachment*, ed. Irwin Altman and Setha Low, 1–12. New York: Plenum.

Anderson, Alan, and George Pickering. 2008. *Confronting the Color Line: The Broken Promise of the Civil Rights Movement in Chicago.* Athens: University of Georgia Press.

Anderson, Margaret. 2003. "Whitewashing Race: A Critical Perspective on Whiteness." In *White Out: The Continuing Significance of Racism*, ed. Ashley Doane and Eduardo Bonilla-Silva, 21–34. New York: Routledge.

Anderson, Monroe. 1984. "Bigotry Appears in a New Guise." *Chicago Tribune*, April 27.

Bailey, Alison. 2007. "Strategic Ignorance." In *Race and Epistemologies of Ignorance*, ed. Shannon Sullivan and Nancy Tuana, 77–94. Albany: State University of New York Press.

Ballard, Richard. 2004. "Middle Class Neighbourhoods or 'African Kraals'? The Impact of Informal Settlements and Vagrants on Post-Apartheid White Identity." *Urban Forum* 15 (1): 48–73.

———. 2007. "Defending Animals; Defending Suburbs; Defending Civilisation." In *Undressing Durban*, ed. Rob Pattman and Sultan Khan, 250–256. Durban, South Africa: Madiba.

———. 2010. "'Slaughter in the Suburbs': Livestock Slaughter and Race in Post-Apartheid Cities." *Ethnic and Racial Studies* 33 (6): 1069–1087.

Beauregard, Robert. 2002. *Voices of Decline: The Postwar Fate of U.S. Cities.* New York: Routledge.

——. 2006. *When America Became Suburban*. Minneapolis: University of Minnesota Press.

Belgrave, Linda Liska, and Kenneth Smith. 1994. "Experiencing Hurricane Andrew: Environment and Everyday Life" In *Studies in Symbolic Interaction*, vol. 6, ed. Norman Denzin, 251–273. Greenwich, CT: JAI.

Bell, Jeannine. 2013. *Hate Thy Neighbor: Move-In Violence and the Persistence of Racial Segregation in American Housing*. New York: New York University Press.

Bellah, Robert N., Richard Madsen, William M. Sullivan, Ann Swidler, and Steven M. Tipton. 1985. *Habits of the Heart: Individualism and Commitment in American Life*. Berkeley: University of California Press.

Bennett, Larry. 1987. "The Dilemmas of Building a Progressive Urban Coalition: The Linked Development in Chicago." *Journal of Urban Affairs* 9 (3): 263–276.

——. 1990. *Fragments of Cities: The New American Downtowns and Neighborhoods*. Columbus: Ohio State University Press.

——. 2011. *Third City: Chicago and American Urbanism*. Chicago: University of Chicago Press.

——. 2013. "Forging Barack Obama: Harold Washington, Chicago, and the Politics of Race." In *Fire on the Prairie: Harold Washington, Chicago Politics, and the Roots of the Obama Presidency*, ed. Gary Rivlin, xiii–xxix. Philadelphia: Temple University Press.

Bentley, Kristina, and Adam Habib. 2008. "Racial Redress, National Identity, and Citizenship in Post-Apartheid South Africa." In *Racial Redress and Citizenship*, ed. Adam Habib and Kristina Bentley, 3-32. Cape Town, South Africa: HSRC Press.

Berlet, Chip. 2001. "Hate Groups, Racial Tension and Ethnoviolence in an Integrating Chicago Neighborhood, 1976–1988." *Politics of Social Inequality* 9:117–163.

Bluestone, Barry, and Bennett Harrison. 1982. *The Deindustrialization of America: Plant Closings, Community Abandonment, and the Dismantling of Basic Industry*. New York: Basic.

Bobo, Lawrence, James Kluegel, and Ryan Smith. 1997. "Laissez-Faire Racism: The Crystallization of a Kinder, Gentler, Antiblack Ideology." In *Racial Attitudes in the 1990s: Continuity and Change*, ed. Stephen Tuch and Jack Martin, 15–44. Westport, CT: Praeger.

Bonilla-Silva, Eduardo. 2001a. "'This Is a White Country': The Racial Ideology of the Western Nations of the World-System." *Sociological Inquiry* 70 (2): 188–214.

——. 2001b. *White Supremacy and Racism in the Post–Civil Rights Era*. Boulder, CO: Lynne Rienner.

——. 2009. *Racism without Racists: Color-Blind Racism and the Persistence of Racial Inequality in America*, 3d ed. Lanham, MD: Rowan and Littlefield.

Bonilla-Silva, Eduardo, and Tyrone Forman. 2000. "'I Am Not a Racist, but . . .': Mapping White College Students' Racial Ideology in the USA." *Discourse and Society* 11 (1): 50–85.

Bonilla-Silva, Eduardo, Carla Goar, and David Embrick. 2004. "When Whites Flock Together: The Social Psychology of White Habitus." *Critical Sociology* 32 (1–2): 229–253.

Bonilla-Silva, Eduardo, Amanda Lewis, and David Embrick. 2006. "I Did Not Get that Job Because of a Black Man . . . : The Story Lines and Testimonies of Color-Blind Racism." *Sociological Forum* 19 (4): 555–581.

Booth, Tim, and Wendy Booth. 1994. "The Use of Depth Interviewing with Vulnerable Subjects." *Social Science and Medicine* 39:415–424.

Bourdieu, Pierre. 1979. *Distinction: A Social Critique of the Judgment of Taste*. New York: Routledge.

Boyd, Michelle. 2010. *Jim Crow Nostalgia: Reconstructing Race in Bronzeville*. Minneapolis: University of Minnesota Press.

Boyer, Brian. 1973. *Cities Destroyed for Cash: The FHA Scandal at HUD*. New York: Follet.

Boym, Svetlana. 2001. *The Future of Nostalgia*. New York: Basic.

Boyte, Harry C. 1980. *The Backyard Revolution: Understanding the New Citizen Movement*. Philadelphia: Temple University Press.

Brantlinger, Ellen. 2003. *Dividing Classes: How the Middle Class Negotiates and Rationalizes School*. New York: Routledge.

Brown, Barbara, and Douglas Perkins. 1992. "Disruptions in Place Attachment." In *Place Attachment*, ed. Irwin Altman and Setha Low, 309–316. New York: Plenum.

Burke, Meghan. 2012. *Racial Ambivalence in Diverse Communities: Whiteness and the Power of Color-Blind Ideologies*. Lanham, MD: Lexington.

Carter, Shannon, Leslie Picca, and Brittany Murray. 2012. "Racialization in Public and Private: Memories of First Racial Experiences." *Race and Social Problems* 4 (3–4): 133–143.

Casey, Edward. 1987. *Remembering: A Phenomenological Study*. Bloomington: Indiana University Press.

Charles, Camille. 2003. "The Dynamics of Racial Residential Segregation." *Annual Review of Sociology* 29:167–207.

Charmaz, K. 1991. *Good Days, Bad Days: The Self in Chronic Illness and Time*. New Brunswick, NJ: Rutgers University Press.

———. 2003. "Qualitative Interviewing and Grounded Theory Analysis." In *Inside Interviewing: New Lenses, New Concerns*, ed. James Holstein and Jaber F. Gubrium, 311–330. Thousand Oaks, CA: Sage.

Chiao, Joan, and Vani Mathur. 2010. "Intergroup Empathy: How Does Race Affect Empathic Neural Responses?" *Current Biology* 20 (11): 478–480.

Coates, James. 1968. "Riots following Killing of Martin Luther King Jr: A City Erupts." *Chicago Tribune*, April 5.

Coffey, Amanda, and Paul Atkinson. 1996. *Making Sense of Qualitative Data: Complementary Research Strategies*. Thousand Oaks, CA: Sage.

Collins, Catherine. 1985. "Legacy of FHA Loan Program: Lost Houses and Shady Deals." *Chicago Tribune*, June 30.

Collins, Patricia Hill. 1998. *Fighting Words: Black Women and the Search for Justice*. Minneapolis: University of Minnesota Press.

———. 2000. *Black Feminist Thought: Knowledge, Consciousness, and the Politics of Empowerment*, 2d ed. New York: Routledge.

Covington, Jeannette and Ralph Taylor. 1991. "Fear of Crime in Urban Residential Neighborhoods: Implications of Between- and Within-Neighborhood Sources for Current Models." *Sociological Quarterly* 32 (2): 231–249.

Cowan, David, and John Kuenster. 1998. *To Sleep with the Angels: The Story of a Fire*. Chicago: Ivan R. Dee.

Cummings, Scott. 1998. *Left Behind in Rosedale: Race Relations and the Collapse of Community Institutions*. Boulder, CO: Westview.

Cuomo, Mario. 1980. "On Keeping the Neighborhood in the Neighborhood." *New York Daily News*, February 26.

Cutler, Irving. 1982. *Chicago: Metropolis of the Mid-continent*. Dubuque: Kendall and Hunt.

Dalmage, Heather. 2000. *Tripping on the Color Line: Black-White Multiracial Families in a Racially Divided World*. New Brunswick, NJ: Rutgers University Press.

———. 2004. "Protecting Racial Comfort, Protecting Racial Privilege." In *The Politics of Multiracialism: Challenging Racial Thinking*, ed. Heather Dalmage. Albany: State University of New York Press.

Davidson, Jean, and Paul Sullivan. 1984. "Police 'Close' to Solution of Firebombing on Southwest Side." *Chicago Tribune*, November 24.

Davis, Fred. 1979. *Yearning for Yesterday: A Sociology of Nostalgia*. New York: Free Press.

Davis, Robert. 1979. "Neighborhood 'White-Flight' Plan Is Rejected." *Chicago Tribune*, October 10.

Decety, Jean, and Yoshiya Moriguchi. 2007. "The Empathic Brain and Its Dysfunction in Psychiatric Populations: Implications for Intervention across Different Clinical Conditions." *BioPsychoSocial Medicine* 1 (November 16): 1–22.

Delgado, Richard. 1999. *Critical Race Theory*. Philadelphia: Temple University Press.

DeSenna, Judith. 1994. "Local Gatekeeping Practices and Residential Segregation." *Sociological Inquiry* 64 (3): 307–321.

Devall, Cheryl. 1988. "Sawyer Has Problem with Equity Plan." *Chicago Tribune*, June 11.

Diamond, Andrew. 2009. *Mean Streets: Chicago Youths and the Everyday Struggle for Empowerment in the Multiracial City, 1908–1969*. Berkeley: University of California Press.

Doane, Ashley "Woody". 2003. "Rethinking Whiteness Studies." In *White Out: The Continuing Significance of Racism*, ed. Ashley Doane and Eduardo Bonilla-Silva, pp. 3-20. London: Routledge.

———. 2006. "What Is Racism? Racial Discourse and Racial Politics." *Critical Sociology* 32 (3–4): 255–274.

Dolby, Nadine. 2001. *Constructing Race: Youth, Identity, and Popular Culture in South Africa*. Albany: State University of New York Press.

Dold, Bruce. 1984a. "Home Equity Insurance: Would It Really Work?" *Chicago Tribune*, May 29.

———. 1984b. "1,000 Whites Call Racist Label Unfair and Ask Mayor for Help." *Chicago Tribune*, April 30.

Drwecki, Brian B., Colleen F. Moore, Sandra E. Ward, and Kenneth M. Prkachin. 2011. "Reducing Racial Disparities in Pain Treatment: The Role of Empathy and Perspective-Taking." *Pain* 152 (5): 1001–1006.

Duncan, Otis, and Beverly Duncan. 1957. *The Negro Population of Chicago: A Study of Residential Segregation*. Chicago: University of Chicago Press.

DuRocher, Kristina. 2011. *Raising Racists: The Socialization of White Children in the Jim Crow South*. Lexington: University Press of Kentucky.

Duster, Troy. 2001. "The 'Morphing' Properties of Whiteness." In *The Making and Unmaking of Whiteness*, ed. B. Brander Rasmussen, 133–137. Durham, NC: Duke University Press.

Dyer, Richard. 1997. *White: Essays on Race and Culture*. New York : Routledge.

Edelman, Bryan. 2006. *Racial Prejudice, Juror Empathy and Sentencing in Death Penalty Cases*. New York: LFB Scholarly.

Edsall, Thomas, and Mary Edsall. 1991. *Chain Reaction: The Impact of Race, Rights, and Taxes on American Politics*. New York: W. W. Norton.

Ehrenhalt, Alan. 1996. *The Lost City: The Forgotten Virtues of Community in America*. New York: Basic.

Ehrenreich, Barbara. 1990. *Fear of Falling: The Inner Life of the Middle Class*. New York: HarperCollins.

Ellen, Ingrid. 2000. *Sharing America's Neighborhoods: The Prospects for Stable Racial Integration*. Cambridge, MA: Harvard University Press.

Erikson, Kai. 1976. *Everything in Its Path: Destruction of Community in the Buffalo Creek Flood*. New York: Touchstone.

Etzioni, Amitai. 1993. *The Spirit of Community: The Reinvention of American Society*. New York: Simon and Schuster.

Feagin, Joe. 2010. *The White Racial Frame: Centuries of Racial Framing and Counter-Framing*. New York: Routledge.

Feagin, Joe, Hernan Vera, and Pinar Batur. 2000. *White Racism: The Basics*. London: Routledge.

Ferrarotti, Franco. 1990. *Time, Memory, and Society*. New York: Greenwood.

Fields, Barbara. 1990. "Slavery, Race and Ideology in the United States of America." *New Left Review* 181:95–118.

Fisher, Robert. 1994. *Let the People Decide: Neighborhood Organizing in America*. New York: Twayne.

Fivush, Robyn. 1994 "Constructing Narrative, Emotion, and Self in Parent-Child Conversations about the Past." In *The Remembering Self*, ed. Ulrich Neisser and Robyn Fivush, 136–157. Cambridge: Cambridge University Press.

Forman, Tyrone, and Amanda Lewis. 2006. "Racial Apathy and Hurricane Katrina: The Social Anatomy of Prejudice in the Post–Civil Rights Era." *Du Bois Review* 3 (1): 175–202.

Formisano, Ronald. 1991. *Boston against Busing: Race, Class, and Ethnicity in the 1960s and 1970s*. Chapel Hill: University of North Carolina Press.

Fox, Roger, and Amy Goldman. 1977. *Marquette Park: A Descriptive History of Efforts to Peacefully Resolve Racial Conflict*. Chicago: Urban League.

Frankenberg, Ruth. 1993. *White Women, Race Matters: The Social Construction of Whiteness*. Minneapolis: University of Minnesota Press.

Freedberg, Sharon. 2007. "Re-examining Empathy: A Relational-Feminist Point of View." *Social Work* 52 (3): 251–259.

Freund, David. 2007. *Colored Property: State Policy and White Racial Politics in Suburban America*. Chicago: University of Chicago Press.

Frey, William. 1979. "Central City White Flight: Racial and Nonracial Causes." *American Sociological Review* 44 (3): 425–448.

Fried, Marc. 1963. *The World of the Urban Working Class*. Cambridge, MA: Harvard University Press.

Frisbie, Margerie. 2002. *An Alley in Chicago: The Life and Legacy of Monsignor John Egan*. Franklin, WI: Sheed and Ward.

Fullilove, Mindy. 2005. *Root Shock: How Tearing Up City Neighborhoods Hurts America, and What We Can Do about It*. New York: One World/Ballantine.

Gallagher, Charles. 1993. "White Reconstruction in the University." *Socialist Review* 94 (1–2): 165–187.

———. 1997. "White Racial Formation: Into the Twenty-First Century." In *Critical White Studies: Looking Beyond the Mirror*, ed. Richard Delgado and Jean Stefancic, 6–11. Philadelphia: Temple University Press.

———. 2000. "White Like Me? Methods, Meaning, and Manipulation in the Field of White Studies." In *Racing Research, Researching Race: Methodological Dilemmas in Critical Race Studies*, ed. France W. Twine and Jonathan V. Warren, 67–92. New York: New York University Press.

———. 2003. "Playing the White Ethnic Card: Using Ethnic Identity to Deny Contemporary Racism." In *White Out: The Continuing Significance of Racism*, ed. Ashley Doane and Eduardo Bonilla-Silva, 145–158. London: Routledge.

———. 2010. "'The End of Racism' as the New Doxa: New Strategies for Researching Race." In *White Logic, White Methods: Racism and Methodology*, ed. Tukufu Zuberi and Eduardo Bonilla-Silva, 163–178. Lanham, MD: Rowman and Littlefield.

Gamm, Gerald. 1999. *Urban Exodus: Why the Jews Left Boston and the Catholics Stayed.* Cambridge, MA: Harvard University Press.

Gans, Herbert. 1982. *The Urban Villagers: Group and Class in the Life of Italian-Americans.* New York: Free Press.

Garb, Margaret. 2005. *City of American Dreams: A History of Home Ownership and Housing Reform in Chicago, 1871–1919.* Chicago: University of Chicago Press.

Garrow, David. 1989. *We Shall Overcome: The Civil Rights Movement in the United States in the 1950's and 1960's.* Brooklyn, NY: Carlson.

Gerdes, Karen, Elizabeth Segal, Kelly Jackson, and Jennifer Mullins. 2011. "Teaching Empathy: A Framework Rooted in Social Cognitive Neuroscience and Social Justice." *Journal of Social Work Education* 47 (1): 109–131.

Goffman, Erving. 1959. *The Presentation of Self in Everyday Life.* New York: Doubleday.

———. 1963. *Stigma.* Englewood Cliffs, NJ: Prentice Hall.

Goodwin, Carole. 1979. *The Oak Park Strategy: Community Control of Racial Change.* Chicago: University of Chicago Press.

Green, Paul M. 1988. "SON/SOC: Organizing in White Ethnic Neighborhoods." *Illinois Issues*, no. 26. Available at http://www.lib.niu.edu/1988/ii880524.html. Accessed June 8, 2012.

———. 1990. "SON/SOC: Organizing in White Ethnic Neighborhoods." In *After Alinsky: Community Organizing in Illinois*, ed. Peg Knoepfle, 23–33. Springfield, IL: Sangamon State University.

Griffiths, Dominic, and Maria Prozesky. 2010. "The Politics of Dwelling: Being White/ Being South African." *Africa Today* 56 (4): 22–41.

Grimes, Ann. 1984. "Community Organizing in Black and White: The 'New Victims' Raise Their Voices." *Chicago Reader*, May 4, 40–41.

Groves, Adam. 2006. "Martin Luther King, Jr., Assassination Riots, Chicago: April 5–8, 1968." Available at https://ideals.illinois.edu/bitstream/handle/2142/92/ Martin+Luther+King?sequence=2. Accessed June 8, 2012.

Guglielmo, Thomas. 2003. *White on Arrival: Italians, Race, Color, and Power in Chicago, 1890–1945.* London: Oxford University Press.

Gutmann, Amy, ed. 1994. *Multiculturalism: Examining the Politics of Recognition.* Princeton, NJ: Princeton University Press.

Habermas, Jürgen. 1984. *The Theory of Communicative Action, Volume One: Reason and the Racialization of Society.* Boston: Beacon.

Halbwachs, Maurice. 1992. *On Collective Memory*, trans. and ed. Lewis Coser. Chicago: University of Chicago Press.

Halpern, Jodi, and Harvey Weinstein. 2004. "Rehumanizing the Other: Empathy and Reconciliation." *Human Rights Quarterly* 26:561–583.

Hamm, Jill. 2000. "Do Birds of a Feather Flock Together? The Variable Bases for African American, Asian American, and European American Adolescents' Selection of Similar Friends." *Developmental Psychology* 36 (2): 209–219.

Harris, Cheryl. 1993. "Whiteness as Property." *Harvard Law Review* 106 (8): 1707–1791.

Hartigan, John. 1999. *Racial Situations: Class Predicaments of Whiteness in Detroit.* Princeton, NJ: Princeton University Press.

Hirsch, Arnold. 1983. *Making the Second Ghetto.* Chicago: University of Chicago Press.

Hobsbawm, Eric. 1972. "The Social Function of the Past: Some Questions." *Past Present* 55:3–17.

Hollinger, David. 2006. "From Identity to Solidarity." *Daedalus* 135 (4): 23–31.

Hooker, Juliet. 2009. *Race and the Politics of Solidarity.* New York: Oxford University Press.

"Housing Discrimination Must Be Dealt with by HUD." 1980. *Journal of Housing* 37 (June): 315–322.

Hughes, Langston. 1994. *The Collected Poems of Langston Hughes.* New York: Vintage.

Hummon, David. 1992. "Community Attachment: Local Sentiment and Sense of Place." In *Place Attachment*, ed. Irwin Altman and Setha Low, 253–278. New York: Plenum.

Irwin-Zarecka, Iwona. 1994. *Frames of Remembrance: The Dynamics of Collective Memory.* New Brunswick, NJ: Transaction.

Jackson, Kenneth. 1980. "Federal Subsidy and the Suburban Dream: The First Quarter-Century of Government Intervention in the Housing Market." *Records of the Columbia Historical Society, Washington, DC* 50:421–451.

———. 1985. *Crabgrass Frontier: The Suburbanization of the United States.* New York: Oxford University Press.

Jacobs, Jane. 1961. *The Death and Life of Great American Cities.* New York: Vintage.

Jacobson, Matthew Frye. 2008. *Roots Too: White Ethnic Revival in Post–Civil Rights America.* Cambridge, MA: Harvard University Press.

Johnson, Richard, and Graham Dawson. 1982. "Popular Memory: Theory, Politics, Method." In *Making Histories: Studies in History-Writing and Politics*, ed. Richard Johnson, 205–252. London: Hutchinson.

Kao, Grace, and Jennifer Thompson. 2003. "Racial and Ethnic Stratification in Educational Achievement and Attainment." *Annual Review of Sociology* 29:417–442.

Kasinitz, Philip, and David Hillyard. 1995. "The Old-Timers Tale: The Politics of Nostalgia on the Waterfront." *Journal of Contemporary Ethnography* 24:139–164.

Katovich, Michael, and Robert Hintz. 1997. "Responding to a Traumatic Event: Restoring Shared Pasts within a Small Community." *Symbolic Interaction* 20:275–290.

Kazin, Michael. 1995. *The Populist Persuasion: An American History.* New York: Basic Books.

Keating, Dennis. 1994. *The Suburban Racial Dilemma.* Philadelphia: Temple University Press.

Kefalas, Maria. 2003. *Working-Class Heroes: Protecting Home, Community, and Nation in a Chicago Neighborhood.* Chicago: University of Chicago Press,

Kelly, Ed. 1973. "Parents Group Opposed Protest in Gage Park: Prefer Learning." *Southtown Economist*, January 7, 1.

Kerner, Otto. 1968. *Kerner Report: The 1968 Report of the National Advisory Commission on Civil Disorders.* Washington, DC: Alfred A. Knopf.

Kinder, Donald, and Lynn Sanders. 1996. *Divided by Color: Racial Politics and Democratic Ideals.* Chicago: University of Chicago Press.

Klinenberg, Eric. 2003. *Heat Wave: A Social Autopsy of Disaster in Chicago.* Chicago: University of Chicago Press.

Kruse, Kevin. 2005. *White Flight: The Strategies, Ideology, and Legacy of Segregationists in Atlanta.* Princeton, NJ: Princeton University Press.

Lassiter, Matthew. 2006. *The Silent Majority: Suburban Politics in the Sunbelt South.* Princeton, NJ: Princeton University Press.

Leibowitz, Brenda, Vivienne Bozalek, Paul Rohleder, Ronelle Carolissen, and Leslie Swartz. 2010. "'Ah, but the Whiteys Love to Talk about Themselves': Discomfort as a Pedagogy for Change, Race, Ethnicity and Education." *Race Ethnicity and Education* 13 (1): 83–100.

Leonardo, Zeus. 2004. "Critical Social Theory and Transformative Knowledge: The Functions of Criticism in Quality Education." *Educational Researcher* 33 (6): 11–18.

———. 2009. *Race, Whiteness, and Education.* New York: Routledge.

———. 2011. "After the Glow: Race Ambivalence and Other Educational Prognoses." *Educational Philosophy and Theory* 43 (6): 675–698.

Lesane-Brown, Chase, Tony Brown, Emily Tanner-Smith, and Marino A. Bruce. 2010. "Negotiating Boundaries and Bonds: Frequency of Young Children's Socialization to Their Ethnic/Racial Heritage." *Journal of Cross-Cultural Psychology* 41 (3): 457–464.

Levin, Hillel, and Lawrence Harmon. 1991. *The Death of an American Jewish Community: A Tragedy of Good Intentions.* New York: Free Press.

Levin, Jack, and Jack McDevitt. 2001. *Hate Crimes: The Rising Tide of Bigotry and Bloodshed.* Boulder, CO: Westview.

Lewinnek, Elaine. 2006. "Better than a Bank for a Poor Man? Home Financing Strategies in Early Chicago." *Journal of Urban History* 32 (2): 274–301.

———. 2014. *The Working Man's Reward: Chicago's Early Suburbs and the Roots of American Sprawl.* Chicago: University of Chicago Press.

Lewis, Amanda. 2004. "'What Group?' Studying Whites and Whiteness in the Era of 'Color-Blindness.'" *Sociological Theory* 22 (4): 623–646.

Lipset, Seymour, and Earl Rabb. 1970. *The Politics of Unreason: Right Wing Extremism in America, 1790–1970.* New York: Harper and Row.

Lipsitz, George. 1995. "The Possessive Investment in Whiteness: Racialized Social Democracy and the 'White' Problem in American Studies." *American Quarterly* 47 (3): 369–387.

———. 2006. *The Possessive Investment in Whiteness: How White People Profit from Identity Politics.* Philadelphia: Temple University Press.

Lofland, Lyn. 1982. "Loss and Human Connection." In *Personality, Roles, and Social Behavior,* ed. William John Ickes and Eric S. Knowles, 219–242. New York: Springer-Verlag.

———. 1985. *A World of Strangers: Order and Action in Urban Public Space.* Prospect Heights, IL: Waveland.

Low, Setha. 2007. "Whiteness and Niceness." In *The Way Class Works: Readings on School, Family, and the Economy,* ed. Lois Weis, 44–59. New York: Routledge.

Lowenthal, David. 1985. *The Past Is a Foreign Country.* Cambridge: Cambridge University Press.

Lyons, Arthur, Kathleen McCourt, and Philip Nyden. 1986. *Preserving Home Values in Chicago through a Home Equity Program.* A report submitted to the Chicago Neighborhood Organizing Project, Chicago, January 31.

Maly, Michael. 2005. *Beyond Segregation: Multiracial and Multiethnic Neighborhoods in the United States.* Philadelphia: Temple University Press.

Manzo, Lynne. 2003. "Beyond Home and Haven: Toward a Revisioning of Emotional Relationships with Places." *Journal of Environmental Psychology* 23 (1): 47–61.

Manzo, Lynne, and Douglas Perkins. 2006. "Finding Common Ground: The Importance of Place Attachment to Community Participation and Planning." *Journal of Planning Literature* 20 (4): 335–350.

Marris, Peter. 1986. *Loss and Change.* London: Routledge and Kegan Paul.

Massey, Douglas, and Nancy Denton. 1993. *American Apartheid*. Cambridge, MA: Harvard University Press.

May, Ruben. 2000. "Race Talk and Local Collective Memory among African American Men in a Neighborhood Tavern." *Qualitative Sociology* 23 (2): 201–214.

McCarron, John. 1987. "Taxpayers Tour Their Money: Neighborhood Coalition Views Downtown Subsidies. *Chicago Tribune*, April 5, A3.

McClory, Robert. 2010. *Radical Disciple: Father Pfleger, St. Sabina Church, and the Fight for Social Justice*. Chicago: Chicago Review Press.

McCourt, Kathleen. 1977. *Working-Class Women and Grassroots Politics*. Bloomington: Indiana University Press.

McDermott, Monica, and Frank Samson. 2005. "White Racial and Ethnic Identity in the United States." *Annual Review of Sociology* 31:245–261.

McGreevy, John. 1996. *Parish Boundaries: The Catholic Encounter with Race in the Twentieth-Century Urban North*. Chicago: University of Chicago Press.

McIntosh, Peggy. 1992. "White Privilege and Male Privilege: A Personal Account of Coming to See Correspondences through Work in Women's Studies." In *Race, Class, and Gender: An Anthology*, ed. Margaret L. Anderson and Patricia Hill Collins, 70–81. Belmont, CA: Wadsworth.

McKinney, Carolyn. 2007. "Caught Between the 'Old' and the 'New'? Talking about 'Race' in a Post-Apartheid Classroom." *Race Ethnicity and Education* 10 (2): 215–231.

McMahon, Eileen. 1995. *What Parish Are You From? A Chicago Irish Community and Race Relations*. Louisville: University of Kentucky Press.

Meyer, Stephen Grant. 2000. *As Long as They Don't Move Next Door: Segregation and Racial Conflict in American Neighborhoods*. Lanham, MD: Rowman and Littlefield.

Milligan, Melinda. 1998. "Interactional Past and Potential: The Social Construction of Place Attachment." *Symbolic Interaction* 21:1–33.

———. 2003. "Displacement and Identity Discontinuity: The Role of Nostalgia in Establishing New Identity." *Symbolic Interaction* 26:381–403.

Mills, Charles 1997. *The Racial Contract*. Ithaca, NY: Cornell University Press.

———. 2007. "White Ignorance." In *Race and Epistemologies of Ignorance*, ed. Shannon Sullivan and Nancy Tuana, 11–38. Albany: State University of New York Press.

Molotch, Harvey. 1972. *Managed Integration*. Berkeley: University of California Press.

Morris, Edward. 2007. "Researching Race: Identifying a Social Construction through Qualitative Methods and an Interactionist Perspective." *Symbolic Interaction* 30 (3): 409–425.

Myers, Kristen. 2005. *Racetalk: Racism Hiding in Plain Sight*. Lanham, MD: Rowman and Littlefield.

Myrdal, Gunnar. 1944. *An American Dilemma: The Negro Problem and Modern Democracy*. New York: Harper and Brothers.

Nakayama, Thomas, and Robert Krizek. 1995. "Whiteness: A Strategic Rhetoric." *Quarterly Journal of Speech* 81 (3): 291–309.

Neenan, John. 1972. "Board Votes to Allow 800 Gage Pupils to Transfer to Englewood or Harper: Won't." *Southtown Economist*, September 10, 4.

Neenan, John, and Ken Masson. 1972. "Mrs. Preston Hears Gage Hi Hassle Again." *Southtown Economist*, September 20, 1.

Nicolaides, Becky. 2002. *My Blue Heaven: Life and Politics in the Working-Class Suburbs of Los Angeles, 1920–1965*. Chicago: University of Chicago Press.

Novak, Michael. 1972. *The Rise of the Unmeltable Ethnics*. New York: Macmillan.

Nussbaum, Martha 1997. *Cultivating Humanity: A Classical Defense of Reform in Liberal Education*. Cambridge, MA: Harvard University Press.

———. 2007. *Frontiers of Justice: Disability, Nationality, Species Membership*. Cambridge, MA: Harvard University Press.

Nyden, Philip, Michael Maly, and John Lukehart. 1997. "The Emergence of Stable Racially and Ethnically Diverse Urban Communities: A Case Study of Nine U.S. Cities." *Housing and Policy Debate* 8 (2): 491–534.

Ocejo, Richard. 2011. "The Early Gentrifier: Weaving a Nostalgia Narrative on the Lower East Side." *City and Community* 10 (3): 285–310.

O'Gorman, Hubert. 1975. "Pluralistic Ignorance and White Estimates of White Support for Racial Segregation." *Public Opinion Quarterly* 39 (3): 313–330.

Olson, Philip, and Laura Gillman. 2013. "Combating Racialization and Gendered Ignorance: Theorizing a Transactional Pedagogy of Friendship." *Feminist Formations* 25 (1): 59–83.

Omi, Michael, and Howard Winant. 1994. *Racial Formation in the United States: From the 1960s to the 1990s*, 2d ed. New York: Routledge.

Orfield, Gary. 1978. *Must We Bus? Segregated Schools and National Policy*. Washington, DC: Brookings Institution.

Osbourne, Brian. 2001. "Landscapes, Memory, Monuments, and Commemoration: Putting Identity in Its Place." *Canadian Ethnic Studies* 33 (3): 39–77.

Oser, Edward. 1994. *Blockbusting in Baltimore: The Edmondson Village Story*. Lexington: University Press of Kentucky.

Osman, Suleiman. 2008. "The Decade of the Neighborhood." In *Rightward Bound: Making America Conservative in the 1970s*, ed. Bruce J. Schulman and Julian E. Zeilzer, 106–127. Cambridge, MA: Harvard University Press.

Pacyga, Dominic. 2003. "Moving on Up: Chicago's Bungalow and the American Dream." In *The Chicago Bungalow*, ed. Dominic A. Pacyga and Charles Shanabruch, 117–138. Chicago: Arcadia.

———. 2010. *Chicago: A Biography*. Chicago: University of Chicago Press.

Patillo-McCoy, Mary. 1999. *Black Picket Fences: Privilege and Peril among the Black Middle Class*. Chicago: University of Chicago Press.

———. 2007. *Black on the Block: The Politics of Race and Class in the City*. Chicago: University of Chicago Press.

Patterson, James. 1996. *Grand Expectations: The United States, 1945–1974*. New York: Oxford University Press.

Pedwell, Carolyn. 2012. "Economies of Empathy: Obama, Neoliberalism, and Social Justice." *Environment and Planning D: Society and Space* 30:280–297.

Podair, Jerald E. 2004. *The Strike That Changed New York: Blacks, Whites, and the Ocean Hill–Brownsville Crisis*. New Haven, CT: Yale University Press.

Putnam, Robert. 2000. *Bowling Alone: The Collapse and Renewal of American Community*. New York: Simon and Schuster.

Ralph, James. 1993. *Northern Protest: Martin Luther King, Jr., Chicago, and the Civil Rights Movement*. Cambridge, MA: Harvard University Press.

Ramachandran, V. S. 2010. "Mirror Neurons and Imitation as the Driving Force behind 'the Great Leap Forward' in Human Evolution." Edge: The Third Culture. Available at http://www.edge.org/3rd_culture/ramachandran/ramachandran_p1.html.

Rast, Joel. 1999. *Remaking Chicago: The Political Origins of Urban Industrial Change*. DeKalb: Northern Illinois University Press.

Renfrow, Daniel. 2004. "A Cartography of Passing in Everyday Life." *Symbolic Interaction* 27 (4): 485–506.

Revill, George. 1993. "Reading Rosehill: Community, Identity, and Inner-City Derby." In *Place and the Politics of Identity*, ed. Michael Keith and Steve Pile, 114–138. London: Routledge.

Rieder, Jonathan. 1985. *Canarsie: The Jews and Italians of Brooklyn against Liberalism.* Cambridge, MA: Harvard University Press.

———. 1989. "The Rise of the Silent Majority." In *The Rise and Fall of the New Deal*, ed. Steve Fraser and Gary Gerstle, 243–268. Princeton, NJ: Princeton University Press.

Ring, Dave. 1984. "Chicago Mayor Blasted: Called Insensitive; 1000 Vote on White Agenda." *Boston Globe*, April 30.

Rivlin, Gary. 1988. "The Night Chicago Burned." *Chicago Reader*, August 25.

———. 2013. *Fire on the Prairie: Harold Washington, Chicago Politics, and the Roots of the Obama Presidency.* Philadelphia: Temple University Press.

Roberts, Gene. 1966. "Rock Hits Dr. King as Whites Attack March in Chicago: Felled Rights Leader Rises and Continues Protest as Crowd of 4,000 Riots." *New York Times*, August 6.

Rosen, Louis. 1999. *South Side: The Racial Transformation of an American Neighborhood.* Chicago: Ivan R. Dee.

Rothman, Barbara Katz. 2001. *The Book of Life.* Boston, MA: Beacon Press.

Ryback, David. 2001. "Mutual Affect Therapy and the Emergence of Transformational Empathy." *Journal of Humanistic Psychology* 41 (3): 75–94.

Saltman, Juliet. 1990. *A Fragile Movement: The Struggle for Neighborhood Stabilization.* New York: Greenwood.

Sampson, Robert. 2012. *Great American City: Chicago and the Enduring Neighborhood Effect.* Chicago: University of Chicago Press.

Scales-Trent, Judy. 1995. *Notes of a White Black Woman: Race, Color, Community.* University Park: Pennsylvania State University Press

Schwalbe, Michael, and Douglas Mason-Schrock. 1996. "Identity Work as Group Process." *Advances in Group Process* 13:113–147.

Schwartz, Barrie. 1996. "Memory as a Cultural System: Abraham Lincoln in World War II." *American Sociological Review* 61 (5): 908–927.

———. 1997. "Collective Memory and History: How Abraham Lincoln Became a Symbol of Racial Equality." *Sociological Quarterly* 38 (3): 469–496.

Sears, David, and P. J. Henry. 2003. "The Origins of Symbolic Racism." *Journal of Personality and Social Psychology* 85 (2): 259–275.

Seligman, Amanda. 2005. *Block by Block: Neighborhoods and Public Policy on Chicago's West Side.* Chicago: University of Chicago Press.

Silverstein, Jason. 2013. "I Don't Feel Your Pain: A Failure of Empathy Perpetuates Racial Disparities." Available at www.slate.com/articles/health_and_science/science/2013/06/racial_empathy_gap_people_don_t_perceive_pain_in_other_races.html.

Smith, Kenneth, and Linda Liska Belgrave. 1995. "The Reconstruction of Everyday Life: Experiencing Hurricane Andrew." *Journal of Contemporary Ethnography* 24:244–269.

Sokol, Jason. 2007. *There Goes My Everything: White Southerners in the Age of Civil Rights, 1945–1975.* New York: Vintage.

Soudien, Crain. 2010. "The Reconstitution of Privilege: Integration in Former White Schools in South Africa." *Journal of Social Issues* 66 (2): 352–366.

Southern Policy Law Center. 1987. "'Move-In' Violence: White Resistance to Neighborhood Integration in the 1980s." Montgomery, AL: Southern Policy Law Center.

Soutner, Susan Blanche. 1980. "The Boston Banks Urban Renewal Group Homeowner-ship Program: A Study of Racial Discrimination in an Urban Housing Market." Cambridge, MA: Department of City and Regional Planning, Harvard University.

Spelman, Elizabeth. 2007. "Managing Ignorance." In *Race and Epistemologies of Igno-rance*, ed. Shannon Sullivan and Nancy Tuana, 119–131. Albany: State University of New York Press.

Squires, Greg, Larry Bennett, Kathleen McCourt, and Philip Nyden. 1987. *Chicago: Race, Class, and the Response to Urban Decline*. Philadelphia: Temple University Press.

Steyn, Melissa. 2001. *Whiteness Just Isn't What It Used to Be: White Identity in a Chang-ing South Africa*. Albany: State University of New York Press.

———. 2012. "The Ignorance Contract: Recollections of Apartheid Childhoods and the Construction of Epistemologies of Ignorance." *Identities: Global Studies in Culture and Power* 19 (1): 8–25.

Street, Paul. 2007. *Racial Oppression in the Global Metropolis: A Living Black Chicago History*. Lanham, MD: Rowman and Littlefield.

Suarez, Ray. 1999. *The Old Neighborhood: What We Lost in the Great Suburban Migra-tion, 1966–1999*. New York: Free Press.

Sugrue, Thomas. 1996. *The Origins of the Urban Crisis: Race and Inequality in Postwar Detroit*. Princeton, NJ: Princeton University Press.

Sugrue, Thomas, and John Skrentny. 2008. "The White Ethnic Strategy." In *Rightward Bound*, ed. Bruce J. Schulman and Julian E. Zeilzer, 171–192. Cambridge, MA: Har-vard University Press.

Sulzer, Glenn. 1988. "Racist Equity?" *Chicago Tribune*, July 5.

Suttles, Gerald. 1972. *The Social Construction of Communities*. Chicago: University of Chicago Press.

Swan, Elaine. 2010. "States of White Ignorance, and Audit Masculinity in English Higher Education." *Social Politics: International Studies in Gender, State and Soci-ety* 17 (4): 477–506.

Swanstrom, Todd. 1985. *The Crisis of Growth Politics: Cleveland, Kucinich, and the Chal-lenge of Urban Populism*. Philadelphia: Temple University Press.

Taub, Richard, Garth Taylor, and Jan Dunham. 1984. *Paths of Neighborhood Change*. Chi-cago: University of Chicago Press.

Tayler, Marianne. 1985. "Firebombs Greet Black Family." *Chicago Tribune*, June 27.

Taylor, Charles. 1994. "The Politics of Recognition." In *Multiculturalism: Examining the Politics of Recognition*, ed. Amy Gutmann. 25–74. Princeton, NJ: Princeton Univer-sity Press.

Teaford, Jon. 1990. *The Rough Road to Renaissance: Urban Revitalization in America, 1940–1985*. Baltimore: Johns Hopkins University Press.

Terkel, Studs. 1992. *Race: How Blacks and Whites Think and Feel about the American Obsession*. New York: New Press.

Terry, Don. 2006. "Northern Exposure: Nothing He'd Seen in the South Prepared Martin Luther King for the Streets of Marquette Park in 1966." *Chicago Tribune*, January 15.

Townley, Cynthia. 2006. "Toward a Revaluation of Ignorance." *Hypatia* 21 (3): 37–55.

Tuan, Yi-Fu. 1974. *Topophilia*. Englewood Cliffs, NJ: Prentice-Hall.

———. 1977. *Space and Place: The Perspectives of Experience*. Minneapolis: University of Minnesota Press.

Tuana, Nancy. 2006. "The Speculum of Ignorance: The Women's Health Movement and Epistemologies of Ignorance." *Hypatia* 21 (3): 1–19.

Van Ausdale, Debra, and Joe Feagin. 2001. *The First R: How Children Learn Race and Racism*. Lanham, MD: Rowman and Littlefield.

Vera, Hernan, Joe Feagin, and Andrew Gordon. 1995. "Superior Intellect? Sincere Fictions of the White Self." *Journal of Negro Education* 64 (3): 295–306.

Vitebsky, Piers. 1993. "Is Death the Same Everywhere? Contexts of Knowing and Doubting." In *An Anthropological Critique of Development: The Growth of Ignorance*, ed. Mark Hobart, 100–115. London: Routledge.

Waghid, Yusef. 2001. "Globalization and Higher Education Restructuring in South Africa: Is Democracy Under Threat?" *Journal of Educational Policy* 16 (5): 455–464.

Walley, Christine. 2013. *Exit 0: Family and Class in Postindustrial Chicago*. Chicago: University of Chicago Press.

Warren, Mark. 2010. *Fire in the Heart: How White Activists Embrace Racial Justice*. Cambridge: Oxford University Press.

Wellman, David. 1993. *Portraits of White Racism*, 2d ed. London: Cambridge University Press.

———. 1997. "Minstrel Shows, Affirmative Action Talk, and Angry White Men: Marking Racial Otherness in the 1990s." In *Displacing Whiteness: Essays in Social and Cultural Criticism*, ed. Ruth Frankenberg. 311–331. Durham, NC: Duke University Press.

Werelo, Terry. 1974. "Redlining Will Strangle Neighborhood Stability, Commission Probe Told." *Southtown Economist*, July 28.

Wernick, Andrew. 1997. "Resort to Nostalgia: Mountains, Memories, and Myths of Time." In *Buy this Book: Studies in Advertising and Consumption*, ed. Mica Nova, Andrew Blake, Iain MacRury, and Barry Richards, 207–223. New York: Routledge.

White, Walter. 1995. *A Man Called White: The Autobiography of Walter White*. Athens: University of Georgia Press.

Wiese, Andrew. 1995. "Neighborhood Diversity: Social Change, Ambiguity, and Fair Housing since 1968." *Journal of Urban Affairs* 172: 107–129.

Wilson, Janelle. 2005. *Nostalgia: Sanctuary of Meaning*. Lewisburg, PA: Bucknell University Press.

Wilson, William J., and Richard P. Taub. 2006. *There Goes the Neighborhood: Racial, Ethnic, and Class Tensions in Four Chicago Neighborhoods and Their Meaning for America*. New York: Alfred A. Knopf.

Winant, Howard. 1997. "Behind Blue Eyes: Contemporary White Racial Politics." *New Left Review* 225 (September–October): 73–88.

Woldoff, Rachael. 2011. *White Flight/Black Flight: The Dynamics of Racial Change in an American Neighborhood*. Ithaca, NY: Cornell University Press.

Young, Michael, and Peter Willmott. 1957. *Family and Kinship in East London*. London: Routledge and Kegan Paul.

Zerubavel, Eviatar. 1996. "Social Memories: Steps to a Sociology of the Past." *Qualitative Sociology* 19 (3): 283–299.

Ziemba, Stanley. 1975. "Probe Urged of 'Kickbacks' on FHA Loans." *Chicago Tribune*, January 3.

———. 1978. "S.W. Side Maps Home Equity Plan." *Chicago Tribune*, July 15.

Zukin, Sharon. 2010. *Naked City: The Death and Life of Authentic Urban Places*. New York: Oxford University Press.

Index

Michael T. Maly is Associate Professor of Sociology and Director of the Policy Research Collaborative at Roosevelt University in Chicago. He is the author of *Beyond Segregation: Multiracial and Multiethnic Neighborhoods in the United States* (Temple).

Heather M. Dalmage is Professor of Sociology and Director of the Mansfield Institute for Social Justice and Transformation at Roosevelt University in Chicago. She is the author of *Tripping on the Color Line: Black-White Multiracial Families in a Racially Divided World.*

www.ingramcontent.com/pod-product-compliance
Lightning Source LLC
Chambersburg PA
CBHW020001290326
41935CB00007B/263